K-12 CLASSROOM TEACHING

A Primer for New Professionals

Second Edition

Andrea M. Guillaume
California State University, Fullerton

PEARSON

Merrill
Prentice Hall

Upper Saddle River, New Jersey
Columbus, Ohio

Library of Congress Cataloging-in-Publication Data

Guillaume, Andrea M.
    K-12 classroom teaching : a primer for new professionals / Andrea M. Guillaume.-- 2nd ed.
      p. cm
    Rev. ed. of: Classroom teaching. 2000.
    Includes bibliographical references and index.
    ISBN 0-13-049694-4 (pbk.)
      1. First year teachers--United States. 2. Teaching--United States. I. Guillaume, Andrea
M. Classroom teaching. II. Title.

    LB2844.1.N4G85 2004
    371.102--dc21   2003052725

Vice President and Executive Publisher: Jeffery W. Johnston
Executive Editor: Debra A. Stollenwerk
Associate Editor: Ben Stephen
Editorial Assistant: Mary Morrill
Production Editor: Kris Robinson
Production Coordination: Carlisle Publishers Services
Photo Coordinator: Sandy Schaefer
Design Coordinator: Diane C. Lorenzo
Cover Designer: Thomas Mack
Cover Image: Superstock
Production Manager: Pamela D. Bennett
Director of Marketing: Ann Castel Davis
Marketing Manager: Darcy Betts Prybella
Marketing Coordinator: Tyra Poole

This book was set in Korinna by Carlisle Communications, Ltd. It was printed and bound by Banta Book Group.
The cover was printed by Phoenix Color Corp.

Photo Credits: Scott Cunningham/Merrill, pp. 2, 23, 43, 99, 114, 184; Valerie Schultz/Merrill, p. 6; Barbara
Schwartz/Merrill, pp. 7, 32, 102; Anthony Magnacca/Merrill, pp. 19, 84, 149, 161, 220; Tom Watson/Merrill, p. 57;
Anne Vega/Merrill, pp. 78, 196, 214; Parvin/Texas Memorial Museum/Silver Burdett Ginn, p. 103; Modern
Curriculum Press/Pearson Learning, p. 142; Karen Mancinelli/Pearson Learning, p. 170.

Pearson Education Ltd.   Pearson Education Australia Pty. Limited
Pearson Education Singapore Pte. Ltd.   Pearson Education North Asia Ltd.
Pearson Education Canada, Ltd.   Pearson Educación de Mexico, S.A. de C.V.
Pearson Education—Japan   Pearson Education Malaysia Pte. Ltd.

10 9 8 7 6 5 4 3 2 1
ISBN: 0-13-049694-4

For my husband, Darrell, and for my mother,
Lu Ann Munns Berthel, with gratitude.

PREFACE

By learning you will teach; by teaching you will learn.

—Latin proverb

K–12 Classroom Teaching: A Primer for New Professionals, Second Edition, is a core text for elementary and secondary preservice teachers who are taking introduction to teaching courses, field experience courses, or general methods courses. It is also a quick but thorough core text for inservice teachers who are gaining certification at the same time they are beginning to teach. Instructors of specialized methods courses or foundations of education courses will find this primer a useful supplemental text.

K–12 Classroom Teaching presents useful, practical points of view that can provide meaning and direction behind new teachers' actions related to a number of central educational issues. It uses clear, reader-friendly language to concisely explore key aspects of classroom teaching, including the context of teaching today; strategies for learning about students; educational stances; planning and assessment; instruction and instructional strategies; classroom management and discipline; and professional growth. Chapters include a balance of up-to-date discussions of educational issues, recent research findings, and practical advice. The selection and presentation of topics is guided by a conceptual approach that emphasizes the active nature of learning to teach.

CONCEPTUAL APPROACH

K–12 Classroom Teaching: A Primer for New Professionals is based upon the premise that teaching is goal-directed, interactional, and mindful of the local setting in its efforts to encourage learners' growth. Two core convictions are that classroom teaching is complex and that today's teachers face special difficulties given current demands and events at home and abroad. It takes the conceptual approach that, in the face of these challenging conditions, teachers at their best are guided by:

- a clear sense of what they hope to accomplish
- an understanding of what research shows to be effective
- a set of professional knowledge and skills
- a sense of ethics concerning what is right
- a sense of responsibility to value and enhance the learning of every student

---

Note: The pronouns *she, he, her,* and *his* are used variously throughout the text to represent either teacher or student.

Building these dispositions, commitments, and understandings is hard work, so this text approaches the process of learning to teach (and of learning in general) as an active, social one. Through its content and through its approach, the text encourages readers to reflect on past experience, to question assumptions, to consider multiple sources of information, and to commit to enacting well-defined notions of good practice that address learners' diverse needs and honor the dignity of the human experience.

ORGANIZATION OF THE TEXT

Chapters are arranged topically, and content of later chapters draws from the work the reader accomplishes in earlier chapters. In Chapter 1, the text begins with an exploration of the distinct character of classroom teaching. Chapter 1 explores this character through six propositions of teaching that lay a foundation for the entire text through their content and their implications for chapters' presentation of information. These propositions include:

1. Teaching looks easy . . . from the outside.
2. Every teacher is part of a system.
3. Teaching is directed toward the goal of fostering change.
4. Teaching is more than telling.
5. There is agreement on what teachers need to know and be able to do.
6. Teachers can be effective and yet not just alike.

Chapter 2 stresses the importance of understanding the philosophical bases found in educational practice and of developing one's own stance toward education. Subsequent chapters ask readers to use their stance to guide their decisions related to the chapters' content. Chapter 3 explores the growing range of strengths and needs exhibited by students in American schools and urges new teachers to use knowledge of specific students as a starting point for their instructional decisions. Chapter 4 addresses instructional planning both in the long range and in the short term. It presents a variety of unit planning approaches and objectives-based lesson planning. Chapter 5 presents six pieces of general advice for instruction using the mnemonic device COME-IN: Connect, Organize, Model, Enrich, Interact, and consider Nature and Needs. Chapter 6 shares instructional strategies and discusses the strengths and potential drawbacks of models such as direct instruction and inquiry. Chapter 7 explores principles of assessment and offers a variety of assessment strategies in keeping with those principles. Special attention is given to current concerns about school accountability and its focus on student achievement as measured through standardized tests. Chapter 8 addresses classroom management, and Chapter 9 focuses on encouraging appropriate student behavior in ways that respect students, prevent misbehavior, and encourage self-control. The final chapter, Chapter 10, addresses issues of professional involvement and growth for new teachers.

FEATURES OF THE TEXT

Readers and reviewers of the first edition of *K–12 Classroom Teaching* commented positively on a variety of the text's characteristics, and those have been retained in the second edition. They include the text's condensed format, its readable style, its useful ideas, and its personal approach.

In keeping with the text's active approach to learning, a number of special features can also be found throughout the text.

- *Warm-Up Exercises:* Because past experience influences present learning, chapters begin with warm-up activities that help readers access their thinking related to major points about to be explored.

- *Presentation of Information:* Key concepts are presented in clear language. Tables are often used to present information in a succinct format.
- *Teaching Tips:* Practical classroom suggestions are given in boxes throughout the chapters.
- *Words From Teachers:* The voices of previous readers, now teachers, offer advice and writing samples that are presented in many chapters. Examples include a metaphor for teaching, sample stances, daily schedule structures, and poems.
- *Quotations:* Words to inspire thought and appreciation are offered throughout.
- *Parting Words:* Rather than concluding with a traditional summary, chapters conclude with some final words of advice related to the issues at hand.
- *Links to Research, Theory and Practice:* The links found at the close of each chapter give not only reference citations for the chapter, but citations for classic works and for other current research and practical references.
- *Web Sites:* Internet Web sites related to the chapter's content are provided. Web sites provide connections to professional organizations and instructionally related resources and materials.
- *Opportunities to Practice:* Application exercises conclude each chapter. They are meant to extend readers' connections with the content in a variety of ways that directly relate to world of the classroom.
- *Blank Forms:* Opportunities to practice, along with many figures throughout the text, provide for structured practice and application of the chapters' key ideas. Examples include blank observation guides, lesson plan forms, and assessment and management plans.

  Readers and reviewers suggested some special features that have been incorporated into the second edition. These include:
- *Photographs and Illustrations:* Visual displays enhance the presentation of the chapters' ideas.
- *Glossary:* Boldface terms presented in each chapter are defined in a glossary at the end of the text.
- *Fast Facts:* Statistical information from across the nation is presented in Fast Fact boxes in many chapters.

NEW TO THIS EDITION

The second edition of *K–12 Classroom Teaching: A Primer for New Professionals* responds to the dynamic conditions teachers today face. It also responds to the suggestions of previous readers and reviewers. In addition to the new features already discussed in the second edition, a number of content shifts are also evident.

- Content has been updated to reflect *current trends and research.* Examples of current topics include:
  - Differentiated instruction (Chapter 3)
  - Backwards planning (Chapter 4)
  - Graphic organizers and concept maps and a nationwide focus on standards-based instruction and student achievement (Chapter 7)
- *Issues related to secondary teachers* (middle school, junior high school, and high school teachers) have been incorporated more directly. Research and perspectives addressing the special conditions faced by secondary students and teachers are incorporated throughout the text. Two examples include:
  - Instructional planning concerns (Chapter 4)
  - Classroom management concerns (Chapter 8)

- *Issues that face teachers and students across our nation* have been more directly addressed. These include:
  - Federal legislation such as the No Child Left Behind Act of 2001
  - Teacher induction
  - Standards for teachers
  - Academic content standards for students
- *Family-school connections* are addressed in several chapters, drawing tighter links among the team members who work together on behalf of students
- Issues related to *instructional technology* are incorporated throughout this edition. Examples include:
  - Issues of access to technology (Chapter 1)
  - Evaluating lesson plans found on the Internet (Chapter 4)
  - Management of the one-computer classroom (Chapter 8)

There is one change in the organization of chapters in the second edition. Information related to students and their needs was included in the first edition's Chapter 9, "Professional Responses to Learner Diversity." The second edition more forcefully recognizes the centrality of the student in the educative process and thus includes information on learning about students and their needs much earlier in the text. Chapter 3, "Starting With Students," reflects the text's key propositions of teaching: Teaching is interactional, and it is directed toward the goal of fostering growth for learners. These propositions necessitate that readers first consider their learners and then plan, instruct, and assess in ways that incorporate this vital knowledge of students.

SUPPLEMENTS

An instructor's manual is available without cost to instructors using *K–12 Classroom Teaching: A Primer for New Professionals* as part of their courses. The comprehensive instructor's manual includes the following components:

- *Chapter overview and key outcomes:* An at-a-glance preview of the chapter and a listing of some outcomes students should be able to demonstrate after reading the chapter
- *Chapter outline and graphic organizer:* Two different presentations of the chapter's key points
- *Sample class activities:* Activities that can be used to access students' prior knowledge, connect the text's main points to their lives and practice, and extend their practice
- *Transparency masters:* Main points from the chapter and supplemental information ready for duplication
- *Portfolio entries:* Possible artifacts and reflections to include in readers' professional portfolios
- *Test bank items:* Assessment tasks and traditional test items

The test bank items in the Instructor's Manual are available in TestGen software in both Macintosh and PC formats. TestGen also provides a user-friendly interface for instructors wishing to create their own tests.

ACKNOWLEDGMENTS

I am grateful to my colleagues in the profession of education for their wisdom and assistance in the continuing evolution of this text.

- Thanks to my students and students around the nation who have provided frank feedback that helps me to consider (and reconsider) what it means to teach well and how best to write about our work.

- Thanks to the teachers who continue to show me what it means to be excellent. These teachers include the many masterful teachers I see daily in the field and my university colleagues.
- Thanks to Loretta Zarow for her help in conducting research for the second edition.
- Thanks to those who reviewed the first edition and provided valuable insights and directions for development of the second edition: Amy Cox-Petersen, California State University–Fullerton; Donna Strand, Baruch College–NYC (CUNY); Leigh Chiarelott, Bowling Green State University; Adele Sanders, University of Northern Colorado; Beatrice Fennimore, Indiana University of Pennsylvania; Allan F. Cook, University of Illinois–Springfield; Ivan W. Banks, Jackson State University; Mary Lou Brotherson, Nova Southeastern University; Sharon Hobbs, Montana State University–Billings; Scott Willison, Boise State University; and Jean Deller, Tri-State University.
- Thanks to the professionals who shaped the development and production of this work: Debbie Stollenwerk for her continued faith in the project, Ben Stephen for his firm support of the second edition and for sending junk food at just the right time, Jean Pascual for her assistance in copyediting the text, Emily Hatteberg for her skillful oversight of its production, and Paula Keck for her careful illustration.
- Thanks to my children, who thus far continue to tolerate my telling of their stories.

Educator Learning Center: An Invaluable Online Resource

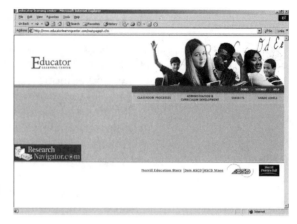

Merrill Education and the Association for Supervision and Curriculum Development (ASCD) invite you to take advantage of a new online resource, one that provides access to the top research and proven strategies associated with ASCD and Merrill—the Educator Learning Center. At **www.EducatorLearningCenter.com** you will find resources that will enhance your students' understanding of course topics and of current educational issues, in addition to being invaluable for further research.

HOW THE EDUCATOR LEARNING CENTER WILL HELP YOUR STUDENTS BECOME BETTER TEACHERS

With the combined resources of Merrill Education and ASCD, you and your students will find a wealth of tools and materials to better prepare them for the classroom.

Research

- More than 600 articles from the ASCD journal *Educational Leadership* discuss everyday issues faced by practicing teachers.
- A direct link on the site to Research Navigator™ gives students access to many of the leading education journals, as well as extensive content detailing the research process.
- Excerpts from Merrill Education texts give your students insights on important topics of instructional methods, diverse populations, assessment, classroom management, technology, and refining classroom practice.

Classroom Practice

- Hundreds of lesson plans and teaching strategies are categorized by content area and age range.
- Case studies and classroom video footage provide virtual field experience for student reflection.
- Computer simulations and other electronic tools keep your students abreast of today's classrooms and current technologies.

LOOK INTO THE VALUE OF EDUCATOR LEARNING CENTER YOURSELF

Preview the value of this educational environment by visiting **www.EducatorLearningCenter.com** and clicking on "Demo." For a free 4-month subscription to the Educator Learning Center in conjunction with this text, simply contact your Merrill/Prentice Hall sales representative.

BRIEF CONTENTS

CONTENTS

Note: Every effort has been made to provide accurate and current Internet information in this book. However, the Internet and information posted on it are constantly changing, it is inevitable that some of the Internet addresses listed in this textbook will change.

Before you begin reading Chapter 1

Learning is an active process. What you already know influences what you will learn. Use the first column of the knowledge chart below to jot down some of the things that you know right now about teaching. In the second column, write down some of the questions you have about teaching. Revise your chart as you read, completing the third column as you gain experience.

Knowledge Chart on Teaching		
Know	**Want**	**Learned**

CHAPTER *One*

The Nature of Teaching

American children play school, spend many years as students in classrooms, and encounter countless media images of teachers. All these sources push us toward the conclusion that, before we ever become adults, we know all there is to know about teaching. However, a more careful look suggests that our earlier experiences with teaching may not provide information that, after all, helps us to *teach* well. What is teaching? How is it different from other things people do? How does one teach well? The following six propositions help to distinguish teaching from other activities and to combat common misconceptions about teaching:

1. Teaching looks easy . . . from the outside.
2. Every teacher is part of a system.
3. Teaching is directed toward the goal of fostering change.
4. Teaching is more than telling.
5. There is agreement on what teachers need to know and be able to do.
6. Teachers can be effective and yet not just alike.

TEACHING LOOKS EASY . . . FROM THE OUTSIDE

The prevailing perception is that good teaching is easy. Unlike medicine or law, the profession of teaching does not inspire awe by conjuring up visions of a scary knowledge base or of harrowing training experiences. Because each of us has had, as a child, years of classroom experience, we may assume that we know all that teachers know. Not until we step in front of a classroom for the first time do we realize how difficult teaching can be.

Teaching is difficult partly because classrooms are complex (Doyle, 1986). First, teachers are required to serve in several roles. They need to serve as coach, activities director, supply master, evaluator, and confidante, for instance. In their varied roles, teachers make many decisions about different kinds of issues. Some estimate that teachers make more than a thousand decisions a day. Teachers need to think about students' safety, their learning, and their other needs simultaneously, all while they also consider their own personal and professional issues.

Second, classrooms are complex because events tend to overlap: Many things happen at once, and they happen quickly. As the number of learners increases or the learners' maturity level decreases, the challenges can increase, but in all classrooms teachers must make quick judgments without the benefit of time to reflect and weigh the consequences of their actions. Third, although particular classrooms have common elements, every learning situation is different. The physical,

Fast Facts 1.1

Survey Says . . .

3	Average number of hours per week teachers report working with students outside of regular school hours.
9	Average number of hours per week teachers report working on school-related activities not involving students.
"Seventy-one percent agree that . . .	. . . routine duties and paperwork interfere with their teaching" (from a national survey of public elementary and secondary teachers).

Source: U.S. Department of Education, National Center for Education Statistics. Schools and Staffing Survey, 1999–2000: Overview of the Data for Public, Private, Public Charter, and Bureau of Indian Affairs Elementary and Secondary Schools. *http://nces.ed.gov/pubs2002/2002313_1.pdf*

Teaching looks easy . . .
from the outside.

sociocultural, and historical setting of the class, as well as individual learners' experiences and needs, affect the nature of the class. Consequently, as teachers and their students spend time together, they build a shared history. That is why an outside observer may miss inside jokes, be confused by a class's accepted procedures, or fail to see why a single comment could irritate others.

A fourth way in which classrooms are complex is that, because people affect each other, the act of teaching is inherently uncertain. It is difficult for even an experienced teacher to predict with certainty how a class will respond to a lesson. Classrooms are also unpredictable because as teachers we may pursue goals that are unclear, our base of authority may be in question, and we are usually unsure of the outcomes of our efforts, especially long-range outcomes (Jackson, 1986). What happens to students after they leave us? What did they learn? Did they learn *because of us* or *in spite of us?* Finally, teaching is an act that reaches into time both before and after face-to-face interaction with students. It requires preparation, and it requires reflection and revision.

- Preparation
- Teaching
- Reflection and revision

Exercise 1 in Opportunities to Practice at the close of this chapter presents the words of a prospective teacher as he considers his many roles and responsibilities as a teacher. Take a look, and think about your own vision for accomplishing these many roles.

*G*ood teaching is neither obvious nor simplistic.

—National Board for Professional Teaching Standards (1998)

Have you seen the television commercial that hawks deodorant by admonishing us to "never let them see you sweat"? That commercial seems to capture the first aspect of teaching: Teaching looks easy . . . from the outside. Seldom are the daily events of teaching witnessed by the public. Few people witness the conditions under which teachers are expected to encourage learning and to manage the complexity of the classroom without a drop of perspiration. Further, classroom complexity is compounded because classrooms exist as part of a larger system.

EVERY TEACHER IS PART OF A SYSTEM

No teacher serves as an island; no teacher teaches solely for his own purposes. Instead, a teacher serves at the center of a set of nested circles of influence, as shown in Figure 1.1. Imagine an archery target. You, the teacher, are in the bull's-eye, and the outermost ring contains society in the broadest sense. As a teacher, you are expected to act in ways that are consistent with the rules and goals of society. These rules guide your actions as a citizen, and, more specifically, they direct you as a teacher. Laws govern many aspects of your behavior (as summarized in Figure 1.2) as well as your professional practice. A recent example of legislative influence on educators' practice is the federal **No Child Left Behind Act of 2001,** which is designed to improve **student achievement** and **school accountability.** Its requirements for annual student testing, academic progress targets, and teacher quality may well touch lives in every public school in the United States.

In addition to legal influences, society also exerts influence on classrooms through its professional organizations such as the National Board for Professional Teaching Standards, the National Council of Teachers of Mathematics, and the National Council for the Social Studies. Organizations like these shape professional practice by recommending standards for teachers, students, and schools. (Examples of professional societies are found in the Web sites listed at the chapter's close.)

By moving toward the center of the target, you travel through rings that represent increasingly local and specific settings. The settings found in these rings usually have narrower and more explicitly defined purposes and expectations.

FIGURE 1.1 *Circles of influence that affect classroom teachers.*

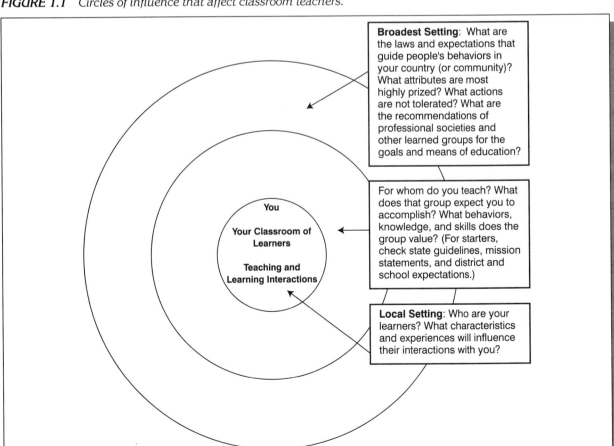

_ *1.2* *Teachers and the law.*

Source: Adapted from McDaniel (1979), and corroborated and updated with Fischer, Schimmel, and Kelly (1999) and McCarthy, Cambron-McCabe, and Thomas (1998).

1. *Public schools must not promote worship.* Schools may teach *about* religion if the intent is not to worship. Students cannot be required to salute the flag if their religious convictions or matters of conscience (in some states) prohibit it (Fischer, Schimmel, & Kelly, 1999).

2. *Academic freedom has limits.* Teachers are permitted to address controversial topics and use controversial methods if they are educationally defensible, appropriate for the students, and are not disruptive. School boards have authority to set curriculum and methods.

3. *Teachers' private activities must not impair their teaching effectiveness.* Although teachers hold the same rights as other citizens, their conduct is held to a higher standard. When teachers' private lives weaken their classroom effectiveness, it is possible that they may be dismissed. Sexual relationships with students are cause for dismissal (Fischer, Schimmel, & Kelly, 1999).

4. *Students have rights to due process.* Teachers' and schools' rules and procedures must be fair and reasonable, and justice must be administered evenhandedly. Due process is important for such issues as search and seizure, suspension, and expulsion (McCarthy, Cambron-McCabe, & Thomas, 1998). Families of students with disabilities have additional due process procedures related to special education services (Fischer, Schimmel, & Kelly, 1999).

5. *Teachers must not use academic penalties to punish behavior.* Students' academic grades cannot be lowered as a result of disciplinary infractions. Students must be allowed to make up work that accumulates during suspensions or other disciplinary periods (McCarthy, Cambron-McCabe, & Thomas, 1998).

6. *Corporal punishment must not be misused.* About half the states prohibit corporal punishment. In states where it is allowed, corporal punishment must be delivered while the teacher is not in a state of anger, it must fit the crime and the students' age and condition, and it must not lead to permanent injury or run the risk of such (McCarthy, Cambron-McCabe, & Thomas, 1998). Disciplinary actions that serve to humiliate a child may be illegal too.

7. *Teachers must protect children's safety.* Teachers must act in place of the parents, providing prudent, reasonable supervision to protect children from harm. They can be held negligent if they do not do so. Teachers and schools can protect children's safety by establishing and enforcing rules pertaining to safety and by providing prudent, reasonable care in their supervision (Fischer, Schimmel, & Kelly, 1999).

8. *Teachers must not slander or libel their students.* Teachers must say and write only things about students that they know objectively to be true. Even confidential files must not contain statements that demean a student's character, background, or home life. Statements should be based on relevant observable behavior (Fischer, Schimmel, & Kelly, 1999). Teachers must share information only with personnel who have a right to such information.

9. *Teachers must copy instructional materials in accordance with copyright laws.* The reproduction without author's permission of copyrighted instructional materials, including print sources, visual images, videotape, and computer software, is restricted to conditions of fair use. Examples of fair use are a single copy of a book chapter for a teacher's own use, or a copy of a poem. Teachers may not make copies to replace collected works, nor may they make copies of consumable materials. Teachers may not make copies of computer software, and they are greatly restricted in their use of videotape in the classroom (Fischer, Schimmel, & Kelly, 1999; McCarthy, Cambron-McCabe, & Thomas, 1998).

10. *Teachers need to know the law.* Ignorance is no excuse.

11. *Teachers must report suspected child abuse.* All states require teachers to report suspected physical or sexual abuse, and no state requires certainty, only reasonable cause to believe that abuse is present (Fischer, Schimmel, & Kelly, 1999).

For example, states develop **content standards** across the curriculum, and these standards influence **textbook adoptions,** professional development activities for teachers, and learning opportunities for students. Another local source of influence on classrooms is the family. Effective teachers respond to the values and dreams of the families they serve and make use of the resources offered by families and their communities (Gonzalez, Andrade, Civil, & Moll, 2001; Moll, Amanti, Neff, & Gonzalez 1992).

FIGURE 1.3 *Contrasting poverty rates for school-aged children within the same states.*

Source: National Center for Educational Statistics (2002).

State	Percentage of Students Aged 5–17 Living in Poverty, 1996–1997			
California	San Bernardino City Unified	44%	San Juan Unified	14%
Georgia	Atlanta City	42%	Gwinnett County	8%
Maryland	Baltimore City	32%	Montgomery County	8%

Some people who affect new teachers in particular are the experienced educators who direct and supervise their growth. Examples include university supervisors, **mentors,** and site administrators. These individuals can hold a powerful influence on teachers and represent the interests and values of the profession by serving the school or university as an institution.

Figure 1.1 should not, however, imply that the relationship between circles of influence is static or unquestioned. Throughout history, the interactions among rings have often been emotionally, culturally, and politically charged.

Sources of influence in the various rings offer opportunities: The United States is a wealthy nation with relatively high literacy rates, for instance. We are leaders in technology and in medical innovations. These are potentially positive sources of influence. However, sources of influence also offer constraints. Although the United States is a wealthy nation, Kozol (1991) painfully documented the experiences of public school students who, even as the twentieth century drew to a close, experienced institutionalized racism in unsafe, dirty, and woefully understocked inner-city schools. Although citizens of the same state and country as their peers in better maintained schools, students in many urban and less affluent suburban schools, Kozol reported, could expect funding rates half those of nearby affluent schools. We can continue to find disparate levels of wealth in American schools (e.g., Kozol, 2000). Figure 1.3 presents poverty rates for students in relatively large, contrasting districts in three states. Despite our hopes that the United States is a country rich with opportunities, patterns of inequity exist, and those patterns affect what happens in classrooms.

The general direction of influence for these rings or sources of influence, then, seems to be inward: Each of these layers can shape what happens in classrooms so that many forces press teachers to act in certain ways and to accomplish certain ends. Examples include legislation that governs education, public interest in standardized test scores and in policies and procedures of **teacher testing** and **certification,** and local economic and cultural conditions. Historical influences at every level can also shape what happens in individual classrooms. Imagine for a moment how different life is for Americans since the horrific events of September 11, 2001. These differences have shaped policies and procedures in schools, and they have affected the outlooks of many students and their families. We are a different people now.

However, despite the profound influences inward on the diagram, the direction of influence can be from the center outward as well. As a poignant example, many students in schools across the nation responded to the September 11th tragedies with humanitarian efforts to ease the suffering of New Yorkers and of the nation at large. Thus, as students examine local conditions, challenge existing practices, and participate in **social action** or **service learning** projects (e.g., Bomer & Bomer, 2001; Darling-Hammond, French, & Garcia-Lopez, 2002; Stephens, 1995), they shape their communities. When teachers participate in the professional and societal community, they too influence what happens in the outer rings. There are broader, historical examples of the influence

Differences in achievement or educational experience based on gender, race, or **socioeconomic status** *may be exacerbated by the* Digital Divide, *or disparities in access to high-quality technology, the Internet, and effective computer-assisted instruction (Lazarus & Mora, 2000).*

of students and schools outward as well. In the 1930s, one movement of educational reform, **Social Reconstructionism,** held schools as an instrument to reshape society.

You, as a teacher, not only teach toward your own ideals and aims but also toward the goals of the nested groups—rings on the target—to which you belong. No doubt you will have opportunities to witness and manage tensions that result from the competing goals found in different rings. Part of your job will be to negotiate at least temporary solutions for the dilemmas found in competing goals. Take a few minutes to consider the goals and expectations of the circles of influence that envelop you. What influence do you hope to have in each of the rings? Try jotting your notes on Figure 1.1.

Also, because teachers are part of a system, they must recognize the influence of other elements of their local setting. The bull's-eye includes not only you, the teacher, but also your learners. Learners exert influence. Teaching is **interactional.** Although you as the teacher may be awarded more status and power, students are participants who must be considered in your instructional decisions. In fact, students are at the center of your instructional decisions; teaching is meant to encourage learning. A body of literature on **democratic classrooms** (e.g., Allen, 1999; Bomer & Bomer, 2001; Charney, 1997; Hoover & Kindsvatter, 1997; Kohn, 1998) seeks to harness the influence of students in molding classrooms that reflect the goals, interests, and spirit of each student as a caring member of the learning community.

Teaching is more than telling.

TEACHING IS DIRECTED TOWARD THE GOAL OF FOSTERING CHANGE

Teachers are expected to nudge learners toward improvement. Learners should come to know more, to know more deeply, or to have enhanced skills, abilities, or attitudes through their classroom interactions. Although certainly teachers are affected by their learners, and effective teachers must continue to grow over time, instructor improvement is not the universal goal of teaching. The goal of teaching is change for the learner. What changes are expected? Who creates the change? Which methods are used? The answers to these questions vary by teacher and circumstance, but in every case we expect that learners will leave the setting different from when they entered it. The hope of a teacher is to make a positive difference in learners' lives.

Teaching becomes complicated by the fact that teachers usually pursue many—and sometimes conflicting—goals. For instance, although a teacher may strive to help learners become more independent, she also needs to encourage order, and she may do so by praising conformity ("I like the way that Sung is sitting so nicely!"). Learners also pursue their own agendas, including ones that may contradict the teacher's goals. My son Alex provides an example. When his first-grade teacher stepped into the hall for a brief conversation with a colleague, Alex immediately seized the moment and leapt onto his chair. Fists and face raised to the sky, he screamed "Let's party!" No matter how reluctant the learners, teaching is directed toward the goal of fostering change for the learners.

TEACHING IS MORE THAN TELLING

Teaching ≠ telling

Part of the perception that teaching is easy stems from the mistaken notion that teaching and telling are the same thing: If a teacher says it, students will know it. Certainly a well-delivered lecture can be a powerful learning tool, but we cannot presume that knowledge travels directly from the mouth of the teacher to the mind of the learner. What students learn is affected by their physical characteristics, their perspectives, their preferences, and their prior experiences. Knowledge is constructed as learners bring their perspectives and experiences to bear on new information. Teachers need to help students connect new information to their own lives.

FIGURE 1.4   *Current views on how people learn.*

- *Behaviorist theories of learning* focus on observable behaviors and how they can be shaped through rewards and punishments, or consequences. Learning occurs continuously and can be intentional or unintentional. Teachers often shape students' behavior through behaviorist strategies like reinforcers. Examples of positive reinforcers include grades, praise, and tangible items. Punishment can take the form of time-outs and names on the board for misbehavior. Names associated with behaviorist models include Thorndike, Skinner, and, more recently, Bandura (Slavin, 1997).

- *Information processing models* address how information is selectively perceived and stored in memory. Information is received through the senses and then is perceived by the mind. It enters short-term memory either from the process of sensation or from long-term memory. If concepts are stored through schemata (systems of linked concepts), teachers must be careful to access students' background knowledge and clarify the conceptual models by which content is organized. Another direct classroom application is the use of meaningful practice to aid retention (Slavin, 1997).

- *Constructivist approaches* hold that students build information rather than receiving it intact from environmental stimuli. By continually checking new information against their mental rules, learners act on new information and internalize it in idiosyncratic ways. Piaget (1952) and Vygotsky (1978) are heavy influences on constructivist theories. Both emphasize the social nature of learning and the importance of "disequilibration," of unsettling experiences that cause learners to reorganize cognition at higher levels. Teaching approaches that facilitate learning include those in which students are actively engaged in testing and refining their thinking and cooperative approaches in which students interact in heterogeneous groups, thus challenging and supporting each other's thinking and discoveries (Eggen & Kauchak, 1999).

- *Multiple intelligence theory* by Gardner (1983) challenges the long-held notion that intelligence is a single construct. Instead, multiple intelligence theory suggests that people can be smart in many different ways. The intelligences include (1) logical or mathematical, (2) linguistic, (3) musical, (4) spatial, (5) bodily or kinesthetic, (6) interpersonal, and (7) intrapersonal intelligence. An eighth intelligence, naturalist intelligence, has also been added to the list (Checkley, 1997). Although the empirical research to support multiple intelligence theory is currently sparse, the power of multiple intelligence theory is that it cautions teachers not to assume that a certain level of performance in one area is necessarily associated with a similar level of performance in another area, and it urges schools and teachers to broaden the kinds of experiences offered to children (Eggen & Kauchak, 1999; Slavin, 1997).

- *Brain-based research* (e.g., Caine & Caine, 1994) holds that school experiences should be directly guided by how the brain functions. Caine and Caine posit a three-level brain that functions holistically, processing many kinds of information (such as emotions and facts) at once. They hold that the search for meaning and pattern making is innate. As a result, school experiences should provide numerous complex and concrete experiences that are rich in sensory stimulation and embedded within human contexts.

Because classrooms are interactive and dynamic, "teaching as telling" does not capitalize on the learners' goals or on the power of their experiences. It also does not draw directly from current theories on how children learn. Figure 1.4 summarizes current views on how people learn.

One trend that emerges from these views on how people learn is that learning seems not a simple matter of reception. Instead, it appears to be about active engagement, about questioning, and about facing misunderstandings and building better understandings by organizing information in meaningful ways (Bransford, 2000; Gagnon & Collay, 2001; Marlowe & Page, 1998). Because human learning appears to be a complicated affair, teaching as purely telling can short-circuit learning by ignoring the large variety of strategies that teachers can use to help encourage growth. That is why skilled teachers have rich repertoires of **instructional strategies** from which they select as they consider their goals, their learners, and the settings in which they teach. A teacher does more than deliver a monologue (see Figure 1.5).

> Skilled teachers have rich repertoires of instructional strategies.

Teaching is more than telling, too, because it involves listening. When people are learning, they are trying to figure things out, to make sense of new information. One effective way to help learners understand things is to listen to

FIGURE 1.5 *Teacher's cannot pour knowledge into students' needs.*

their points of view, their musings, and their questions. *Listening* is an important strategy that teachers can employ to slow down the presentation of new information, to give learners an opportunity to sort things out, and to help learners discover what they think. Finally, because teaching is interactional, listening gives us information about the learners' reasoning that can be used to guide our moment-by-moment and longer-range instructional decisions. The fact that teaching is more than telling is reflected in the agreement on what teachers need to know and be able to do.

THERE IS AGREEMENT ON WHAT TEACHERS NEED TO KNOW AND BE ABLE TO DO

Despite the perception that most people who have attended school understand teaching, and although some individuals may appear to be "born teachers," there is a body of knowledge, attitudes, and skills that teachers can acquire with effort and experience. National and state panels codify the domains that teachers consider in their work. One of the most influential boards that has considered what it means to be an excellent teacher is the **National Board for Professional Teaching Standards (NBPTS).** The NBPTS sets forth five propositions of effective practice, and these domains are assessed as experienced teachers pursue **National Board certification** (an optional, advanced certification that is meant to delineate excellent teachers). Domains of competence are assessed also for prospective and beginning teachers. One or more of the three **Praxis** series of examinations administered by the **Educational Testing Service (ETS),** for example, is used in more than half of the United States as a measure of new teachers' academic skills, subject matter knowledge, or teaching competence. Figure 1.6 synthesizes general conclusions about excellent teaching, drawn largely from the National Board for Professional Teaching Standards (2002) and the Praxis domains (Educational Testing Service, 2002).

FIGURE 1.6 *Domains of teacher expertise.*

Source: In part synthesized and adapted from National Board for Professional Teaching Standards (2002) and Praxis III Domains (Educational Testing Service, 2002).

Subject Matter Knowledge	• Understanding human learning and the many factors (e.g., culture and context) that affect it • Holding rich, organized understanding of the content and how it is used • Using specialized knowledge to help students build accurate and deep understandings of the content
Planning	• Assessing and using students' background knowledge and incorporating it into instruction • Setting and communicating clear learning goals • Creating and selecting learning experiences appropriate for students and goals • Creating and selecting a rich variety of resources to enrich learning
Instruction	• Committing to students and their ability to learn • Providing instruction aligned with communicated goals • Building connections with previous learning • Making content understandable for all students • Teaching for meaning, critical thinking, problem solving, and creative thinking • Monitoring student responses and adjusting instruction
Assessment	• Creating or selecting assessment strategies consistent with learning goals and student needs • Measuring learning for groups and individuals • Using multiple measures to assess growth
Classroom Management and Discipline	• Creating safe climates that promote fairness, autonomy, and respect • Setting norms for social interaction • Establishing and maintaining standards of student behavior • Using routines, procedures, and time effectively
Professional Growth	• Modeling traits of an educated person • Reflecting on goals and practice • Building professional relationships • Working with families, communities, and the profession

In general, effective teachers understand their subject matter, human development, diversity, and learning; they use their knowledge to plan meaningful instruction; they create productive and humane learning environments; they teach in ways that help students learn deeply; and they assess students' growth carefully and use results to modify their instruction. They also engage in their profession by working with families, communities, and other educators to reflect on and improve teaching and learning. Does this sound like plenty to learn? Compare the row headings of Figure 1.6 with the chapter titles of this text and you will note that we have a whole text to begin exploration of these domains of competence together.

Large bodies of research examine schooling practices, both to capture the experiences of teachers and learners and to determine promising teaching practices. Research has provided some insights into how students and teachers make sense of the schooling experience, and it has provided some directions for practice (e.g., Marzano, Pickering, & Pollock, 2001; Reynolds, 1992). The search for understanding and for prediction continues as educators and researchers examine questions related to the domains of teacher expertise.

The questionnaire in Figure 1.7 presents an entry-level self-assessment that you can use to consider your current knowledge and skills. Mark areas that may figure prominently in a plan for your professional growth. If you like, formulate questions to capture these areas and record your areas on your knowledge chart from the beginning of the chapter. You may wish to flip ahead to chapters that will address your questions.

FIGURE 1.7 Questionnaire for self-analysis of teaching.

	Strongly Disagree			Strongly Agree
1. I can describe how people learn.	1	2	3	4
2. I know my subject matter.	1	2	3	4
3. I can list some ways to find out who my students are and what they know.	1	2	3	4
4. I can plan a lesson related to a goal or outcome.	1	2	3	4
5. I can demonstrate more than one instructional strategy or technique that helps makes the content clear to students.	1	2	3	4
6. I can assess students' learning based on traditional tests and at least one other measure.	1	2	3	4
7. I can modify my instruction based on what I discover about students' learning.	1	2	3	4
8. I know how to help students treat each other and me respectfully during class.	1	2	3	4
9. I can structure my time and materials so there is little wasted time.	1	2	3	4
10. I can describe two ways to involve parents beyond conferences and in-class volunteer time.	1	2	3	4

TEACHERS CAN BE EFFECTIVE AND YET NOT JUST ALIKE

> *What* better or greater gift can we offer the republic than to teach and to instruct our young?
>
> *—Cicero*

Although there are documented domains of expert teaching, few prescriptions hold in every circumstance. Teaching is uncertain and interactional. Part of teaching well is using a combination of one's own talents, insights, skills, and professional judgments to encourage students' learning and development.

Cicero's sentiment underscores the personal and giving nature of teaching: When we teach, we offer gifts to our students—gifts that depend on our traits and triumphs as givers. Think back to two teachers who had a powerful effect on your learning. What were their gifts? If you make lists of strengths for those two teachers (Figure 1.8), you may find areas of overlap; the teachers probably shared some common strengths and abilities. These instructors probably also made unique contributions to your learning. Your lists will probably contain both personal attributes and professional skills, attitudes, and abilities.

When asked to consider their memorable teachers, my students often find commonalities such as passion for the subject matter and genuine regard for the learner. However, the idiosyncratic contributions that their teachers offered are many. Some mention humor, others reserve. Some mention competitive learning activities, others mention collaborative ones. Teachers bring themselves and their abilities to their students. What do you bring to the classroom? Use Figure 1.9 to display your gifts.

PARTING WORDS

Common misconceptions hold that teachers work toward a single set of unquestioned goals, usually by standing in front of a calm classroom and talking. Instead, this chapter suggests that teaching is a far more complicated act. It argues that teachers must encourage learner growth of many kinds while weighing often-competing demands and carefully considering their learners and the local context. Despite the complexity of teaching, we find some agreement in the literature about the kinds of things teachers should know and be able to do, and we know that there are many ways to practice the craft of teaching well.

FIGURE 1.8   *Characteristics of effective teachers I have known.*

Personal Attributes	Professional Skills, Attributes, and Abilities
Teacher One: *Pam* *People people* *friendly / firm —* *Creative, wacky* *Structure*	*Motivational Master* *Organization*
Teacher Two: *Gayle*	

FIGURE 1.9   *Personal characteristics that I bring to learners.*

My Personal Attributes	My Professional Skills and Abilities

One place to start is by forming an educational philosophy, a personal stance toward teaching, as is encouraged in Chapter 2.

Between here and Chapter 2 you will find a number of end-of-chapter features. "Links to Research, Theory, and Practice" provides references for the works cited throughout the chapter and a number of resources that can provide additional information and points of view. "Web Sites" provides an opportunity for you to join a larger community conversation about teaching. Finally, "Opportunities to Practice" asks you to apply what you know and to connect chapter ideas with your own thoughts and practice.

LINKS TO RESEARCH, THEORY, AND PRACTICE

Allen J. (1999). *Class actions: Teaching for social justice in elementary and middle school.* New York: Teachers College Press.

Bomer, R., & Bomer, K. (2001). *For a better world: Reading and writing for social action.* Portsmouth, NH: Heinemann.

Bransford, J. (2000). *How people learn: Brain, mind, experience, and school.* Washington, DC: National Academy Press.

Caine, R. M., & Caine, G. (1994). *Making connections: Teaching and the human brain.* Menlo Park, CA: Addison-Wesley.

Charney, R. S. (1997). *Habits of goodness.* Greenfield, MA: Northeast Foundation for Children.

Checkley, K. (1997). The first seven . . . and the eighth. *Educational Leadership, 55,* 8–13.

Darling-Hammond, L., French, J., Garcia-Lopez, S., Eds. (2002). *Learning to teach for social justice.* New York: Teachers College Press.

Doyle, W. (1986). Classroom organization and management. In M. Wittrock (Ed.), *Handbook of research on teaching* (3rd ed., pp. 392–431). New York: Macmillan.

Educational Testing Service (2002). *Pathwise/Praxis III Domains.* Retrieved February 13, 2003, from http://www.ets.org

Eggen, P., & Kauchak, D. (1999). *Educational psychology: Windows on classrooms* (4th ed.). Upper Saddle River, NJ: Merrill/Prentice Hall.

Fischer, L., Schimmel, D., & Kelly, C. (1999). *Teachers and the law* (5th ed.). New York: Longman.

Gagnon, G. W., Jr., & Collay, M. (2001). *Designing for learning: Six elements in constructivist classrooms.* Thousand Oaks, CA: Corwin Press.

Gardner, H. (1983). *Frames of mind: The theory of multiple intelligences.* New York: Basic Books.

Gonzalez, N., Andrade, R., Civil, M., & Moll, L. (2001). Bridging funds of distributed knowledge: Creating zones of practices in mathematics. *Journal of Education for Students Placed at Risk (JESPAR), 6*(1–2), 115–132.

Hoover, R. L., & Kindsvatter, R. (1997). *Democratic discipline: Foundation and practice.* Upper Saddle River, NJ: Merrill/Prentice Hall.

Jackson, P. (1968). *Life in classrooms.* New York: Holt, Rinehart & Winston.

Jackson, P. (1986). *The practice of teaching.* New York: Teachers College Press.

Kohn, A. (1996). *Beyond discipline: From compliance to community.* Alexandria, VA: Association for Curriculum and Supervision.

Kohn, A. (1998). Beyond bribes and threats: How not to get control of the classroom. *NAMTA Journal, 23*(1), 6–61.

Kozol, J. (1991). *Savage inequalities: Children in America's schools.* New York: Crown.

Kozol, J. (2000). An unequal education. *School Library Journal, 46*(5), 46–49.

Lazarus, W., & Mora, F. (2000). *Online content for low-income and underserved Americans: The digital divide's new frontier. A strategic audit of activities and opportunities.* Children's Partnership, Santa Monica, CA. (ERIC Document Reproduction Service No. ED 440 190)

Marlowe, B. A., & Page, M. L. (1998). *Creating and sustaining the constructivist classroom.* Thousand Oaks, CA: Corwin Press.

Marzano. R. J., Pickering, D. J., & Pollock, J. E. (2001). *Classroom instruction that works: Research-based strategies for increasing student achievement.* Alexandria, VA: Association for Supervision and Curriculum Development.

McCarthy, M. M., Cambron-McCabe, N. H., & Thomas, S. B. (1998). *Public school law: Teachers' and students' rights* (4th ed.). Boston: Allyn & Bacon.

McDaniel, T. R. (1979). The teacher's ten commandments: School law in the classroom. *Phi Delta Kappan, 60*(10), 703–708.

Moll, L. C., Amanti, C., Neff, D., & Gonzalez, N. (1992). Funds of knowledge for teaching: Using a qualitative approach to connect homes and classrooms. *Theory into Practice, 31*(1), 132–141.

National Board for Professional Teaching Standards. (1998). *The five propositions of accomplished teaching.* Retrieved February 13, 2003, from http://www.nbpts.org/about/coreprops.cfm

National Center for Educational Statistics. *Digest of educational statistics.* (2002). Retrieved February 13, 2003, from http://nces.ed.gov/pubs2002/digest2002/tables/dt094.asp

Piaget, J. (1952). *Origins of intelligence in children.* New York: W. W. Norton.

Reynolds, A. (1992). What is competent beginning teaching? A review of the literature. *Review of Educational Research, 62*(1), 1–35.

Slavin, R. (1997). *Educational psychology: Theory and practice* (5th ed.). Boston: Allyn & Bacon.

Stephens, L. S. (1995). *The complete guide to learning through community service: Grades K–9.* Boston: Allyn & Bacon.

Vygotsky, L. S. (1978). *Mind in society: The development of higher psychological processes* (M. Cole, Ed.). Cambridge: Harvard University Press.

WEB SITES

Research and Current Events

http://www.ericsp.org
  ERIC Clearinghouse on Teaching and Teacher Education

http://www.prgaustin.com
  Publishers Resource Group, Inc.: National and state education news, adoption schedules, calendars of important meetings and conferences, and links to a variety of education-related Web sites

http://www.edweek.com
  Edweek newspaper: Current events with links to Teacher Magazine and other relevant sources

http://www.ed.gov
  The U.S. Department of Education. Read more about the No Child Left Behind Act

National Subject Matter and Standards Organizations

http://www.nbpts.org
  National Board for Professional Teaching Standards

http://www.ncss.org
  National Council for the Social Studies

http://www.ncate.org
  National Council of Teachers of English

http://www.enc.org/
  Eisenhower National Clearinghouse: Resources on Mathematics and Science education

http://www.nap.edu/readingroom/books/nses/html
  National Science Education Standards

http://www.ira.org
  International Reading Association

http://www.nctm.org
  National Council of Teachers of Mathematics

http://www.nsta.org
  National Science Teachers Association

OPPORTUNITIES TO PRACTICE

1. Read prospective teacher Jason Ross's words as he considers the importance of managing many roles well. Try composing your own metaphor that conveys your understanding of the important work of classroom teaching.

2. Think back on the chapter you just read. Use Figure 1.10 to write one point that you found especially worthwhile and write one point with which you disagree. How is teaching different for you than it is for me?

3. Revise your knowledge chart on teaching. Take special note of the surprises you encountered along the way.

4. Connect the work you did in Figures 1.1 and 1.6. In what ways have various sources of influence affected your perceived abilities as a teacher thus far? How might they influence your growth as a teacher in the future? Discuss the questionnaire in Figure 1.7 with a relatively new teacher and with an experienced one. You may wish to compare the value they place on the content of each question.

5. Go to one of the Web sites listed at the close of Chapter 1. First, find sources that influence what happens in classrooms. Add them to your work in Figure 1.1. Second, connect what you read on the Web sites with one or more of the six propositions of

---

TEACHERS AS PILOTS

. . . "Children in a classroom are a lot like passengers on a commercial airliner. They may feel confined by the small area that they are allowed to call their personal space; however, in the end, everyone arrives at his destination. Teachers play the role of the flight attendant. We keep the passengers well-fed and comfortable, while making their experience informative and even fun.

. . . "We, as pilots, have a great influence on our passengers. The passengers need to know that their flight crew has everything under control, regardless of turbulence. We control what attitudes they may have about flying with our company, or even about flying at all. The children who develop a fear of flying are the ones whom teachers have failed to reach, and future pilots will have a hard time convincing them to fly again."

—Jason H. Ross
Prospective Teacher, 2002
(Used with permission)

FIGURE 1.10 *Analysis of Chapter 1.*

One point that I found interesting or useful:

One point with which I disagree:

teaching. Talk with an experienced colleague about recent history related to that issue.

6.   Interview a non-teacher about her views on effective teaching. Consider speaking with a parent, a student, or a professional who works outside of education and has little contact with students or schools. What do good teachers do? What do students wish teachers knew? How closely do your interviewee's insights match the propositions from the chapter?

Before you begin reading Chapter 2

In his popular treatise, Robert Fulghum (1988) asserts that everything he ever really needed to know about the world, and how to be a good person in it, he learned at school . . . in kindergarten. In kindergarten he learned, for example, to share, to play fair, and to clean up his messes. Each of these could be considered a "big lesson" that applies not only to five-year-olds, but to fifty-five-year-olds as well.

Take a few minutes to consider the influence you hope to have on students. If they could learn only two or three things with you, what would those things be? What are the big lessons in life that you hope to help teach?

Warm-Up Exercise for Developing a Personal Stance toward Education

I hope to help students learn or become . . .

CHAPTER *Two*

Developing a Personal Stance Toward Education

"Now in teaching, as in several other things, it does not matter what your philosophy is or is not. It matters more whether you have a philosophy or not. And it matters very much whether you try to live up to your philosophy or not. The only principles of teaching which I thoroughly dislike are those to which people pay only lip service."

—George Polya, *Mathematical Discovery*

The operative goal of classroom teaching seems obvious: Teachers teach subject matter to students. That goal appears to go largely unquestioned. However, no matter how clearly defined or matter-of-fact a classroom situation may seem, no teacher can escape the burden of personal and professional judgment. Take another look at that operative goal: Teachers teach subject matter to students. Who should teach our students? What subject matter should be taught? How? To which students? Under which conditions? Toward what end? According to which standards? With which expectations of success?

Important questions such as these make it imperative that teachers know what they think and take guidance from a larger vision of what should be (Duffy, 1998). I urge you to form a stance—a vision of education or educational philosophy—that sets out what you believe to be (1) the purposes of your work, (2) the nature of humans and learning, and (3) your view of what it means to teach well. (Figure 2.1 continues the urging.) Captured in words, these notions can serve as a guide for your actions. Your efforts to plan lessons, instruct, and assess students can be richer and more cohesive when shaped by a thoughtful, carefully constructed vision of education.

What good is a philosophy when the **curriculum** is prescribed? "Curriculum" turns out to be a multifaceted notion. Eisner (1979) argues convincingly that schools teach three kinds of curricula:

1. The explicit curriculum
2. The implicit curriculum
3. The null curriculum

The **explicit curriculum** is that content which is intentionally selected and addressed through instruction. Examples include traditional subject areas such as reading, mathematics, and physical education. The explicit curriculum also

---

Fast Facts 2.1

Survey Says . . .

83% agree that . . .	. . . Goals and priorities for the staff at their site are clear
84% agree that . . .	. . . Most of their colleagues share beliefs and values about what the central mission of the school should be.

From a national survey of public elementary and secondary teachers. Responses of private school teachers are different. Take a look: *http://nces.ed.gov/pubs2002/digest2001/tables/dt074.asp*

Source: U.S. Department of Education, National Center for Education Statistics *Schools and Staffing Survey, 1993–94.*

FIGURE 2.1   *Yes, personal stance is philosophy in disguise.*

Three (Not Good Enough) Reasons to Skip This Chapter	Four (Really Good) Reasons to Work Hard in This Chapter
1. I know what I need to teach; the ____ tells me. 2. The _____ has methods I am required to use. 3. I'm just trying to get through this _____ (lesson/day/month/year). 4. I have it on my "to do list."	1. Teaching can be overwhelming, especially for the novice. So many decisions need to be made. A stance toward education provides a compass for decision making. 2. Everyone appears to be an expert in education . . . with plenty of free advice. A well developed stance allows you to carefully select the advice you accept. 3. Classrooms are so busy that it is easy to lose sight of the long-term consequences of our actions. A stance can help you remember to maintain your focus on the long range. 4. Having your own stance and understanding the stances of others allows you to understand their perspectives and the kinds of criteria and evidence they would accept. It can allow you to understand why you fit/don't fit and the language to use in speaking about issues with someone with a different stance.

> As with all great teachers, his curriculum was an insignificant part of what he communicated. From him you didn't learn a subject but life. . . . Tolerance and justice, fearlessness and pride, reverence and pity are learned in a course on long division if the teacher has those qualities.
>
> —William Alexander Percy

includes skills or habits that teachers purposefully select and teach. Examples may include neatness, politeness, and cooperation. The **implicit curriculum,** or hidden curriculum, is not purposefully selected. Rather, it includes the lessons taught tacitly through actions and through unconsidered consequences. Some say that the hidden curriculum is "caught" rather than "taught." Examples of the hidden curriculum may include competition and deference to authority. In Gatto's (1992) eyes, compulsory schooling in the United States has a hidden curriculum that encourages conformity, deadens the spirit, and weakens students' ability to think creatively and independently. Positive aspects of the implicit curriculum include outcomes such as kindness, respect, and the notion that people believe in one's abilities to succeed. Finally, the **null curriculum** refers to what we learn because of the subject matter *not* taught. Examples may include lessons about the relative importance of content areas such as art and music that often lose funding or receive low instructional priority.

These concepts of implied and null curricula suggest that not only planned lessons influence learners but subtle, often unintended, methods do as well. For example, what do elementary students learn as their teacher asks them to form two lines: one for girls and one for boys? What message is sent about the value of a high-school student's writing when the paper is covered with a teacher's red marks? What does a middle school teacher teach when he allows students to laugh at each other?

Eisner's three curricula warn that every action a teacher takes—or does not take—can teach. Even instantaneous decisions and fleeting behaviors convey our stance to our learners and to our communities. Think about the powerful things you learned in school that were probably not recorded in your teachers' daily plan books. I remember, for instance, a teacher's lesson almost 30 years ago. When I was a new sixth grader, I crumpled up a half-finished art project and threw it away as I ran out to recess. The next morning, I found that wrinkled work hanging alongside my classmates' dazzling finished products. My teacher, Mr. G., had removed it from the trash, smoothed it, and placed it in the gallery of masterpieces. Taken aback, I reassured him that I truly had intended for the piece to stay in the trash. When a second version of the project was finished, Mr. G. promised, it would replace the forlorn original. I took great care to finish another work, and I rushed it to my teacher. Down came the creased and

What are these students learning through their interactions with their teacher?

smudged object of embarrassment. Up went a work of which I was proud. No 20-minute lecture could have been as effective for me as Mr. G.'s simple, quiet lesson on persistence and pride.

Because every action—or *in*action—can teach, a coherent philosophy or stance toward education can be a helpful guide and a reminder for us to be intentional with our words and actions. How can you develop a stance toward education that can direct you as you teach? One way is by considering a set of enduring questions.

 QUESTION FOR THOUGHT

Teaching is difficult, in part because different students can learn different lessons from teachers' actions. Would your response to Mr. G.'s actions have been the same as mine? Was Mr. G.'s lesson an example of good teaching?

CONSIDERING THE QUESTIONS OF EDUCATION: DEVELOPING YOUR OWN STANCE

Philosophy as a field of study addresses questions about beauty, logic, ethics, morality, the nature of reality, and the character of knowledge. Of the many sets of questions proposed by educational theorists, an especially useful one was proposed by the ancient Greeks and suggested to me by James T. Dillon (1987). These questions, which parallel the concerns of the sixteenth century's famous philosopher John Comenius (Sadler, 1966), ask the following:

1. What is the good? Who is the good person living in the good society?
2. What is the purpose of education?
3. What should everyone learn? Why?
4. What is the nature of learning?
5. What is (excellent) teaching?
6. What does school do?

Do you recall the saying, "The last one to see the water is the fish?" Answering these seemingly simple questions may put you in the position of the fish, exploring the world that has been your home and thus has many aspects that may be transparent to you. Considering these questions of education means exposing some of your tacit notions about how the world is and should be. It also entails considering the fact that your perspectives have alternatives. Here are a few tips related to the questions to get you started composing your stance.

> *E*very science and every inquiry, and similarly every activity and pursuit, is thought to aim at some good.
>
> —*Aristotle*

1. As you consider the questions of *"What is the good? Who is the good person living in the good society?"* consider your own upbringing. If you were raised as part of the **dominant culture** in the United States, you no doubt were exposed to American core values. These values are not universal. Some American ideals include (Pai & Adler, 2001):

- The Puritan morality (which emphasizes delayed gratification, respectability, and duty)
- The belief that people should work hard to succeed and that unsuccessful people do not work hard
- Individualism and its emphasis on self-reliance and originality
- An achievement orientation (we should all try to achieve higher goals through hard work)
- Future time orientation (saving for tomorrow)

2. In thinking about the *purpose of education,* consider carefully how it is that society brings its people to "the good." How is it that education serves as a vehicle to create "the good society"? One possible answer to this question is given in an excerpt of Martin Luther King, Jr.'s (1947) essay on the purpose of education, which he wrote as an undergraduate student:

> "The function of education, therefore, is to teach one to think intensively and to think critically. . . . We must remember that intelligence is not enough. Intelligence plus character—that is the goal of true education."

3. Considering *what everyone should learn and why* gives you an opportunity to think about the subject matter that is important enough for each person in the society to learn. As you consider subject matter, remember that what is considered "basic" in one part of the world or at one time in history may be superfluous in another. In your response, remember to think not just about what might be considered traditional content but issues of character, skills, values, and abilities as well. Be able to explain why people should learn what you suggest, and not something else. Remember, too, that "everyone" means every person; this question addresses the common core of learnings to be mastered in the society.

> *T*he role of the teacher remains the highest calling of a free people. To the teacher, America entrusts her most precious resource, her children; and asks that they be prepared . . . to face the rigors of individual participation in a democratic society.
>
> —*Shirley Hufstedler*

4. The *nature of learning* includes both the nature of the learner (are people inherently bad? inherently good?), the nature of knowledge (is it unchanging? tentative?), and the processes by which we learn.

5. You have begun to think about *excellent teaching* through your work in Chapter 1. Think about the professional knowledge, skills, and abilities that teachers have and also about the personal attributes required of excellent teachers. For example, must a teacher serve as a model of "the good person"?

6. *What does school do?* As you consider this question, keep in mind that "school" is just one of the educative institutions in a society. Cortes (2000) explores "the social curriculum" through its branches, including the media, the family and neighborhood, and institutions such as religion and youth groups. What unique contribution does schooling provide, for better and for worse?

When you consider the answers to these questions as a set, you will have developed for yourself a stance, a conception of education. To address these questions, think solely about your own ideas—no need to quote famous people

Fast Facts 2.2

How Well Do Schools Fulfill Different Purposes?

Survey Says . . .

What percentage of secondary teachers and students say that their schools are doing extremely well at preparing students to . . .

	Percentage of *Teachers* Who Said "Extremely Well"	Percentage of *Students* Who Said "Extremely Well"
. . . go to college?	29	15
. . . get a good job?	18	15
. . . learn how to learn?	17	22
. . . be good citizens?	21	17
. . . get along well with others?	21	19

Source: From a national survey of secondary school teachers and students. Findings vary based on many factors, such as students' gender. Take a look at the results yourself by downloading the report from *http://www.metlife.com/Applications/Corporate/WPS/CDA/PageGenerator/0,1674,P2817,00.html The Metlife Survey of the American Teacher. Student life: School, Home and Community. New York.* (2002). Metropolitan Life Insurance Company.

or to write a term paper. Instead, write no more than a page to answer each of the questions, taken in order. You may stumble a bit in interpreting the questions. Interpret them any way you like, as long as they guide you in discovering what you think. After you compose a first draft, check your answers to see that you are consistent from question to question. Revise so that answers are coherent. Take out extra words. Read your answers aloud to yourself and then to a friend to be sure that your answers truly communicate your convictions. You will know when you have finished when not a word can be cut and when each reading convinces you more fully of the soundness of your stance.

If you need a push, Figure 2.2 gives brief phrases from two teachers' philosophies. Both Rae Anne and Jaime stress the importance of people working and living in groups and of the power of education to help them do so. They also both emphasize the need for teachers to draw on students' prior experiences to connect to new information. They differ, however, in the fine points of their conceptions. For instance, Jaime emphasizes dignity for the learner and a safe learning environment, whereas Rae Anne focuses more on teachers needing flexibility and openness to new teaching methodologies. Although the differences between these two teachers' philosophies are relatively minor, they reflect some major philosophical differences put forward and practiced in the past.

CONCEPTIONS OF EDUCATION FOUND IN PRACTICE

Though each of us must wrestle with our own vision of what teaching should be, two things are also true. First, visions change over time, and second, there are similarities found across stances. Examining those patterns of change and constancy may provide further insights into your own thinking.

Curriculum researchers have traced society's views toward education over time, finding that visions of education are fluid and responsive to the historical, cultural, and social contexts of the people who create them (e.g., Chartock, 2000). Events such as the Industrial Revolution and the race for space changed the trajectory of the nation's views of education.

Along with change over time, we can also find similarities across stances. Prakash and Waks's (1985) analysis summarizes four broad families of conceptions of educational excellence, as shown in Figure 2.3. As you study the figure, notice that each of the stances (technical, rational, personal, and social) have distinct visions of what we should accomplish and how to go about accomplishing it. The technical conception of education tends to be prevalent in K–12 public education, whereas the rational model tends to prevail in universities. With its emphasis on the individual, the personal stance is less frequently found in public schools and more often occurs in private, or independent, schools. Which way of thinking is most prevalent in your area?

Where would you place Rae Anne and Jaime in this family of stances? See if you can place Rae Anne's and Jaime's stances in one of the rows within Figure 2.3. They view their jobs as helping young people value each other and work well in groups. They see themselves as facilitators who will match their methods to students' needs and help students take an active stance in solving

FIGURE 2.2 *Excerpts from two teachers' philosophies.*

	Rae Anne	Jaime
Who is the good person living in the good society?	Considers actions before committing them Lives harmoniously and gains knowledge from his or her surroundings in order to improve the present quality of life	Recognizes cultural differences and takes pride in diversity People work, socialize, mingle with kindness and respect Actively participates in the life of the community Passionately engages in the pursuit of knowledge
What is the purpose of education?	To create equal opportunities To provide the power to obtain one's goals and dreams To broaden one's thinking To build self-esteem and character	To draw from the lives of participants To encourage social development To provide the opportunity to discover individual passions To prepare participants for active engagement in the community To encourage lifelong learning
What should everyone learn?	That which will create citizens who can contribute new ideas and understanding to society Problem solving	Positive attitudes toward challenging subject matter Real-world applications of the subject matter That which will allow citizens to participate
What is the nature of learning?	Building on previous information through interaction Asking questions Understanding, not memorizing Varies by person: doing, observing, reading	Comparing new experiences with information from previous endeavors Trial and error Watching Examining physical representations Interacting in groups Fostered by safe environment
What is (excellent) teaching?	Reaches greatest number of students possible Is flexible and willing to change methods to enrich students' learning Creates many alternate plans Searches for new information and improvement as teacher	Holds passion for education and children Models actions and behaviors desired by the society Commits to reaching every student and meeting the needs of all Plans to incorporate different ways and rates of learning Respects the dignity of the learner Taps into background knowledge

important problems. These positions are consistent with the social realm. Their stances are relatively conservative within the social school of thinking, however, because both Rae Anne and Jaime plan to teach core academic areas as a focus and to infuse problem solving within the schooling context. Some proponents of the social stance suggest that we use schools to reconstruct society into a system with more equitable patterns of interaction. Had they fallen within the technical stance, Rae Anne and Jaime would have placed greater emphasis on mastery of basic skills and far less emphasis on group dynamics.

How might this teacher's vision of education differ from those of today?

FIGURE 2.3 *Prakash and Waks's description of different conceptions of education.*

Source: Adapted from Prakash M. S., & Waks, L. J., 1985.

	What is the good?	What is the purpose of education?	What is learning?	What is teaching?
Technical	Efficiency Proficiency	To produce high achievement To adjust productive means to measurable ends	Memorizing Problem solving: applying facts to routines	Provides information for rote acquisition
Rational	Disciplined thinking Initiation Imagination	To transmit values by involving students in worthwhile activities Cognitive socialization of youth	Problem solving: higher-order creative and logical abilities Building complex schema	Presents ideas and concepts in a way that allows learners to see the structure of the subject Leads discussions and projects
Personal	Self-actualization (reaching individual potential)	To create opportunities so that individuals can develop along unique paths	Learning through own mistakes and experiences Introspection Being "centered" (in touch with self)	Independent, aware individuals Provides resources and space for exploration
Social	Individual development within the context of the common good Social responsibility	To provide skills for competence in civic life To teach the ability to identify and solve problems related to societal issues To foster the dispositions needed to take action	Interacting with a group Thinking beyond "I" to "we" Focusing on the disciplines only so far as they relate to relevant problems	Provides choices for group projects and actions Facilitates problem identification and solution Provides leadership

Prakash and Waks (1985) argue that there is no neutral philosophy. What are the benefits of the stance you see as most prevalent? What are the drawbacks? Who wins? Who loses?

The usefulness of examining current conceptions of education lies in the fact that conceptions expose very different answers to oft-unexamined questions. We all seem to say that we want what is best for the next generation and for the nation. Examining conceptions of education helps us to realize that "best" is a matter requiring much deliberation. Bringing about the "best" requires even more. Our stances toward education are not disembodied ideals, but rather, important matters that play out daily, with great implications for the nation's children. *Please* develop a stance and use it regularly to guide and examine the work you do.

USING YOUR STANCE

> *A* philosophy is to a teacher what a bus schedule is to a traveler. A philosophy provides guidance, clarification, and consistency. A teacher with a philosophy has a purpose and vision for how her classroom will function, as well as clear goals for what will be taught.
>
> —Amy Jordahl,
> California State
> University, Fullerton
> (1997)

Your stance should be reflected in your year-long plans, in your lessons, and in your minute-by-minute interactions and decisions. Further, a conception of education offers *should* statements to direct you. Questions such as "What 'should' we teach?" and "How 'should' we group students?" are answered in terms of both philosophy and empirical evidence. Use what you know about findings from educational research to enrich your stance and guide your professional decisions. Four suggestions can guide you in using and revising your stance, as follows:

1. In writing your stance, do not be tempted to include a little of every way of thinking. If you were to do so, elements would probably contradict each other and would not provide guidance when you need it.

2. Use your stance to guide your instructional decisions. Remind yourself that when you choose one course of action, you necessarily reject others. For instance, if you emphasize only basic facts, you preclude other kinds of learning opportunities. Conversely, if you include primarily small-group projects, students have fewer experiences in working on skills as individuals. Make sure your choices are in line with achieving excellence in the long view.

3. Write a shortened version of your stance—a one-page credo. Keep your credo where you can refer to it often. Use it as the organizing principle for your professional portfolio.

4. Revise your stance. You are an adult with many years of life experience, so your stance may not change radically over time. On the other hand, it may. Thoughtful teachers engage in frequent reflection on their experience and seek to improve their thinking as their thinking changes.

PARTING WORDS

Today's demands upon teachers' attention are great. Time is short, lists of standards or outcomes to be mastered are long, and priorities sometimes conflict. Maintaining a clear sense of focus about what you consider central to your work as a teacher can help you decide at the close of a hectic day whether you have contributed to the world through your efforts as a teacher. Having a well formulated educational stance can help you to say "yes" to the school policies, instructional practices, committees, and co-curricular duties that are most likely to bring about your vision of life's big lessons.

With the completion of these first two chapters, you will have built a foundation for understanding the nature of teaching and your own vision of education. This foundation will come to life in each of the dimensions of your professional decision making: planning, instruction, assessment, management, and—as the following chapter shows—basing decisions on a solid understanding of your students.

LINKS TO RESEARCH, THEORY, AND PRACTICE

Brann, E. (1979). *Paradoxes of education in a republic.* Chicago: University of Chicago Press.

Chartock, R. K. (2000). *Educational foundations: An anthology.* Upper Saddle River, NJ: Merrill/ Prentice Hall.

Cooper, D. E. (1991). *Authenticity and learning: Nietzsche's educational philosophy.* Brookfield, VT: Gregg Revivals.

Cortes, C. E. (2000). *The children are watching: How the media teach about diversity.* New York: Teachers College Press.

Dewey, J. (1998). My pedagogic creed. In K. Ryan and J. M. Cooper (Eds.), *Kaleidoscope: Readings in education* (8th ed.). Boston: Houghton Mifflin. [Dewey's credo was originally published as a pamphlet in 1897.]

Dillon, J. T. (1987). Unpublished course syllabus for Education 139: Curriculum and Instruction, University of California at Riverside.

Duffy, D. G. (1998, June). Teaching and the balancing of round stones. *Phi Delta Kappan, 79,* 777–80.

Eisner, E. (1979). *The educational imagination: On the design and evaluation of school programs* (3rd ed., pp. 87–107). Upper Saddle River, NJ: Merrill/ Prentice Hall.

Fulghum, R. (1988). *All I really need to know I learned in kindergarten: Uncommon thoughts on common things.* New York: Villard Books.

Gatto J. T. (1992). *Dumbing us down: The hidden curriculum of compulsory schooling.* Philadelphia: New Society Publishers.

Heslep, R. D. (1997). *Philosophical thinking in educational practice.* Westport, CT: Praeger.

hooks, b. (1994). *Teaching to transgress: Education as the practice of freedom.* New York: Routledge.

King, M. L., Jr. (1947). *The purpose of education.* Excerpted in The Papers of Martin Luther King, Jr. *The Martin Luther King, Jr. Papers Project, Stanford University.* Retrieved December 10, 2002, from http://www.stanford.edu/group/King/publications/papers/vol1/470100-The_Purpose_of_Education.htm

Noddings, N. (1995). *Philosophy of education.* Boulder, CO: Westview Press.

Pai, Y., & Adler, S. A. (2001). *Cultural foundations of education.* Upper Saddle River, NJ: Merrill/Prentice Hall.

Prakash, M. S., & Waks, L. J. (1985). Four conceptions of excellence. *Teachers College Record, 87*(1), 79–101.

Sadler, J. E. (1966). *J. A. Comenius and the concept of universal education.* New York: Barnes & Noble.

Spring, J. H. (1994). *Wheels in the head: Educational philosophies of authority, freedom, and culture from Socrates to Paulo Freire.* New York: McGraw-Hill.

Wynne, E. A., & Ryan, K. (1997). *Reclaiming our schools: Teaching character, academics, and discipline* (2nd ed.). Upper Saddle River, NJ: Merrill/Prentice Hall.

WEB SITES

http://kerlins.net/bobbi/research/theorists/
This site includes a timeline of theorists who influenced educational thought. It also contains definitions of key terms in psychology and philosophy and links to sites that allow for greater exploration of those terms.

Theorists & Philosophers
http://people.morehead-st.edu/fs/w.willis/fourtheories.html
This site describes progressivism, perennialism, essentialism, and reconstructionism.

Use the search words "My Philosophy of Education" to search and view philosophies of education students from around the nation.

OPPORTUNITIES TO PRACTICE

1. Four imaginary teachers (each with a different conception of education) are being interviewed. Label each teacher with the appropriate stance from Figure 2.3: technical, rational, personal, or social.

   a. "In my classroom I try to include lots of

   Abigail: "opportunities for kids to choose their own activities. They need to be able to follow their own interests."

   Ben: "resources for kids to learn about current, real-life issues. Then they need experience in addressing those issues."

   Cara: "opportunities for kids to memorize important facts. These facts will help them all their lives!"

   Diego: "chances for kids to think like experts in the field, like artists or scientists, for example."

   b. "You will know children are solving problems in my class when

   Abigail: "they have a clearer view of themselves and use that information to confront challenges. *That's* problem solving!"

   Ben: "they find something that is happening right now in the real world and I see them actually show the heart and courage to do something about it!"

   Cara: "children use their facts to solve more complex exercises. The lightbulbs just glow!"

   Diego: "children use their creativity and logic to solve classical problems or to create something new. You should see what they come up with!"

   c. "Assessment of student learning

   Abigail: "too often interferes with individual students' dignity and sense of self."

   Ben: "is done in groups, with the criteria developed by the students."

   Cara: "is valid only when it is an objective measurement of children's accuracy."

   Diego: "should include student portfolios, in which students display their own style and approach to the subject matter."

   d. "As a teacher, I try hard to

   Abigail: "place the learner at the center of all of my choices. If an activity does not meet my students' individual needs, we do not do it."

   Ben: "put my money where my mouth is. I show commitment to charitable causes."

   Cara: "make it fun for children to learn the skills from the book."

   Diego: "emphasize that the students and I embark on an exciting adventure together."

   e. "My metaphor for teacher is 'teacher as

   Abigail: " 'a lens through which students can better know themselves.' "

   Ben: " 'a spark who can ignite the fire of action for the common good.' "

   Cara: " 'a factory leader who uses resources efficiently for the best product possible.' "

   Diego: " 'a sage who helps students learn to judge performance.' "

Were you drawn toward any cluster of responses from the first exercise? These imaginary statements may provide specific examples to help you pin down your own stance toward education.

Key: Technical: Cara; Rational: Diego; Personal: Abigail; Social: Ben.

2. Stretch your thinking by imagining the implications of different stances on some common issues in classroom teaching. Try to imagine how these different conceptions would play out for the elements listed in Figure 2.4. Note that your own stance provides the final entries in the table. Check back to your row in Figure 2.4 as you read subsequent chapters . . . you may already know the punch lines!

3. Analyze school mission statements, beginning with your own school's statement if one is available. Or go to the Internet and locate some using the search term "school mission statements." Is it possible to place the statement in one of the families of educational thought from Chapter 2? Look for areas of agreement and disagreement with your own stance. Talk with experienced teachers about how mission statements are written and discuss issues such as group consensus, conceptual coherence, and enacting the mission statement.

4. Why does the United States have local control over education? Why do we divide students into chronological age groups at school? Why do we study discrete subject areas? The answers to each of these questions are rooted in history. Spend some time examining the historical context of schooling. Use "history of education" as a search term either in your university's library or on the Internet and examine some of the events that have shaped our current educational practices.

FIGURE 2.4   *Daily implications of conceptions of education.*

	Common Learning Experiences	Prevalent Teaching Methods	Assessment Instruments	Homework Assignments	Expectations for Parents
Technical					
Rational					
Personal					
Social					
My own stance					

5. The circumstances of classroom teaching sometimes present obstacles for enacting one's teaching stance. For instance, you may want students to be the ultimate judges of their work, but you are required to give standardized tests. Use Figure 2.5 to help structure your thinking and to consider how to address potential obstacles. Hint: You will need this chart in Chapter 5.

6. Ask students with whom you work to help you find what is hidden: the implicit and null curriculum. Secondary students are often able to articulate their experience without much prompting. For example, one secondary student told me recently that, through his school's **tracking** practices, he has learned that some kids are smarter than others: different classes for different kids, better teachers for more advanced students. Younger students may respond to more specific questions such as, "How do you know whether you have done a good job at school? What behaviors do teachers like? What have you not learned in school that you would like to learn?" Do you find patterns in students' responses? Is the news good?

FIGURE 2.5 *Enacting my stance toward education.*

	My Convictions	**Possible Obstacles**	**Strategies to Consider**
A good society			
What education (and school) should do			
What everyone should learn			
How I should teach			

Before you begin reading Chapter 3

Warm-Up Exercise for Starting With Students

Engage in a bit of personal introspection by writing an "I am from" poem. There is only one simple rule: Each line must begin with the words "I am from." As you compose your poem, think about all the factors that make you who you are. You may wish to think about features such as your unique qualities, your values, your ethnic heritage, your family experiences, your spiritual identity, significant events, and about your favorites in life. There are no rules about length, rhyme, meter, or sharing it with an audience.

I Am From

Read it aloud. Now reflect on your poem. What new insights (if any) did you gain? Excerpts from some recently composed poems are found at the end of this chapter. As you read them over, look for themes: Who are we? What matters to us? Themes such as immigration experiences, ethnic and national identity, conflict, the importance of family regardless of its structure, and a sense of growth seem to speak clearly. *Now imagine a world where schools knew where we were from and embraced us.*

CHAPTER *Three*

Starting With Students

"The secret in education lies in respecting the student."

—Ralph Waldo Emerson

This chapter is predicated on my belief that who your students are matters deeply to you. It is based on a teacher's moral commitment to honoring each of the people who cross the classroom's threshold every morning. And it is guided by the conviction that when we know and respect our students, we can teach them. To help you *start with the students,* this chapter is organized according to the following five sections:

Students as the Basis for Your Decisions
Learning About Students
Mutual Accommodation
Providing Appropriate Instruction
Locating and Using Resources

STUDENTS AS THE BASIS FOR YOUR DECISIONS

You enter the teaching profession at a time when the demands upon teachers are high. You and your school will be held accountable for students' achievement in some very distinct ways. The pressure that accompanies today's emphasis on **standards-based instruction** and **high-stakes testing** is palpable in some schools I visit today, and I suspect that, given recent federal requirements, you may be observing similar trends . . . wherever you are in the United States.

One of the most important aspects of your job may be the uniting of rigorous academic standards with your individual students. The nation's students evince a vast array of experiences, needs, and strengths. Knowing your students—starting with your students—can help you fulfill the promise of providing **access to the core curriculum** and fostering learning for each student.

Who Are America's Students?

Trends vary by region and by subgroup, but one generalization is that American students are an increasingly diverse group. One in three students nationwide is identified as a minority, and in the most populous states, rates of minority students can be far higher than that, as shown in Fast Facts 3.1.

Fast Facts 3.1

Minority Student Rates in the States With the Most Students

State	Number of Students K–12	Percentage of Students Who Are Minorities
California	6,142,348	63%
Texas	4,059,619	58%
New York	2,882,188	45%
Florida	2,434,821	47%
Illinois	2,048,792	40%

Minority students in these states live primarily in cities, or on the fringes of cities.

Source: U. S. Department of Education, National Center for Education Statistics, Common Core of Data, *Public Elementary/Secondary School Universe Survey, 2000–01* and *State Nonfiscal Survey of Public Elementary/Secondary Education, 2000-01. http://nces.ed.gov/pubs2002/overview/table11.asp*

Fast Facts 3.2

Gifted and Talented Education (GATE) Services in Public K–12 Schools

Programs

Number of states mandating gifted programs: 31

Number of states with discretionary state
support of gifted programs: 16

Gifted Populations

- In one report, half of all states identified between 1% and 5% of their total student population as gifted.

- The percentage of the total state student population identified as gifted and talented ranged from 1% to 15%.

Source: Council of State Directors of Programs for the Gifted, The 1994 and 1996 State of the States Gifted and Talented Education Reports. Reported by the National Center for Educational Statistics. *http://nces.ed.gov/pubs2002/ digest2001/tables/dt054.asp*

Some of your students may also be identified as **gifted** and may receive Gifted and Talented Education (GATE) program services. Although intelligence is increasingly being conceived of as a multidimensional construct, many states use traditional intelligence tests to qualify students for GATE programs. Fast Facts 3.2 shows that most states offer GATE programs and that a small percentage of our nation's students are identified as gifted and receive special services.

Chances are, you will also be working with students who have identified disabilities, or special needs. That is because approximately 13% of all of America's students are so identified, and about half of students with special needs spend a good portion of their school day in **general education** classrooms. By far the most prevalent disabilities are **specific learning disabilities** and **speech or language disorders.** Students with specific learning disabilities have adequate cognitive functioning, learn some skills well, and struggle in one or more others. For instance, I might learn mathematics with ease but struggle greatly with reading text. Students with speech or language disorders have trouble processing the language they hear or producing oral messages.

Your work will be made more complex and interesting by the fact that students display not just one type of characteristic, but overlapping characteristics and needs. That is, it would not be unusual for you to work with a student who

Students in the United States bring complex constellations of characteristics to the classroom.

Fast Facts 3.3

When it Comes to How Well Prepared Teachers Feel About Working With Students, Did You Know That . . .

. . . teachers feel best prepared to maintain discipline and control?

. . . teachers feel least prepared to address the needs of students with diverse cultural or linguistic backgrounds?

	Percent Feeling Well Prepared	Percent Feeling Not At All Prepared
maintain order and discipline in the classroom	71	1
address the needs of students with limited English proficiency or diverse cultural backgrounds	20	17

Source: U.S. Department of Education, National Center for Education Statistics, Fast Response Survey System, Teacher Survey on Professional Development and Training, FRSS 65, 1998. http://nces.ed.gov/quicktables/Detail.asp?Key=272

Fast Facts 3.4

Conflicting Opinions?

What percentage of secondary teachers and students strongly agree that . . .

	Percentage of *Teachers* Who Strongly Agreed	Percentage of *Students* Who Strongly Agreed
. . . Teachers are interested in what's best for the students?	50	24
. . . Teachers think about students as individuals and not as part of some group?	44	20
. . . Teachers respect all their students?	33	18
. . . Teachers know a lot about students' community or neighborhood?	47	9

Source: The Metlife Survey of the American Teacher. Student life: School, Home and Community. New York. (2002). Metropolitan Life Insurance Company. Downloaded from http://www.metlife.com/Applications/Corporate/WPS/CDA/PageGenerator/0,1674,P2817,00.html

meets the federal classification of "minority," is identified as gifted, and who exhibits a specific learning need. Additionally, students vary in terms of their gender, their family structure, their academic interests and development, their learning preferences, and their background experiences. For all these reasons, you can expect to be greeted with wonderfully complex constellations of learners.

Though such diversity can bring richness to the learning community, it also requires thorough preparation and diligent ongoing professional development so that teachers can encourage learning for all. Whereas teachers in one national survey felt very well prepared to maintain classroom discipline, they felt least prepared to meet the needs of learners from diverse cultural and language backgrounds, as Fast Fact 3.3 shows.

What Difference Does Diversity Make?

Teachers worry, with good reason, about meeting students' needs. A convincing body of research indicates that despite many teachers' good intentions and caring natures, typical schooling practices tend to parallel larger patterns of societal injustice. Race, ethnicity, and poverty, for example, have direct effects on students' schooling experiences. For instance, if you are a child whose family is minority or low income (and the two descriptors often are linked in the United States), you will be less likely to (National Center for Education Statistics, 2002):

- have a science center in your kindergarten classroom
- use the Internet at school
- be in a reduced-size class (despite the fact the minority and low-income students benefit the most from lower class sizes)
- have teachers with high expectations for your success (Harris Interactive, 2001)
- receive high quality instruction (Cole, 1995; Harris Interactive, 2001)
- perform well on standardized tests (Kohn, 1999)
- attend a well-funded school (Cole, 1995)

Differences in educational experiences based on students' gender and culture are also well documented in the literature (e.g., Cole, 1995; Kohn, 1999). First, for instance, teachers tend to unknowingly favor boys and encourage their achievement while they encourage girls' compliant behavior (Wellesley College Center for Research on Women, 1992). Also, classroom structures reflect the interests of the dominant culture, sometimes making them unfriendly places for students from cultures other than the dominant culture (Nieto, 1996; Pai & Adler, 2001).

These findings seem to suggest that we, as a nation, have not entirely succeeded in starting with our students. Take a look at Fast Fact 3.4 for junior and senior high school students' and teachers' perceptions of teachers' thoughts on students. You and I are not in charge of changing the whole world . . . but we can almost certainly improve life and learning within our own local realm. Perhaps study of the poem you composed a bit ago and those found at this chapter's close reaffirm for you that all of us have unique experiences that factor into who we are, and we each have commonalties that make us members of certain groups. Each of us is a dynamic product of the many painful and sweet experiences life has to offer. Recognizing that many students face a variety of conditions outside of their control that directly enhance or impede their success is a good first step in starting with students. A next step is to learn about our specific learners.

LEARNING ABOUT STUDENTS

Learning about students and their families includes questioning our assumptions and gathering information.

Questioning Assumptions

Ronald, one of my middle school students, was struggling with medical and home-life issues, so I made a special point to make personal contact with him during class each day, to look him in the eye and converse with him about his life. At a conference a few months into the school year, his mother told me that Ronald *hated* my daily conversations. The shock and discomfort I still feel in recounting Ronald's episode reflect the extent of my surprise in discovering what a horrible job I had done in discovering my student's actual needs and preferences. My assumptions about what I thought would be right for my student were deeply rooted and unquestioned. I *assumed* that my effort to engage him personally would be a good and helpful thing. In Ronald's experience, my personal interest was anything *but* helpful. Ronald taught me a difficult yet productive lesson about working with others: Question assumptions.

Part of our intelligence as humans stems from our ability to draw inferences from experience: We attach meaning to sensory data. Because we can draw inferences, we can learn and we can act, even when given only limited information. Unfortunately, when inferences are based on limited information and assumptions about people's physical conditions, character, or home life, we run the risk of making faulty and counterproductive decisions. Instead, we need to realize that our assumptions may be incorrect and that we can sensitively collect information to enrich or replace our original faulty information.

As an example, one prevalent faulty assumption is that parents—especially those of certain groups of students such as students of color—just do not care about their students' progress or teachers' efforts. Educators' work is so difficult that it is easy to see why some may become discouraged. However, the research on parent participation indicates solidly that parents in different ethnic groups *do care* about education and their students' success. One example is the work of Valencia and Block (2002), who review many studies documenting Mexican American families' participation in schools and the value they place on education. Fast Facts 3.5 gives another such example.

How do we go about gathering information about our students? We first commit to admitting that our own knowledge is necessarily limited and to asking, in gentle and respectful ways, questions that will help us learn.

Fast Facts 3.5

What Is the Most Important Issue Facing Your Community?

When surveyed, members of the three largest ethnic or racial groups in America said . . .

		Percent Citing Issue
Education	African Americans	45%
Education	Hispanics	36%
Education	Asian Americans	29%

Source: Cole (1995), reporting a survey conducted in 1993 by Market Segment Research.

> *T*each thy tongue to say "I do not know," and thou shalt progress.
>
> —*Maimonides*

WHAT ELSE?

Try this: When you are tempted to draw a conclusion, try listing several alternative explanations for what you see. Try asking students to do the same. It can help them learn to take other perspectives.

Here is one for practice: Your teammate did not get you the list of readings your students are to finish by next month. One explanation: She purposely sabotaged your students so hers will look better. What else might explain it? She forgot. What else? She put it in the wrong mailbox. What else? It's at the bottom of your stack of mail.

Gathering Information

Experts (e.g., Horgan, 1995) offer general approaches for teachers to gather systematic information about their particular students. Grant and Sleeter (1998), for example, suggest that teachers explore the home community and interpersonal communication styles. Similarly, Kottler (1997) argues that teachers often expect to function as junior psychologists. Armed with theories of learning and development, we are prepared to look into the minds of students to teach what we think they should know. He suggests an additional role for us: Teaching as if we are anthropologists. As anthropologists, we would focus not so much on individual motivations as on people's cultural practices, on the knowledge base they share with others in their group that guides their thoughts, feelings, and actions. Kottler (1997, p. 98) urges us as anthropologists to address a number of questions, all of which help us challenge our assumptions:

- What is it about where this student comes from that leads him or her to respond to others they way he or she does?
- What is it that I do not know or understand about this child's background that might help me make sense of what is happening?
- How might I investigate further the customs of this child's family?
- What are the interactive effects of having so many cultures represented in this classroom?
- How are my cultural values and biases getting in the way of honoring those among my students who are different from what I am used to?

In addition to attending to issues of culture, you will want to gather information on students' **learning styles** and preferences. Nieto (1996, p. 374) recommends, for instance, that teachers ask for instructional feedback from students: "What do they like? What do they dislike? How would they change the classroom? the materials? What would they do to make it more interesting to them?" Students can provide this information anonymously in writing, or they may be open to responding to small-group or individual interviews. Figure 3.1 contains background information on learning styles and provides some suggestions for assessing them.

Other techniques for gathering information include some of the assessment strategies addressed in Chapter 7. Examples include:

- Attitude surveys ("Please rank subjects in order of your preference.")
- Interviews ("Bring in an object that represents your family and be ready to tell us about it.")

ANDREA:	"If there was one thing you wish your teachers knew about you, what would it be?"
ALEX (14):	"That I have a life."

FIGURE 3.1   *Learning styles: What are they? How do I know? How do they help?*

What Are Learning Styles?

Learning styles refers to the ways in which individuals perceive, process, store, and retrieve information (Grant & Sleeter, 1998). Individuals' responses to educational experiences tend to fall into consistent, stable patterns that reflect differences in cognitive, affective, and physical styles of response (Bennett, 1995). In plain language, learning styles are the activity preferences students pursue when given the choice. Learning styles are conceptualized in different ways, as summarized by Bennett:

1. *Field dependence versus field independence.* Learners vary in their ability to separate information from the background in which it is embedded. Field-independent learners tend to be intrinsically motivated, good at analytical thought, and individualistic. Field-dependent learners rely more on extrinsic motivation, are attuned to the social environment, are poor at analytical problem solving, and use global perception.

2. *High versus low structure requirements.* Students who require low external structuring of their time and tasks rely on themselves to organize their materials and time. They need few directions from a teacher and can handle long-term assignments without much support. Students who require greater structure need more frequent direction and feedback from the teacher. They need help in organizing time and materials and need support in assuming self-responsibility.

3. *Perceptual modalities.* Modalities are the ways in which students perceive input. Four modalities include visualization, written words, listening, and activities. Students are thought to learn best when input matches their preferred modality.

4. *Learning style inventory.* Dunn and Dunn's inventory (reviewed in Dunn, 1990) focuses on five kinds of stimuli: the immediate environment, the student's emotionality, the learner's preference for group size, the learner's physiological characteristics, and the learner's cognitive processing inclinations.

How Do I Know?

Once you select a scheme (e.g., one of Bennett's four schemes), discover your students' learning styles through two general strategies. First, ask them specific questions about the ways in which they prefer to learn. Second, give them choices and observe their selections in action. The references from this figure present observation guides that can be used, but some students' choices are clear enough for you to devise your own check sheets. For instance, you can allow students to work alone or with partners or small groups and then tally students' choices as they work. You can also record how many and which students come to you to receive additional directions while others keep working.

How Do They Help?

Bennett (1995) presents convincing arguments for considering learning styles:

- Learning styles allow us to pinpoint student differences when students struggle to learn. This information can be particularly helpful to secondary school teachers who have less time to get to know their many students.
- By placing emphasis on *how* students learn, we assume that students *can* learn.
- Learning styles encourage educational equity by reminding teachers that we may not reach our learners if we teach only in the ways we ourselves learn and that differences are not the same as deficits.

Caveats

Research has not clearly demonstrated that teaching according to students' preferences positively affects their learning. Further, although culture appears to play some role in learning preferences, you run the risk of overgeneralizing and stereotyping if you rely on group generalizations rather than gathering information about your particular students' learning preferences. Perhaps the primary strengths of the notion of learning styles is that they remind teachers to

- Question assumptions about how people learn
- Provide rich and varied input
- Provide students with meaningful choices

FIGURE 3.2 *Understanding a student through observation.*

Source: Pat Keig, California State University, Fullerton. Used with permission.

1. Select a student who does not immediately attract notice. This student may quietly pass the days without much demand for your attention.
2. Unobtrusively observe the student for a sustained period of time. Better yet, select varied times over the course of several days.
3. Take notes that describe the student's behavior:
   a. What does this student care about?

   b. Does this student show discomfort or fear? Of what?

   c. Does he have any skills or behaviors for avoiding notice?

   d. Does he initiate contact with peers? Which ones? How do they respond?

   e. How does he interact with the content? Is he on task? What evidence is there that he understands?

4. Analyze your observations:
   a. Would this student be learning more if he were more actively engaged?

   b. What forms of active engagement can you use that might show this student that you are teaching him as well as others?

   c. In what ways is this student exceptional?

   d. What could you do to get to know the student better?

- Journal entries ("What is the best thing that happened in class this week?")
- Drawings and diagrams ("Draw a picture of yourself studying biology.")
- Teacher observations

A sample classroom observation intended to surface facets of a single student's style and interactions is found in Figure 3.2. It may help you to gain information about a student whose particular strengths and struggles may otherwise go unnoticed. Keep your eyes open for experienced teachers' methods of getting to know students. Some use lunch with the students, home visits (e.g., Faltis, 2001) and community social events. When my son Zachary was in first grade, his teacher came to watch one of his soccer games. In addition to these strategies for learning about students, teachers may learn much about students by simply listening to their stories and perspectives (e.g., Thorson, 2003).

MUTUAL ACCOMMODATION

Part of starting with the students is perceiving students in terms of the contributions they can make to your classroom. Starting with the students means that you view each student as an individual with personal experiences and qualities that will enrich students' learning and your own experience.

Look one more time at your stance toward education. Does it mention equity? Equal opportunity? Development for all toward full potential? If so, then the prevalent attitude that certain students are deficient and need to adapt is not enough for you. Professional educators see learning as a shared responsibility. Certainly students and their families have responsibilities for fostering learning, but they are not alone. Teachers and schools, too, have a responsibility to grow and change to meet students' needs.

Starting with the students means that you must adjust for your learners and provide, in Nieto's (1996) words, **mutual accommodation.** When you watch a student struggle, ask yourself, "What can I do better to help the student learn?" I urge you to respond to this question in many ways and at different levels. Figure 3.3 suggests some strategies you can employ as a professional educator to meet your learners' needs. Notice that these strategies focus on several avenues: improving your knowledge of students and forging tighter connections with their community, gaining professional knowledge and skills, and providing meaningful curriculum and responsive instruction.

PROVIDING APPROPRIATE INSTRUCTION

Meeting students' needs within the confines of a classroom setting is challenging, especially given the multiple demands placed on you and the pressure of a tight time schedule.

A first step in providing appropriate instruction is knowing the legal rights that your students have. Federal and state legislation provides a number of protections for your students. Figure 1.2 provided a summary of some of these protections. Further, students with identified special needs are granted the right to a free and appropriate education in the least restrictive environment via the Individuals with Disabilities Education Act (IDEA). If you have students with identified special needs in your class, you will serve as an important part of a team of professionals who work to meet those students' educational needs. Your **English learners** (students who are acquiring English in addition to the home language), similarly, have federal rights to equal access to education. Do some research now on how federal and state legislation regarding students' needs is implemented in your locale.

Another key step in providing appropriate instruction is to treat students as individuals. Though this may seem obvious, many teachers proudly proclaim that their goal is to *treat everyone the same.* The danger in treating the students the same, according to Grant (1995), lies in the fact that it does not enhance students' learning about themselves as members of many groups. Look back at the poems at this chapter's close. The poets show their memberships in ethnic, pop-cultural, national, spiritual, and family groups. Grant (1995, p. 10) urges: "The individual diversity and humanness that each and every student brings to school must be accepted and affirmed. Those who tend to see (or want to see) every group, and every member of that group, as the same, miss or deny the beauty of human diversity and variety."

Although all students deserve high expectations and deserve to be treated fairly and with respect, different students need different things. Teachers' emphasis on sameness often translates to their classroom practice. Research indicates that, in the vast majority of general education classrooms, students are indeed treated *the same.* Students pursue the *same* objectives using the *same* activities at the *same* pace and demonstrate their knowledge using the *same* assessment. According to Cole (1995, p. 12), "Instead of being presented in a variety of modes, instruction in U.S. schools tends to be abstract, barren of application, overly sequential, and redundant."

Two opposing themes become clear: Statistics cited earlier in this chapter indicate that students have very different experiences in school based on certain

*W*hether we speak of traditional democratic ideals of equality, equity, and opportunity or of the emergent democratic ideals of empowerment and emancipation as the conscious and purposeful outcomes of schooling, we must face the critical reality of our own cultural experience and bias. . . . Our personal blindness to the traditions of cultures other than our own binds us to convention, to the belief that there is one standard of conduct for all.

—*Hoover and Kindsvatter (1997, p. 67)*

FIGURE 3.3 *Strategies for mutual accommodation.*

Assess the students' needs and interests	1. Gather information from the students: • Interviews • Observations • Informal conversations • Interest and attitude surveys • Journal entries 2. Gather information from the family. Treat parents as experts on their children: • Beginning-of-the-year survey or conversations on students' prior experiences, hopes, and goals • Informal conferences and telephone conversations throughout the year 3. Check information gathered by the school: • Previous formal testing results • Previous successes
Provide a meaningful curriculum that incorporates aspects of the life of the children	1. Use materials and topics of interest to the students. 2. Use problem-centered approaches. 3. Provide opportunities for student choice in what and how they study.
Make classroom adjustments for student differences	1. Watch and listen carefully to determine necessary physical and temporal modifications. 2. Trust students when they tell you about their needs. 3. Alter the physical setting to encourage success. Many physical modifications require a bit of resourceful thinking but are not expensive or difficult. For instance, students who are left-handed cannot see a handwriting model on the left side of the page because their hands block it as they write. Tape two pages together so that a second model appears on the right.
Build your own knowledge and skills	1. Gain information about your students' life experiences. Some strategies include the following: • Read about their cultures. • Tour their community if you are not a member of it. • Listen to music that is popular with them. • If you work with young children, study the action figure and doll aisles at the toy store. • Watch their cartoons and favorite television programs. You need not be one of the students, but understanding what is important to them will help you teach them better. 2. Read the professional literature. 3. Ask expert teachers for strategies. 4. Seek out additional training opportunities.
Build connections to the home and the community	1. Invite parents or other family members to school and provide a range of activities for participation. Expect that some parents will bring younger siblings. Suggestions for participation include the following: • Guest lessons • Read alouds • One-on-one instruction • Materials preparation and clerical assistance • Room environment assistance (e.g., with pets or special centers) 2. Include other means for families to participate in school as well, such as picnics, garden projects, and field trips. 3. Send home a classroom newsletter or email, in more than one language if necessary. Be sure to include students' work and a brag section that over time mentions good news about every student. 4. Contact each family (by phone, note, or in person) with good news at least once during each grading period.

Teaching Tips

WHEN SPEAKING AND THINKING ABOUT STUDENTS, PUT THE PERSON FIRST
For example, "I am thinking of my student with ADHD," not "She's my ADHD student." Putting the exceptionality second staves off the tendency to define a person entirely in terms of a single exceptionality. (ADHD stands for Attention Deficit Hyperactivity Disorder.) (Established by the Individuals with Disabilities Education Act, 1990)

of their characteristics. However, those outcomes are usually the result of insidious, long-term exposure to a hidden curriculum that reinforces differential expectations and maintains inequities. The overt curriculum is different. Through its objectives, materials, assessments, and instructional methodologies, the explicit curriculum tends to be a univocal one.

Treating each student the same can thus be inherently unfair. You can meet individual needs best if you have many instructional strategies in your repertoire, build an enriched learning environment, provide for student choice, and use ongoing assessment of each student's progress. To meet the needs of your students, you need to accomplish both big things that take much time (for instance, develop a range of assignments and activities for a single outcome, learn new instructional strategies, set long-range goals, or change your interactional style for particular students) and smaller things that can be implemented quickly (for instance, shorten homework assignments for those who take more time or move a student toward a helpful peer).

Figure 3.4 gives you a preview of Chapter 5 (Advice on Instruction: COME IN) as it relates to starting with students. The figure presents strategies related to six guidelines for instruction (Connecting to the life the learner, Organizing instruction, Modeling, Enriching learning, Interacting, and considering human Nature and Needs). The figure is meant to serve as a resource, not as a prescriptive list to be memorized, that can support you as you begin to think about providing instruction that meets a variety of student needs.

A promising integrated approach to providing instruction based on students' needs and interests is **differentiated instruction** (Tomlinson, 2001). Teachers who use this approach gather and use frequent assessment data to understand their students and then build instruction based on the conviction that students learn differently and have different needs. In Tomlinson's words:

> [I]n a differentiated classroom, the teacher proactively plans and carries out varied approaches to content, process, and product in anticipation and response to student differences in readiness, interest, and learning needs. (p. 7)

In a differentiated classroom, the class might start out by asking questions about the topic under study, pursuing different kinds of learning activities to address those questions (for instance, some may conduct interviews of experts while others read and others conduct Internet research), then come back together to share results before splitting again to refine their studies and prepare for presentations on their learning. Individual, small group, and whole class instruction are utilized. Wormeli (2001) provides vivid examples of differentiated instruction in middle school.

Differentiating instruction is hard work. It runs contrary to what most of us have experienced in classrooms, and it is not yet a prevalent model. I introduce it here, early in our travels together, to remind us both that classroom instruction can indeed start with the students and engage them in rich and meaningful ways. As you watch experienced teachers and work in their classrooms,

FIGURE 3.4 *Providing appropriate instruction for learner diversity.*

Connect to the life of the learner	• Build a cooperative community. Encourage student interactions through a variety of heterogeneous small groups and larger groups. • Increase your own knowledge about things valued by your students. • Include students' voices and choices. • Use attitude surveys to determine students' interests and preferences. • Listen and respond to students' stories. • To the extent possible, select content that has immediate usefulness or interest. One strategy is to begin with real-world events. • Be explicit in showing how the content is useful today and will be useful later as well. • Assess students' background experiences, being certain to tap into the cultural aspects of those experiences. • Expect that students have relevant experiences and bring those experiences to the surface during your instruction. • Be willing to spend time with your students out of class to develop connections. Some teachers, for example, attend their students' sporting events. • Invite students to bring in artifacts (photographs, letters, and awards) that represent their broader realms of competence. • Provide opportunities for students to think about their thinking through journals and informal discussions. • Send home projects that students can complete with their families. Popular examples include "book in a bag," in which teachers send works of children's literature home for parents and children to read and respond to together, and science activities with simple materials. These projects have proven successful even with parents who do not read.
Organize your instruction	• Study the content carefully and analyze each of its components so that you can adjust your instruction in response to student understanding. **Task analyze** the concepts and skills you expect students to learn by breaking tasks into their components and considering prerequisite knowledge. • Be prepared to present information in a variety of formats to accommodate students' learning preferences. • Use predictable organizational patterns for your instruction, and draw students' attention to those patterns. • For students who need explicit structure, teach your directions for activities explicitly and check for understanding of those directions. Review the teaching tips in Chapter 5 for some pointers on providing clear directions. • Use charts and previews to make the organization of the lesson and the classroom itself very clear to the learner. • Use highly organized instructional strategies for students who have difficulty with a barrage of environmental stimuli. Direct instruction is one suggestion. • Keep the learning environment orderly, safe, and structured. • Teach self-management skills for students who need help in organizing their own time and behaviors.
Model	• Most importantly, model your respect for human dignity. Through your words and interactions, model your care for each student and your expectation that learners will respect and care for each other. • Model careful listening. • Model thinking processes. For instance, help learners find the main idea in a reading passage by thinking aloud as you find the main idea. • Use repeated and simplified models for students who are in the early stages of acquiring English. Students with developmental differences may benefit from clear modeling as well. • Use student models in small groups. • Model often for students who rely less on auditory or written explanations.

continued

FIGURE 3.4   Continued

Enrich (see more ideas in Figure 5.6)	• Begin with meaningful problems. Allow students to select issues or topics that are relevant, either to individuals or to the class. • Teach for understanding, not purely rote recall. Teach a limited number of ideas well by developing them thoroughly. • Use more than one form of input. Use auditory, visual, and tactile input to increase students' chances to form ideas. • Build background knowledge and a common knowledge base by providing real examples of concepts under study. • Use concrete materials to present and reinforce concepts. Examples include using mathematics manipulatives such as bean sticks and fraction bars. • Use visual displays to support auditory input. • When you use inquiry strategies, be prepared to vary the focus from broad to narrow in response to student needs. Some students may need help in structuring their investigations by studying a limited number of variables. • Use community resources that are valued by the students, perhaps including family visitations and contributions. • Provide within-class and out-of-class opportunities for independent study. • Do not equate sticking to the basics with parched learning environments. All learners deserve rich learning opportunities.
Interact	• Select your instructional strategies so that they foster student–student interactions and teacher–student interactions. Figure 5.3 describes active participation devices. • Monitor students' progress in the lesson carefully and provide specific feedback through verbal and nonverbal messages. • Expect different levels of interaction to be appropriate for different students. For example, new English learners should not be expected to produce lengthy English responses, especially in public. • Pair students so that they can help each other. Vary partner arrangements so that all learners have opportunities to work with different members of the class. For instance, English learners can work with fluent English models and with students who use the same language. • Use cross-age and peer tutoring and invite volunteers to work with individuals. • Allow for student choice throughout the lesson. • Use what you know about learning styles to provide a variety of learning experiences. • Provide opportunities for students to evaluate your teaching and their learning. • Capitalize on interactions to provide ongoing assessment information about students' progress in the cognitive, social, and physical realms.
Consider human **n**ature and developmental **n**eeds	• Observe students carefully and ask students and their families about the physical and environmental conditions that will best support their learning. • Expect to see interstudent and intrastudent differences in physical, cognitive, social, and language development. • Expect that different students will have different requirements for physical space and proximity, noise, and other conditions. Arrange your classroom to include places where students can escape the crowd. • Take learners' physical and mental conditions into consideration. For instance, will your student tire easily? Become distracted by peers? Structure your classroom and instruction to foster students' success. • Build-in opportunities for immediate success. For instance, if you have students who speak no English, provide them with opportunities to quickly master facts and skills. One example is flash cards with color words or math facts. Emphasis on quickly mastered facts and skills accomplishes three things: (1) it establishes that you have learning expectations for all students, (2) it establishes an immediate record of success, and (3) it builds a foundation for concepts and principles for later instruction. • Be prepared to extend or simplify your input and provide regular changes in activities. • Provide lessons that allow for physical movement and that use music and the visual arts.

Interactions with a variety of materials and people can help address students' learning needs.

look for ways in which they differentiate instruction, and be thinking about ways to extend that differentiation even more deeply.

Linguistic diversity is prevalent and on the rise. Many students are working to acquire English as they are also learning school subject matter. **Sheltered instruction** (or Specially Designed Academic Instruction in English) is aimed at making content accessible to English language learners by providing "a refuge from the linguistic demands of mainstream instruction" (Echevarria & Graves, 1998, p. 54). Sheltered instruction addresses grade-level curriculum but makes it accessible by focusing meaningfully on a small number of key concepts, providing an enriched learning environment, embedding information in context, and modifying oral and printed language. Echevarria and Graves's suggestions for providing sheltered instruction in the content areas are given in Figure 3.5. Again, meeting the needs of English learners will take extensive study and practice.

Gender is another student difference that, in our society, tends to limit the range of options available to students. In subtle ways, despite efforts to be fair, schools treat male and female children differently in ways that limit members of both groups. For instance, boys are criticized and referred for special education more often than girls. Girls are often praised for behavior but are less often encouraged to meet high academic expectations. Even the best-intentioned teachers can unwittingly encourage these differences. Horgan (1995) provides a comprehensive set of strategies for teachers who strive to create a better learning environment. Figure 3.6 is an adaptation of some of Horgan's strategies.

Clearly, each of these areas of providing appropriate instruction will require deep and sustained inquiry and practice. I introduce them here for two reasons. First, I hope to help you build an initial awareness and a limited repertoire of strategies to use now, in your early days as a professional. More importantly, I introduce them in the hope of helping you to build a mind-set that is very different from what may exist currently for many teachers. Your students' learning needs related to gender, giftedness, exceptionality, language, or culture are not layered upon those of their "regular" (what's that?) needs. You build instruction from the ground up that supports the variety of needs that each of your students possesses.

FIGURE 3.5 *Sheltering content instruction.*

Source: Adapted from Echevarria & Graves, 1998

Planning

Sheltered instruction begins with a vision of what content is to be taught to all, most, and some students. Thematic approaches to sheltered unit planning make material more understandable because the theme, woven across the curriculum, creates ties to hold the material together. Academic learning time should be the first priority in planning for time management for sheltered instruction.

Sheltered Approaches

1. *Provide a positive affective environment,* including frequent positive reinforcement for legitimate success.
2. *Focus instruction on a few key concepts.* Develop meaning for those concepts.
3. *Display and preview key concepts.*
4. *Introduce and display key vocabulary terms,* balancing explicit instruction with contextual presentation.
5. *Keep the activities focused on students.* Activities should be relevant and purposeful.
6. *Provide for high levels of student interaction,* which allows for meaningful language practice.
7. *Embed material in context.* Suggestions include **realia**, graphs, word banks, manipulatives, bulletin boards, multimedia, overhead projector slides, maps, demonstrations, commercially prepared pictures, teacher- and student-prepared pictures, and time lines.
8. *Make explicit connections to background knowledge,* including prior experiences and cultural background.
9. *Use real-life activities.* (Examples include conducting surveys and writing letters to a real audience.)
10. *Reduce the linguistic load of your speech.* Use slower but natural speech. Enunciate. Use shorter sentences with simpler syntax. Pause between phrases. (Try counting two seconds.) Use consistent vocabulary and appropriate repetition. Use extralinguistic cues such as gestures and body language to support your verbal message.
11. *Adapt text materials.* Outline the text. Use live demonstrations of text information. Rewrite the text. Use alternative books. Provide graphic depiction of ideas (e.g., Venn diagrams, semantic maps). Provide audiotapes of the text.

FIGURE 3.6 *Strategies for achieving gender equity.*

Source: Adapted from Horgan, 1995

1. *Study your classroom to assess your own gender biases.* Check the physical environment, activities, feedback received by students, classroom management, and classroom interactions, including praise and criticism, to ensure that opportunities and the messages children receive for their efforts and behaviors do not vary based on gender.
2. *Foster students' willingness to take risks and their ability to set goals.* When students set their own goals, they are more apt to feel ownership and the sense that goals are achievable. Focus on learning goals (not performance goals) to encourage intrinsic motivation and include intermediate as well as long-term goals.
3. *Teach students to value their successes and learn from their mistakes.* Classroom activities should encourage legitimate success . . . but not 100% of the time. Students need to be challenged to move forward.
4. *Provide good feedback.* Good feedback (a) focuses students on the relevant aspects of the problem, (b) gives information not just about outcomes but also about processes, (c) challenges incorrect conclusions, and (d) corrects students' flawed self-assessment.
5. *Send positive messages.* Refrain from sending the message that you do not expect success from some students. Keep expectations for learning high and guard against using excessive praise for substandard performance.
6. *Encourage appropriate attributions.* Help students explain success and failure in appropriate ways by linking their performance with their effort, by encouraging internal explanations for success, and by emphasizing specific and temporary explanations for failure. Help students focus on making choices and exercising control.
7. *Challenge stereotypes.* In neutral settings, ask students to think about common stereotypes. Address stereotypes found in the media. Challenge your own stereotypes, too. Model gender-neutral language and behavior. Be careful to value both typically masculine and typically feminine perspectives and activities.
8. *Use groups flexibly.* Do you have a boys' line and a girls' line? Integrate classroom activities. Use flexible groups in which you vary groups' compositions frequently. Encourage children to work well within a variety of settings. Monitor students' interactions and intervene for support.
9. *Teach the null curriculum.* Include readings and other activities that address the contributions of women.

LOCATING AND USING RESOURCES

When professionals in every domain respond to help their clients, they use every resource at their disposal. They consult other experts, they read professional literature, they attend conferences, and they seek to improve their own skills in service of their clients. Although you may be the lone adult in your classroom, you, too, are part of a professional team that is responsible for a group of clients. The resources at your disposal are many and varied, as shown in Figure 3.7.

New teachers are often awestruck by the rich resources experienced teachers have at their fingertips. You, too, will have a large store of professional knowledge and materials if you begin now to investigate the resources available to you. In doing so, you will be in a better position to serve as an advocate for each of your students.

PARTING WORDS

Did I say teaching looks easy . . . from the outside? Addressing the wide range and variety of student needs is one of the most challenging aspects of classroom teaching today. Teachers who are committed to student success run the risk of growing tired as they help struggle to meet so many demands. One way

FIGURE 3.7 *Professional resources for responding to students' needs.*

Classroom resources	• Print sources, including newspapers, magazines, menus, and books of varied reading levels, genres, topics, and languages • Concrete materials for teaching mathematics including objects such as shells or buttons for counting and sorting, tools for measurement, yarn for estimation, and base-10 blocks for teaching place value • Technological resources for aiding in content development and communication: computers for instruction, word processing, and information gathering; calculators for problem solving and computation • Real materials that students may otherwise not see: animal bones, machines to take apart, spider castings, and clothing from around the world • Study aids: audiotape players, cardboard carrels, and headsets
Personnel resources	• Experienced teachers on staff • Administrators • Specialists, including bilingual educators or coordinators, counselors, school psychologists, and special education teachers • Parents and other family members • Community members who wish to contribute to education by volunteering time or services • Educational researchers with expertise in your area of concern
Service resources	• Computer laboratory facilities • Speech and language services • Psychological support through counselors or other services • Special education services for those who qualify • Medical, dental, vision, and hearing services available through outside agencies • Clothing and food services through charitable organizations
Professional resources	• Electronic resources • Professional journals, often found in the school's professional library • University libraries • Professional organizations (for both teachers and groups with particular needs) • University courses or other workshops to provide specialized training

> **O**ne man with courage makes a majority.
>
> *—Attributed to Andrew Jackson*

to avoid premature burnout is to develop an integrated approach to serving students with different needs (Faltis, 2001). If your room environment, your curriculum, your instruction and interactions, and your assessment strategies all respect the dignity of the human experience, adding new strategies and resources to your room will be less overwhelming. It also helps to remember the scope of your duties as a professional. You *must* do your best, but *all* you can do is your best. Your job is to ensure that all your students have a teacher who:

- Values students as people
- Knows them as learners
- Has high expectations for their success
- Questions her or his own biases and assumptions
- Provides meaningful instruction that meets their needs
- Uses every available resource to the benefit of the students
- Continues to grow and learn as a professional

LINKS TO RESEARCH, THEORY, AND PRACTICE

Bennett, C. I. (1995). *Comprehensive multicultural education: Theory and practice* (3rd ed.). Boston: Allyn & Bacon.

Campbell, D. E. (1996). *Choosing democracy: A practical guide to multicultural education.* Upper Saddle River, NJ: Merrill/Prentice Hall.

Cole, R. W. (Ed.). (1995). *Educating everybody's children: Diverse teaching strategies for diverse learners. What research and practice say about improving achievement.* Alexandria, VA: Association for Supervision and Curriculum Development.

Delpit, L. (1995). *Other people's children: Cultural conflict in the classroom.* New York: New Press.

Dunn, R. (1990). Understanding the Dunn and Dunn Learning Styles Model and the need for individual diagnosis and prescription. *Journal of Reading, Writing, and Learning Disabilities International, 6,* 223–247.

Echevarria, J., & Graves, A. (1998). *Sheltered content instruction: Teaching English-language learners with diverse abilities.* Boston: Allyn & Bacon.

Faltis, C. (2001). *Joinfostering: Teaching and learning in multilingual classrooms* (3rd ed.). Upper Saddle River, NJ: Merrill/Prentice Hall.

Grant, C. A. (Ed.). (1995). *Educating for diversity: An anthology of multicultural voices.* Boston: Allyn & Bacon.

Grant, C. A., & Sleeter, C. E. (1998). *Turning on learning: Five approaches for multicultural teaching plans for race, class, gender, and disability* (2nd ed.). Upper Saddle River, NJ: Merrill/Prentice Hall.

Guillaume, A. M., Zuniga, C., & Yee, I. (1998). What difference does preparation make? Educating preservice teachers for learner diversity. In M. E. Dilworth (Ed.), *Being responsive to cultural differences: How teachers learn* (pp. 143–159). Thousand Oaks, CA: Corwin Press.

Hammeken, P. A. (1997). *Inclusion, 450 strategies for success: A practical guide for all educators who teach students with disabilities.* Minnetonka, MN: Peytral Publications.

Harris Interactive. (2001). *Key elements of quality schools: A survey of teachers, students, and principles. The MetLife Survey of the American Teacher.* Available from MetLife Web site, http://www.metlife.com./ Applications/Corporate/ WPS/CDA/PageGenerator /0,1674,P2817,00.html.

Herrell, A. L. (2000). *Fifty strategies for teaching English language learners.* Upper Saddle River, NJ: Merrill/Prentice Hall.

Hoover, R. L., & Kindsvatter, R. (1997). *Democratic discipline: Foundation and practice.* Upper Saddle River, NJ: Merrill/Prentice Hall.

Horgan, D. D. (1995). *Achieving gender equity: Strategies for the classroom.* Boston: Allyn & Bacon.

Kohl, H. R. (1994). *I won't learn from you and other thoughts on creative maladjustment.* New York: New Press.

Kohn, A. (1999). *The schools our children deserve: Moving beyond traditional classrooms and "tougher standards."* Boston: Houghton Mifflin.

Kottler, J. A. (1997). *What's really said in the teacher's lounge: Provocative ideas about cultures and classrooms.* Thousand Oaks, CA: Corwin Press.

Kozol, J. (1991). *Savage inequalities: Children in America's schools.* New York: Crown.

Ladson-Billings, G. (1994). *The dreamkeepers: Successful teachers of African American children.* San Francisco, CA: Jossey-Bass.

National Cener for Educational Statistics. *Digest of educational statistics.* (2002) Retrieved February 13, 2003, from http://nces.ed.gov/pubs2002/digest2002/ tables/dt094.

Nieto, S. (1996). *Affirming diversity: The sociopolitical context of multicultural education* (2nd ed.). White Plains, NY: Longman.

Pai, Y., & Adler, S. A. (2001). *Cultural foundations of education* (3rd ed.). Upper Saddle River, NJ: Merrill/Prentice Hall.

Slavin, R. E. (1997). *Educational psychology: Theory and practice* (5th ed.). Boston: Allyn & Bacon.

Sternberger, R. J. (1996). IQ counts, but what really counts is successful intelligence. *NASSP-Bulletin, 80*(583), 18–23.

Thorson, S. A. (2003). *Listening to students: Reflections on secondary school classroom management.* Boston: Allyn & Bacon.

Tomlinson, C. A. (2001). *How to differentiate instruction in mixed ability classrooms* (2nd ed.). Alexandria, VA: Association for Supervision and Curriculum Development.

Trentacosta, J., & Kenney, M. J. (Eds.). (1997). *Multicultural and gender equity in the mathematics classroom: The gift of diversity.* Reston, VA: National Council of Teachers of Mathematics.

Valencia, R., & Block, M. S. (2002). "Mexican Americans don't value education!": The basics of the myth, mythmaking, and debunking. *Journal of Latinos and Education, 1*(2) 81–103.

Vaughn, S., Bos, C. S., & Schumm, J. S. (2003). *Teaching exceptional, diverse, and at-risk students in the general education classroom* (3rd ed.). Boston: Allyn & Bacon.

Villa, R. A., & Thousand, J. S. (Eds.). (1995). *Creating an inclusive school.* Alexandria, VA: Association for Supervision and Curriculum Development.

Wellesley College Center for Research on Women. (1992). *The AAUW Report: How schools shortchange girls.* Washington, DC: American Association of University Women Educational Foundation.

Westwood, P. S. (1996). *Commonsense methods for children with special needs: Strategies for the regular classroom.* London: Routledge.

Wormeli, R. (2001). *Meet me in the middle: Becoming an accomplished middle school teacher.* Portland, ME: Stenhouse.

LANGUAGE ACQUISITION (INCLUDING BILINGUAL EDUCATION)

Bilingual Education

http://www.ncela.gwu.edu/
National Clearinghouse for English Language Acquisition & Language Instructional Education Programs

http://www.nabe.org
National Association for Bilingual Education

http://www.edb.utexas.edu/coe/depts/ci/bilingue/resources.html
Bilingual Education Resources on the Internet

http://www.ecsu.ctstateu.edu/depts/edu/textbooks/bilingual.html
Electronic Textbook: Bilingual education (links to findings, policy, purposes, and definitions)

http://www.ed.gov/offices/OBEMLA/
The Office of English Language Acquisition, Language Enhancement, and Academic Achievement for Limited English Proficient Students (OELA)

Equity and Social Justice

http://www.nwrel.org
Northwest Regional Educational Laboratory: Research and Development Assistance for Equitable Educational Programs

http://www.teachingforchange.org
Teaching for Change: Building Social Justice Starting in the Classroom

http://www.teachersforjustice.org/
Teachers for Social Justice (An example of teachers working together for change. This group is based in the Chicago area. Other examples, such as

http://t4sj.tripod.com/, *based in San Francisco, also exist)*

Learners With Exceptional Needs

http://ericec.org
ERIC Clearinghouse for Special Education

http://www.ld.org
National Center for Learning Disabilities

www.add.org
National Attention Deficit Disorder Association

http://www.cec.sped.org
The Council for Exceptional Children, an international professional organization

www.ldonline.org
LDOnline includes resources for teachers and parents relating to learning disabilities.

www.ed.gov/offices/OSERS/IDEA
Office of Special Education Programs. Includes explanations of IDEA and the 1997 amendments

Multicultural Education

http://lweb.tc.columbia.edu/rr/mc/columbia.html
Milbank Web: Teachers College Library collection of works related to multicultural education

http://www.gmu.edu/student/mrrc/resources.html
Worldwide Multicultural Resources List of Resources: The Multicultural Home Page

http://www.iteachnet.com
International Education Webzine

OPPORTUNITIES TO PRACTICE

1. Reexamine your stance toward teaching. What is your commitment to principles of equity? How will you enact that commitment? What social and cultural conditions may conspire against you?

2. Select an experienced teacher and conduct an interview to assess her perspectives on student diversity. If she is a secondary teacher, be sure to ascertain how she focuses on individual students despite the large numbers of students she sees each day. Sample questions include the following:

    a. What kinds of student needs are represented in your classroom?

    b. How do you take students' needs, interests, and perspectives into consideration?

    c. What kinds of challenges do you face in addressing students as individuals?

    d. What advice do you have for me as I prepare to teach all students?

3. Figure 3.8 makes use of the general model for addressing issues related to students' characteristics, needs, and issues. Select an issue from your own practice and use Figure 3.8 to address that issue. Keep a blank copy for next time.

4. Read the following actual scenario and give me some advice: One year I sat in the sweltering southern California summer heat and listened to the commencement speaker give projections for tremendous increases in ethnic and linguistic diversity for my state. Two credential candidates sat before me, wearing the robes that marked completion of their teacher training program. In response to the speaker's predictions, one teacher turned to the other and declared: "It's time to move to Minnesota!" [or some other state that she perceived as ethnically and linguistically homogeneous]. The other teacher groaned in agreement. I, in my own black gown and Ph.D. hood, said nothing. In sitting silently aghast, I missed an opportunity to help these new teachers respond to diversity as professionals. What should I have said or done?

5. Delpit (1995) finds that schools may devalue students' home language and thus decrease students' commitment to school. If your home language was not English and you attended an English-speaking school, compare your experiences to Delpit's finding. Otherwise, interview a person who spoke a language in addition to English as a young student. Analyze your school's culture in terms of the acceptance of languages other than English.

6. Use Figure 3.9 to complete a scavenger hunt for resources at your site. Tell people it is for an assignment but take careful notes for later.

FIGURE 3.8 *Examining an issue related to student differences.*

Understand the Issue

1. The issue, in a sentence or question:

2. Personal values related to the issue (What is important to you? What seems wrong?):

3. Gather factual information and opinions related to the issue:

    Family contacts: Results:

    Records examined: Results:

    Classroom assessments: Results:

Make a Plan

4. Possible referrals (if appropriate):

5. Goal (or goals) written with family input:

6. Teaching skills:

    _____useful:

    _____lacking:

7. Potential resources:

Provide Appropriate Instruction

8. Changes to the physical environment:

9. Instructional strategies and curricular innovations:

10. Other efforts:

Analyze Your Work

11. _____ Goal met   _____ Goal partially met   _____ Goal unmet

    Analysis, including information sources:

12. Changes in your

    _____ Teaching skills:

    _____ Values:

    _____ Resources:

    _____ Other:

13. New goals and issues:

FIGURE 3.9   *Scavenger hunt for educational resources.*

At your site, find someone who	
1. Can translate between English and another language	Name: Language:
2. Can give you advice on building home-school connections	Name: Ideas:
3. Has specialized training in an area related to student diversity (e.g., bilingual education, differentiated instruction, special education, or psychology)	Name: Training:
4. Can help you locate reading materials appropriate for a broad range of interest and ability	Name: Materials:
At your site, find materials that can	
5. Help you teach content to students who are just learning English	Materials: Location:
6. Use technology to support learning	Equipment: Location:
7. Help you arrange the classroom for students who need few distractions	Materials: Plans for use:
8. Provide challenges for students who are particularly eager learners	Materials: Plans for use:
9. Help you teach mathematics for students at a wide range of conceptual levels	Materials: Plans for use:
At your site, find services that	
10. Meet the needs of children who are financially needy	Service: Requirements for use:
11. Help children who are working on clear speech	Service: Referral process:
12. Help students with other needs	Needs: Services available:

"I Am From"
(excerpts of poems by prospective teachers, 2002)

I am from New Jersey, Florida, Germany, and Samoa.
I am from California, China, Singapore, Thailand, and
  Australia.
I am from divorces, an immigrant, and a soldier.
I am from opposing forces, wild horses, and fires that
  continue to smolder.
I am from two brutal brothers who helped me to grow.
I am from a single mother, always off to work she'd go.
I am from both good and bad, a fair mix of the two.
I am from . . . hmm I'll need to think more before I'm
  truly through.

—Joseph DeLuca

I am from life's experiences of laughter, pain, and joy.
I am from an Italian, Japanese, German, and
  Czechoslovakian heritage.
I am from the era of the bubble gum, punk, pop music,
  and fluorescent colors.
I am from a mind that yearns and seeks for knowledge.
I am from a universe where mere existence intrigues
  my soul to treasure every breath I take.

—Jennifer Junio

I am from a family that prepares meals from recipes
  brought to America in steamer trunks.
I am from a dysfunctional family that keeps the dark
  issues private.
I am from this same family; we cling to our strengths
  and display them proudly.
I am from this family. It is mine.

—Julie Clark

I am from a salvaged home where all is bright on the
  outside and has been saved on the inside.
I am from a land where no word can speak without a
  beckon, and where no answer can but agree.
I am from a rejection of the self to acceptance of the
  reflection in the mirror.
I am from many places, but headed for only one place.

—Janny Kim

I am from my faith that guides me.
I am from the mother inside me.
I am from the land of the Hispanic.
I am from a coast of diversity.
I am from the love that changed me.
I am from the education that fills me.
I am from the family who cares for me.
I am from the God who made me.

—Trista Matthews

All excerpts used with permission.

Before you begin reading Chapter 4

As an adult who has experienced some success in navigating through life and its opportunities, you already know a bit about planning. Before you read Chapter 4, think about your own life and how you have planned for it thus far. Jot down some first-impression notes in response to these questions.

Warm-Up Exercise for Planning

1. When do you plan? (Hints: Think small and large. Do you plan on a daily basis? Do you plan for the distant future?)

2. What format do you use to capture your plans? (Hints: Do you use to-do lists? Do you build flow charts? Do you store plans in your memory?)

3. What do you notice about your efforts to plan? (Hints: How do plans help? How do you respond to changes?)

As you read Chapter 4, compare what you know about planning in the broader sense to classroom planning. Points of similarity may include, for instance, that teachers plan at different levels and use their plans to ensure that they meet goals and maintain focus on priorities.

CHAPTER *Four*

Planning

"Cheshire Puss . . . Would you tell me, please, which way I ought to go from here?"

"That depends a good deal on where you want to get to," said the Cat.

"I don't much care where—" said Alice.

"Then it doesn't matter which way you go," said the Cat.

—Lewis Carroll, *Alice's Adventures in Wonderland*

This chapter will help you devise plans to increase the likelihood that you and your students end up where you want to be. It has three major points:

1. Instructional plans are driven by what we want to accomplish, by our goals.
2. Long term planning usually precedes short term planning; it provides a structure for daily events.
3. Short term planning, or lesson planning, arranges activities in logical ways for daily instruction.

The approaches to planning recommended throughout this chapter are consistent with Tyler's (1949) rationale for planning curriculum. Goals drive planning, activities address goals, and we need to assess what we teach. Although Tyler's approach is sometimes criticized as being too linear, even today it is the most widely used approach to planning, in part because it allows for shared discussion of goals and ensures systematic treatment of the subject matter for small and large communities of learners.

Careful planning can help you to help students learn and grow as much as possible during the short time they will spend in your classroom. Planning begins with the selection of goals.

GOALS DRIVE PLANNING

As the Cheshire Cat reminds Alice, if we do not have a goal in mind, it does not much matter how we spend our time. But you and your students have places to go! You need a clear set of goals to guide you.

Kinds of Goals

We tend to think of school as a place of "book learning." In math, we learn fractions. In social studies, history. However, the educational community's vision is much broader. Look again at your stance toward education. Your greatest hopes for your students are probably related to attitudes and actions. Are you

FIGURE 4.1   *Taxonomies for the domains of learning.*

Domain	Levels
Cognitive Domain Thinking	Knowledge: recall Comprehension: show understanding Application: use knowledge in a new setting Analysis: identify logical errors; differentiate Synthesis: make something new Evaluation: form judgments; make decisions (Bloom, Englehart, Hill, Furst, & Krathwohl, 1956)
Affective Domain Feeling	Receiving: be aware of certain stimuli Responding: react to stimuli when asked Valuing: act on a belief when not asked to do so Organization: commit to a set of values Characterization: display behaviors that are all consistent with one's set of beliefs (Krathwohl, Bloom, & Masia, 1964)
Psychomotor Domain Doing	Imitation: repeat an action after observing a model Manipulation: perform an action without a model Precision: perform a refined action without a model or directions Articulation: sequence and perform a series of acts with control, timing, and speed Naturalization: perform actions that are now routine and spontaneous (Harrow, 1969)

interested in your students developing empathy? Responsibility? Persistence? Objectivity? These qualities show up on many teachers' lists of goals. In fact, there is increasing interest in an idea entitled emotional intelligence (Goleman, 1995; 1998). Emotional intelligence allows us to do such things as identify and manage our emotions, empathize with others, and persist in the presence of frustration. Educated people not only know things; they also feel things and can do things. For this reason, theorists have divided the world of educational goals into three domains: the cognitive, the affective, and the psychomotor domains. Figure 4.1 presents commonly used taxonomies—or classification systems—for each of these domains.

Note that in each taxonomy, the first entry is the simplest and requires the least from the learner. Higher levels place increasing demands on the learner. The more complex levels require that the learner draw on the lower levels, and each level contributes to a fuller understanding, appreciation, or performance. The value of these taxonomies is that they remind us of two things: First, we teach more than just cognitive information. We need to specify goals related to different kinds of learning. Second, within each of the areas we teach, there are levels of understanding and action. Teachers need to provide opportunities for mastery across many levels. Students need to process information in increasingly deep and complex ways and to respond to their worlds via sophisticated thoughts, feelings, and actions.

The most widely discussed taxonomy in schools is Bloom's taxonomy for the cognitive domain. Some teachers' editions list the level of the tasks or questions it provides, and teachers are expected to help students work at the higher levels of Bloom's taxonomy. Despite the widespread talk of Bloom's taxonomy, however, Anderson (1994) finds that

> Forty years after the development of the Taxonomy, teachers plan classroom activities, not objectives, construct tests that include a preponderance of

FIGURE 4.2 *Goal or objective?*

Set One: Mathematics

1. Given paper and pencil, students will add two-digit numbers with 90% accuracy.
2. Students will improve their computation skills.

Set Two: Science

1. Without reference materials, students will draw a diagram of the water cycle and describe how humans can affect the cycle at two points at least.
2. Students will use scientific principles to make decisions in their own lives.

knowledge level items, and ask questions of their students that in the main require them to recall or recognize what they have been taught. (p. 139)

Apparently our acquaintance with Bloom and his taxonomy may be surface level. Perhaps you will wish to carefully study the levels of Bloom's taxonomy and work with them until they become part of your vocabulary and practice. Exercise 2 at the end of the chapter under Opportunities to Practice can get you started. As you work with the levels of Bloom's taxonomy, you may uncover some of the common criticisms of it. First, the levels are probably not linear; for example, synthesis may not always be predicated on analysis (Marlowe & Page, 1998). Second, a teacher's question or task does not necessarily draw a student response at the same level. Higher level questions can provoke lower level responses and vice versa. Despite these and other drawbacks, Bloom's taxonomy serves an important function: It reminds teachers to provide a solid core of basic knowledge and opportunities to act on that knowledge in more sophisticated ways.

Goals, then, can fall into a number of domains, including cognitive, affective, and psychomotor. Classroom aims also vary in terms of specificity.

Goals Versus Objectives

Aims that are broad or general are typically termed *goals*. Goals drive our long term planning. General goals subsume more specific and detailed statements. Deemed objectives, these specific statements guide daily instruction. See if you can sort the statements from Figure 4.2 into goals and objectives.

Notice that the goal statements are lofty pursuits that are not yet operationalized, or put into a form that specifies students' exact actions. The specific objective statements in Figure 4.2 will help students build toward understanding of the larger goals. Notice that, though the statements in 4.2 differ in terms of specificity they are alike in a very important way: both goals and objectives are worded in terms of what the student should be able to do. Teaching is directed toward the goal of fostering change. As you examine national and state content standards, you will note that they, also, are phrased in terms of student outcomes. This keeps the focus on students and their learning. Here is an example of a twelfth-grade language arts standard from the state of Wisconsin:

Students will analyze and synthesize the concepts and details encountered in informational texts such as reports, technical manuals, historical papers, and government documents (Wisconsin Academic Standards, 1998).

A few objectives related to this standard might include:

1. The learner will be able to state the main idea in an informational passage.
2. The learner will be able to sort sentences from an information passage into two stacks: major concepts and supporting details.

3. The learner will draw a diagram of the concepts and details in a paragraph of informational text.

Teachers develop and implement hundreds of objectives, and the lesson planning portion of this chapter will help you to write instructional objectives. Your objectives, though, will be shaped by your broader vision of what needs to be accomplished, by your set of goals.

Determining Goals

Professional teachers are charged with making important decisions: What should be taught? To whom? When? These decisions need to be guided by a teacher's consideration of the larger system. To develop your classroom goals, you need to examine various sources. Remember the bull's eye of sources of influence from Chapter 1 (Figure 1.1)? As you write a set of goals for student learning, consider the following suggestions:

- Start with the students: What do they know now? How do they learn? What would they like to learn? What are their interests and plans? What support will they need from you as they master challenging standards?
- Review your aims as a teacher: What are your hopes for the students?
- Think again about broader contexts: What national, state, or district content standards are specified for your students? If you have not yet, spend some time reviewing the content expectations to which you and your students will be held.
- Check grade level articulation: What are students expected to learn in the year or years before your grade? What will their teachers in future grades expect them to know?
- Examine your materials: What goals are identified in your adopted curricular materials?

Jot down information from each of these sources. Look for areas of overlap and areas where goals seem dissimilar. Use a critical eye: Whose perspective is left out of your list of goals? Could a different set of goals be used to improve existing practice? Talk with experienced teachers and other colleagues. Prioritize the goals. Check also to see that your set includes different kinds of goals. Then use your goals to focus your long-range planning. Figure 4.3 provides a reminder of these stages.

LONG-RANGE PLANNING

Although teachers plan differently, one reasonable approach is to move from the broadest level of planning down to the most specific. Long-range planning entails using your set of goals to map out the year (or term) and set out a structure for weekly and daily activities. It also includes unit planning.

FIGURE 4.3 *Goals in action.*

1. If you are working with students, gather and analyze information about them (Chapter 3).
2. Reread your stance toward education (developed through Chapter 2). Then set it aside.
3. Make a list of the three things you wish most deeply for your students. If they could walk away from their time with you with only three things, what would those things be? (Hint: check back to your work in the warm-up exercise for Chapter 2 and in Figure 2.5 for a push.)
4. Write goal statements to capture your wishes. Begin with the words, "Students will . . ."
5. Clip your goals onto your plan book and use this list of big goals to inform your planning efforts for individual subjects and students.

Many teachers bring coherence to their long-term plans by planning collaboratively.

Teaching Tips

ADVICE FOR LONG RANGE PLANNING

1. Be sure that your decisions about how to use instructional time reflect your goals and priorities.
2. Remember that most lessons and units take about twice as long as expected.
3. Worry less about "covering" the material than about "uncovering" it.

Yearlong Planning

With your goals in mind, examine your content standards, your **teachers' editions,** and other materials to determine the content you will teach and to develop an appropriate sequence for the content. Most texts include a **scope and sequence** (a chart that gives a suggested layout for the term), which may be helpful to you as you decide what to teach when. As you decide how much time to devote to each area of study over the year, examine a school calendar for months, scheduled breaks, and local traditions. If you are teaching in a departmentalized setting, you may not have the opportunity to do much **curricular integration,** but if you teach more than one subject to the same group of students, it makes sense for you to consider how the outcomes for each subject area might support each other and to group those units together in time. That way the content from one subject can reinforce another. Teachers in all settings can think about whether certain units make more sense at certain times of year as they decide when to teach each topic. Fit your topics into the school calendar by becoming more specific in your planning: Move to unit planning.

Unit Planning

Glance through a teacher's edition and you will see that authors arrange instruction in units. A **unit** is a set of related lessons that address a single topic, theme, or skill. For example, a literature unit might address a particular book

Teaching Tips

UNIT PLANNING
Plan to teach toward the big ideas.

or genre. A social studies unit might address a particular group of people or a time in history. A math unit might include a single skill area such as measurement. Units range in length from just a few lessons (perhaps a week in length) to many lessons (perhaps more than a month). Four to six weeks tends to be a typical length for instructional units.

Which units will you teach? One option is to march through your texts, page by page. In fact, one estimate suggests that 97% of teachers' instructional decisions are governed by the texts they use. Is this good or bad? The answer depends on how well the texts' topics and activities meet students' needs and interests and address the teachers' long-term goals.

Three other approaches to unit planning allow more flexibility in selecting learning activities. The first format is increasingly popular as teachers plan units to meet content standards. It is called **backwards planning** or backward design (Wiggins & McTighe, 1998). This model begins with the conviction that a student's performance is key to determining whether and what the student knows. First, the teacher identifies what students should know and be able to do at the unit's end. Second, the teacher considers what evidence the students would need to provide for the teacher to determine that they have mastered the content. After the end performance is clearly in mind, the teacher develops activities to help students prepare for the performance. To use backwards planning you might:

1. Select content standards or outcomes for mastery.
2. Unify these outcomes through a theme, an issue, or a "big idea."
3. Compose an essential question that students, if they answered, would demonstrate deep thinking about the content. Develop supporting unit questions as well.
4. Determine performance that you would accept as evidence that the students have mastered the content. You may need more than one measure.
5. Select activities that lead students toward mastery.
6. Develop **rubrics,** with the students if possible, or other measures to assess each performance. (Rubrics and other assessments are addressed in Chapter 7.)
7. Review and revise until each component of the unit supports the others.

The power of the backwards planning model is that it turns the "teach my favorite activities" approach that can be so popular on its head and instead focuses on providing instruction that will help students meet the end goal.

The second unit planning format is recommended by experts in content areas such as social studies (Ellis, 1998; Savage & Armstrong, 2000) and science (Gega & Peters, 2002). We will call it the **"big idea" approach.**

1. Begin by determining the major ideas related to the content. Major ideas, or generalizations, are statements that connect facts and concepts. For example, "tree" is a concept, or a class of ideas with identifiable attributes. "Some trees lose their leaves" is a fact. "Trees and other organisms respond to environmental stimuli" is a generalization. It is a more inclusive statement that relates several concepts and has greater explanatory power. A sample generalization in social studies is, "All human societies change." Teachers' editions

often state generalizations under the heading "Chapter Concepts." Chapters typically include three to four big ideas.

2. Once you find generalizations, write objectives and locate activities that can help your students learn the generalizations. In selecting activities, you may draw from your texts and from other sources such as literature, current events, and **trade books** (which are any nontextbook books, including literature and teaching materials devoted to particular topical areas, typically housed in curriculum libraries or offered for sale at teacher supply stores). Chapter 5 will urge you to select different kinds of activities as you search for those that will lead to important generalizations. Examples of enriching experiences include field trips, guest speakers, and **multimedia projects** (Green & Brown, 2002).

3. Then arrange the activities for daily instruction. Lessons often begin with a "bridge" that takes students from their lives into the content via an engaging question, demonstration, or other activity.

Note that, on their way to learning content generalizations, students will learn facts and concepts that should slowly coalesce to form larger understandings. It is indeed important to teach facts and specific information. The big idea method of unit planning ensures that facts build into larger, more coherent structures of understanding.

Another strength of this planning approach is that your focus on big ideas will ease decisions about which daily activities to cut or extend. Most teachers feel pressed for time. Using the big idea method of unit planning, you can drop activities that are less likely to help students build understanding of key concepts and spend more time on productive learning experiences.

A third popular approach to unit planning is **thematic instruction.** Many teachers find that integrating their content through themes allows them to address content standards efficiently and in ways that are interesting to students. Instead of being based solely on core ideas related to particular subject matters, thematic units are interdisciplinary, with learning activities emanating from the theme (Allen, 1995; Kovalik, 1993; Pappas, Kiefer, & Levstik, 1998; Tiedt & Tiedt, 1999). Examples of themes include, for young students, homes, and for older students, discoveries or interdependence. Concepts from different subject areas are surfaced and linked through the use of the theme. Also, thematic units usually include choices for students, allowing students to select at least some of the individual and small-group learning experiences in the unit. The elements of choice and group discussion can develop a sense of ownership and community as students learn together and share their results. Pappas, Kiefer, and Levstik suggest the following steps for planning thematic units:

1. *Select a theme.* The theme needs to be broad enough to encompass information from many subject areas but not so broad that meaningful connections are lost. Keep your larger goals and students' interests in mind.

2. *Create a planning web.* Brainstorm to create a web—a semantic map—that explores the many instances in which the theme arises. Figure 4.4 gives an abbreviated version of a planning web. Notice that it does not include mention of traditional subject areas such as mathematics or history; it should break away from traditional compartmentalized thinking. Webbing with a colleague leads to more divergent thinking. As you web, you will note connections among ideas and can begin to categorize your ideas into groups. Jot down your ideas for resources, including books, technological materials, concrete materials, and community resources as you web.

3. *Select resources.* Chapter 5 argues that teachers should create rich learning environments. As you plan, aim to provide a wealth of resources. Include the arts, literature, other print sources, tangible materials, technology, and community resources; flip ahead to Figure 5.6 for other ideas.

FIGURE 4.4   *Sample planning web.*

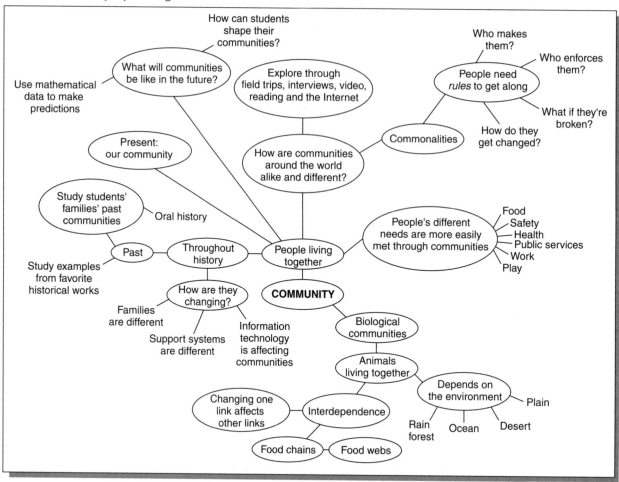

4. *Plan activities.* Choose or create activities that address the theme, utilize rich resources, and encourage students' progress toward learning goals. Remember to include opportunities for students to choose their learning activities.

Experts in multicultural studies advocate thematic approaches to planning because such approaches allow teachers and students to dissolve the traditional subject matter distinctions in favor of content organizations that revolve around topics seen as immediately valuable and powerful. By restructuring the boundaries of curriculum, we may open our classrooms to more democratic and inclusive study.

How do you plan? Some teachers use index cards so they can rearrange activities as necessary. Some keep their plans in a looseleaf notebook so that it is easy to insert other materials. Others create templates and word process their plans so that they can easily copy/paste information such as content standards into their plans. Experiment and see which strategy works best for you.

In his book on ethnic studies, James Banks (1997) presents a unit planning approach that has both an interdisciplinary focus, as does thematic planning, and a focus on key generalizations, as does the big idea approach. This approach allows students to gain information through many diverse examples to build universal, cross-disciplinary generalizations related to such multicultural education topics as ethnicity, socialization, intercultural communication, and power. Banks argues that this planning approach allows learners to gain the knowledge and multiple perspectives required for participation in their increasingly diverse world. Further, Banks and others remind us that the decisions a teacher makes, including decisions about curricular planning, are not purely technical. The ways in which we arrange our content and instruction mirror our visions of what we want for our students.

Whether you use the backwards planning approach, the thematic approach to unit planning, the big idea method, a combination of these, or an entirely different approach, you will teach the units within the confines of your weekly and daily schedule.

Weekly and Daily Schedules

Once you have determined a broad view of what should happen when, devise a schedule of daily and weekly events. A well-designed garden provides an analogy for a thoughtful weekly classroom schedule. According to Benzel (1997) every garden needs plants to serve as "bones," "binders," and "bursts." Bones, permanent and sturdy, provide the structure for the garden. Trees may serve as the bones, for example. Binders connect elements of the garden so that they relate smoothly to each other. Binders might be shrubs and large perennial plants. Bursts infuse the color and excitement. Think colorful flowers. In weekly planning, time structures provide the bones, routines and recurring events provide the binders, and engaging lessons provide the bursts.

Figure 4.5 shows two experienced fourth-grade teachers' classroom schedules, bones only. Notice that both Loretta and Kim have devised structured, stable time schedules to ensure that they use their time well and to provide students with a sense of predictability and direction. Both teachers include similar subject areas, and they have devoted substantial instructional time to the language arts. Both Loretta and Kim struggle to include the visual and performing arts, and both are sometimes frustrated by activities that, though valuable, detract from instructional time. You may notice some differences in the ways these two teachers have chosen to structure the day. Those differences reflect the teachers' professional judgment and local conditions. There are some mandates for instructional time in most public schools, which you can discover by speaking with the principal. Often, though, teachers have much latitude to develop time structures that they judge as best to reflect their educational goals. Remember, time structures provide bones.

Binders are found in the routines and recurring events found during these scheduled time periods. For instance, during the opening in Loretta's classroom, students know they will complete "bell work" (brief review assignments that commence when the morning bell rings), write in their journals, hold a classroom meeting, critique the musical piece they have listened to together, and share important events from outside the classroom. These activities provide a personal and academic focus for the remainder of the day's work. Another example of a binder can be seen during Kim's mathematics time. She

Teaching Tips

WEEKLY PLANNING

Bones
Binders
Bursts

FIGURE 4.5   *Two teachers' daily schedules.*

Loretta's Daily Structure		Kim's Daily Structure	
8:10–8:30	Opening	9:05–9:15	Opening
8:30–10:05	Language Arts	9:15–10:15	Mathematics
10:05–10:20	*Recess*	10:15–10:40	Centers and Small-Group Workshops
10:20–10:45	Read Aloud	*10:40–10:50*	*Recess*
10:45–11:30	Social Studies	10:50–12:15	Language Arts (Bilingual Aide assists; Reading Recovery for 40 minutes twice weekly)
11:30–12:10	Science or Physical Education (alternating days)		
12:10–12:50	*Lunch*	*12:15–12:55*	*Lunch*
12:50–1:05	Silent Reading	12:55–1:10	Read aloud
1:05–2:05	Mathematics	1:10–2:00	Social Studies
2:05–2:25	Center Time	*2:00–2:10*	*Recess*
2:25–2:35	Clean Up, Star of the Day	2:10–3:00	Science or Physical Education (alternating days)
		3:00–3:09	Clean Up, Closure of the Day

Notes	Notes
√ Early dismissal on Wednesday	√ Library or computers on Wednesday during language arts time
√ Music on Wednesdays (10:30)	√ Parent volunteers: one hour per day
√ Work with first-grade buddies on Fridays (9:20)	√ Art is integrated into content areas
√ Art on Thursdays and Fridays (2:00)	√ Need music!

ends every math period with a "mad minute" of drills on basic facts. This brief drill period closes the mathematics period and signals the start of a new activity. Recurring events provide binders.

Within their set schedules, Loretta and Kim provide exciting and unusual learning opportunities, or bursts. One day during her scheduled science time, for instance, Loretta led an engaging lesson on the skeleton. She displayed X-ray films of her back before and after surgery for scoliosis and allowed students to ask her yes–no questions to develop explanations for what they saw on the X-ray films. Students responded enthusiastically to this instructional strategy, called inquiry training (Suchman, 1962; described in Chapter 6), and thereafter asked to lead their own inquiry training sessions. As Loretta's example shows, good bones and binders are not enough. To encourage learning, teachers also need to expend effort in developing meaningful lessons.

Bones, binders, and bursts apply to teachers in departmentalized secondary schools who work within the confines of a tight bell schedule as well. They just compress their usage of bones, binders, and bursts to serve them well during a 55-minute period. Figure 4.6 shows how a 10th-grade teacher structures her time over a day and a week for one period near the beginning of her year.

LESSON PLANNING

A lesson is a relatively brief instructional sequence that focuses on one or a few instructional objectives. When students master the objectives from one lesson, they are a step closer to building more complex ideas, attitudes, and actions related to the overall unit and to your guiding goals. Although lessons vary from

FIGURE 4.6 *A 10th-grade social science teacher's schedule.*

	Monday	Tuesday	Wednesday	Thursday	Friday
binders and bones	For attendance, one person in group raises hand with absences. To review current events, students quiz each other in small groups using **active participation** devices. Record Friday quiz scores on computer grade book and post Monday morning so students can check their scores (using numbers not names). Dismissal: students check their area and copy homework assignment into their planners.				
Period 3	Current events (Teacher and students both share) Geography skill Instruction on current unit	Current events (Teacher and students both share) Geography skill Instruction on current unit	Current events (Teacher and students both share) Geography skill Instruction on current unit	Current events (Teacher and students both share) Students quiz each other in small groups for current events. Instruction on current unit	Current events quiz Read aloud from historical fiction novel Dismissal: "Where in the World" stumper question (an informal check on geography skills)

10 minutes to a week in length, depending on the content and on the age and sophistication of the students, lessons typically last less than an hour. The distinguishing characteristics of a lesson are that

1. It uses a set, logical structure.
2. Activities relate to each other and aim toward exploring ideas or skills related to a very limited set of objectives.

Although objectives take on different forms, a commonly used version is the behavioral objective. A behavioral objective is a specific statement about how students will be different at a lesson's close. Especially in your early days as a teacher, behavioral objectives can push you to focus on students and outcomes: What should students be able to do after your lessons? Without objectives, plans tend to become mere scripts of what teachers do during lessons.

Writing Objectives

Look again at the following objectives, found earlier in Figure 4.2:

1. Given paper and pencil, students will add two-digit numbers with 90% accuracy.
2. Without reference materials, students will draw a diagram of the water cycle and describe how humans can affect the cycle at two points at least.

These objectives have the three components typically specified for behavioral objectives (Popham & Baker, 1970): **behavior, conditions,** and **criteria,** described in Figure 4.7. For more examples of instructional objectives, examine your teachers' editions and other curricular materials. Check to see that each objective includes the three typically identified components of a behavioral objective.

FIGURE 4.7   *Components of a behavioral objective.*

- **Behavior:** What, specifically, should you see the students do as a result of your instruction? (What is the students' observable action on mastery?) In the first objective, students will add. In the second, they will draw and describe.
- **Conditions:** Under what conditions should students perform? (Are there limits on time? What materials may they use?) The conditions of performance are found at the beginning of each of the objectives listed. You can imagine how the conditions would change based on both the students' characteristics and the teacher's expectations for appropriate performance.
- **Criteria:** How well should students perform? (How many? How fast? With what degree of accuracy?) The first objective gives a percentage rate for acceptable performance, and the second sets a minimal number of discussion points. You will need to think carefully about the kind and level of criteria that are appropriate for your students because your definition of success will influence the decisions you make as you plan instruction.

Although many new teachers initially find that writing good objectives is time consuming and may feel artificial, repeated practice streamlines the time required and sharpens their instruction. It is worth the time.

Despite their potential to focus attention on student learning, behavioral objectives are criticized on several grounds. They are criticized, for instance, as being too driven by the teacher and as being so mechanistic that little room is left for spontaneous learning. Opinion is divided in terms of how carefully teachers should compose and adhere to objectives. Many teachers elect to include only the observable behavior, leaving the conditions and criteria implicit. I adopted this approach in a fossil lesson I taught to second graders (Figure 4.8). Until you develop skill at writing objectives and using them to guide your teaching, you probably need to write full objectives. As you become more comfortable with planning, select the format that is most useful for you in encouraging student learning. Once you are clear on what you intend for students to learn, you are ready to make decisions about structuring your lessons.

Teaching Tips

WRITING BEHAVIORAL OBJECTIVES

1. Be sure to focus on the intended outcome of the lesson, not on what students will do throughout the lesson.
2. Focus on the skill or concept involved, not the technique you will use to measure performance. (Why, for instance, have students "complete page 43"?)
3. List only the criteria and conditions that you will actually use. If you will not check to see that all students attain 90% accuracy, do not list it in your objectives.

Lesson Structure

Lessons are composed of activities that are joined meaningfully into a regular structure. Although there are many helpful planning formats, lesson formats share similar components. Every lesson has three sections: *open, body,* and *close.*

To open a lesson, the teacher sets the stage for the lesson to come. It is common for the teacher to state the objective in student-friendly language and give a purpose for the lesson. During the body, he helps students develop con-

FIGURE 4.8 *Fossil lesson.*

Lesson Plan: How Fossils Are Made

Subjects:	Science and Reading
Grade:	Second (7-year-olds)
Students:	20 children; all English speakers, some readers.
Time:	1 hour 35 minutes

Objectives

1. Students will describe the process by which fossils are made in nature.

2. Students will summarize text by sharing two important points from their reading of self-selected portions of a nonfiction text on fossils.

3. Students will explain how the mock fossils they create are the same as and different from real fossils.

Procedure

Reading Portion (35 minutes)

1. Open: On the rug: Complete a five-item opinionnaire on fossils to find out what children know. (In an opinionnaire, respondents mark their agreement with statements such as "Real fossils are made in factories.") Encourage discussion of each item to get kids talking. (8 minutes)

2. Body: Pair up the children (more accomplished readers with newer readers) and pass out multiple copies of the fossil book. Read the introduction together. Glance at the table of contents. Encourage them to read the table of contents to choose the sections that interest them. Draw upon surprises from the opinionnaire. (5 minutes)

3. Release them to partner read anywhere they like in the room. Those who wish to stay and listen to the teacher read may stay and read along. (10 minutes)

4. Back at the rug discuss something surprising that the children learned by reading. Draw from students' ideas to explain the process by which fossils are made. Use illustrations from text as support. (8 minutes)

Science Portion (1 hour)

1. On the rug: Show real fossils. Contrast them with a sample fossil made from plaster of paris.

2. Have students make their own mock fossils. Model procedure, then students work as individuals:

   a) Pass out, soften plasticine (non-hardening) clay.

   b) Release students back to their tables to select items for imprinting: shells, leaves, plastic dinosaurs (already placed at tables).

   c) When ready, have students go to back of room on hard floor to mix their own plaster of paris, pour carefully onto plasticine mold.

   d) When dry, remove fossils.

3. Close: (May need to follow lunch recess.) Reread the text, compare the process and types of real fossils with class's mock fossils.

4. Assign homework: "Tell someone at home what you know about fossils. Use yours as an example."

Assessment: Students describe the fossil-making process, referring to texts and mock fossils.

cepts related to the objective. To close, the teacher and students consolidate and extend what they learned. Figure 4.9 offers some options that may help you as you think about structuring your lessons according to the open-body-close format.

The fossils lesson (shown in Figure 4.8) demonstrates some of these activities in its open-body-close format. Perhaps as you review the lesson, alternative

FIGURE 4.9 *Activities for different lesson stages.*

	Activities for Different Stages of the Lesson Sequence: Open, Body, Close
Open	1. Capture the students' attention: Share a real object, or try using a story, a picture, a book, a video clip, or a song. 2. Present a problem. (Challenge students to solve the problem through the lesson.) 3. Provide warm-up or review exercises to engage students. 4. Elicit students' prior knowledge, experience, or opinions about the content. 5. State your objectives. 6. Preview the lesson. 7. Give your expectations for students' behavior. 8. State the purpose of what they will learn.
Body	1. Present information verbally and through graphic representations. 2. Point out critical attributes, examples, and counter-examples. 3. Model. (Described in Chapter 5.) 4. Read. 5. Discuss. 6. Use hands-on materials. 7. Work in cooperative groups to solve a problem. 8. Make charts and graphs. 9. Use your questions and those of students to explore the content. 10. Do research at the library or on the World Wide Web. 11. Use computer-assisted instruction. 12. Check on students' understanding. Adjust instruction based on their responses.
Close	1. Restate the objective. 2. Gather individual lesson pieces into a coherent whole. 3. Draw conclusions. 4. Summarize what was learned. 5. Give a brief quiz to assess understanding. 6. Ask students to state something they learned. 7. Revisit prior knowledge charts or graphs from the lessons' opening. Revise to reflect new information. 8. Show students how the learning applies to real life, or ask students to make the connections. 9. Ask what students would like to study next, or record their unanswered questions. 10. Write in journals. 11. Connect this lesson to the next by describing the problem to be solved or idea to be explored for tomorrow. 12. Hold a gallery walk (described in Figure 5.7) for students to appreciate each others' work.

ways of opening, developing, and closing the lesson come to mind. What falls into each stage of the sequence indeed depends on the preferences of the teacher and students and also on the particular lesson format being employed. My fossils lesson illustrates not only an open-body-close structure but also elements common to most lesson plans.

Elements of a Lesson Plan

In addition to structuring each of your lessons to include an opening, a development phase, and a closure, you should include in your plans information that will keep you organized and that will help you communicate your intentions to yourself during teaching and to others who may wish to follow your instruction. Figure 4.10 gives a lesson plan format that can be used in many situations. You will see each of these elements evident in the sample lessons in the figures in

FIGURE 4.10 *Elements of a lesson plan.*

Elements of a Lesson Plan

1. **Housekeeping Details**

   Include information about the students, about the materials you will require, and other topics that may affect the lesson.

2. **Concept, Generalization, or Skill**

   Remind yourself of the "big idea" you are working toward. Individual lessons should add up to bigger things.

3. **Objective(s)**

   State the intended outcome(s) of your lesson using an observable student behavior, the conditions for performance, and the criteria for success. Consider listing the content standard.

4. **Procedure**

   Use open-body-close format to structure the lesson.

   List the steps you will follow. Primarily use general descriptions of what you will say and do. Only for important points, or when the content is difficult or new for you, will you include scripted quotations. Include time estimates for good time management and to help you develop realistic expectations for how much time activities will take.

5. **Assessment**

   Include a plan for how you will assess student learning in terms of the objective(s) and other incidental learnings. Consider how you will assess your teaching as well.

6. **Differentiation**

   List specific techniques for differentiating instruction or attending to students' needs and interests, as appropriate for this lesson.

---

the next section. As you review these lessons, you may also notice that I tend to plan in great detail. I am convinced that careful planning enhances teaching, so I encourage you to take great care in preparing good lessons for your students. The more specific and careful your individual lesson plans are, the more confident you can feel in front of the students, the more you will be able to focus on students' learning rather than on your own words and behaviors, and the more quickly you will learn from experience and be able to streamline your planning. Figure 4.11 provides some advice for lesson planning.

Planning Formats

To review, lessons have a predictable structure—open, body, close—and are captured in writing through plans with common elements. Does this mean that lesson planning is as quick as turning out batches of cookies, one indistinguishable from the next? No. Teachers can be effective and yet not just the same. Lessons can take many formats.

The format you select for each lesson will depend on your stance and style and on your understanding of the students and the content. Figure 4.12 gives two lessons. Both lessons use the open-body-close format, both are structured by the same common elements, and both teach toward the same objectives. However, the two lessons employ very different formats to lead students toward the objectives.

What is the primary difference between these lesson plans? In the **directed lesson,** the teacher states the concept near the beginning, and students apply it afterward. In the **inquiry lesson,** students begin with a question, experience a surprising discrepancy through their explorations, and work to develop an explanation of the phenomenon near the end of the lesson. The teacher plays the role of skilled presenter in the directed lesson and

FIGURE 4.11 *Some advice for planning.*

Don't . . .

1. Reinvent the wheel. Begin with existing materials, and check your resources. Modify based upon your own stance, students, and standards. You can develop curriculum as you gain expertise.

2. Let materials make your important decisions. Planning is not the same as finding worksheets to fill the time until lunch, or glossing over lessons so that you can finish the book by June.

3. Be intimidated if the content is new to you. Check out a book or hit the Internet and study the information you will be teaching. All teachers expect to continue improving their subject matter knowledge.

4. Use Internet lesson plans without studying them carefully first. Though there are many excellent resources, the sheer volume of plans and activities available electronically means that they may not have been screened well. Study them carefully to ensure that they are appropriate for your students and are of sufficient quality.

Do . . .

1. Focus on thorough treatment of the content. Most teachers feel as if they are pushed along by the hands of the clock. Rather than simply mentioning topics without exploring them in depth, consider cutting out topics that you cannot fully explore. Devote your planning efforts to encouraging lasting and meaningful learning.

2. Plan with a partner or team. Experience and a rich supply of ideas help.

3. Anticipate students' varying responses. Develop alternate plans to address the things that may possibly go awry. Anticipate!

4. Rehearse, especially if it is the first time you've taught the lesson or if you have a tough audience.

5. Prepare your materials so you are ready to go. Have your materials at your fingertips so that you feel calm and prepared as you begin your lesson.

6. Be prepared to scrap your lesson if you need to rethink it or pursue some other path that is likely to lead to significant learning.

FIGURE 4.12 *Two contrasting lessons.*

Surface Tension Lesson

Grade level:	Upper elementary (grades 4–6)
Time:	See each lesson
Materials:	Picture or CD-ROM segment of a water insect, eyedroppers, paper towels, pennies and other coins, water, and soap
Concepts:	Surface tension is a property of every liquid. The molecules of liquids attract uniformly in all directions, so molecules at a liquid's surface attract mostly toward the center of the liquid. As a result, molecules at the surface form a "skin" and tend toward the shape of a sphere.
Objectives:	1. Using materials of their choice as props, students will describe, in their own words, the phenomenon of surface tension.
	2. Using their knowledge of surface tension, students will predict how many drops of water will fit on the head of a nickel.

	Directed Lesson (50 minutes)	Inquiry Lesson (60 minutes)
Open	1. Teacher displays a picture or video segment of an aquatic insect running across the surface of a pond. Students remark on how strange it would be to run on top of water. 2. Teacher states objective: "Before you leave today, you will be able to give the explanation for this bug's strange ability."	1. Teacher displays the lesson materials and challenges students with a question: "How many drops of water will fit on a penny?" 2. Teacher records students' predictions on the chalkboard.

FIGURE 4.12 *Continued*

	Directed Lesson (50 minutes)	Inquiry Lesson (60 minutes)
Open	3. Teacher states the purpose of the lesson: "Understanding this phenomenon will help you at home in many ways. You may be able to explain how soap works, the characteristics of certain plastics, and the nature of a disease of human lungs. More immediately, you will be able to fill your little brother's cup so full he cannot pick it up without spilling." She smiles. (5 minutes)	3. Teacher leads a discussion of what factors might affect how many drops fit on a penny. Students are unsure.
Body	4. Teacher displays jars full of different liquids. She reminds students that liquids behave as they do based on their molecular structure. Teacher reviews basic characteristics of liquids.	4. Teacher states her expectations for student behavior during experiment time and then distributes materials (eyedroppers, cups of water, and pennies) to pairs of students. (10 minutes)
	5. Teacher holds up a model of a molecule and flashes on the overhead projector: "In liquids, molecules attract each other in every direction." She rephrases and demonstrates with the model.	5. Students conduct their tests and record actual results on the board.
	6. Teacher explains that, because liquid molecules at the surface are not attracted to air in the same manner as they are to other liquid molecules, the molecules' net attraction is toward the center of the liquid. A skin forms.	6. After 15 minutes, teacher leads a discussion on the wide range of students' findings: from 11 drops to 98 drops fit on the pennies.
	7. Teacher labels this phenomenon *surface tension* and has students record the definition in their journals.	7. Now students are able to conclude that all must use a standard drop size and a standard height to release the water from the dropper.
	8. Teacher distributes eyedroppers, paper towels, pennies, and water cups. She states her expectations for student behavior and then encourages them to demonstrate the phenomenon of surface tension by fitting as many drops on the penny as possible. (30 minutes)	8. Students conduct their tests once more. This time the range of their results is smaller.
		9. Teacher questions students: "How can we account for the difference between our predictions and our actual results, which were much higher than our predictions?" Students respond that they had not expected the water to bulge so much at the surface.
Close	9. After they work with the materials, students share their results. Teacher questions students about what they saw (a mounded surface of water on the penny).	10. Teacher directs students to formulate, with their partners, an explanation for the bulging. She urges them to use what they know about liquids to infer what is happening at the molecular level.
	10. Teacher directs students to talk in pairs to apply the concepts of surface tension to explain why the water bubbled over the surface without spilling. She circulates and takes notes on students' explanations.	11. After circulating and listening, teacher develops a group explanation, drawing pictures and supplementing students' ideas with concepts found in the plan. (40 minutes)
	11. Teacher directs students to now explain the phenomenon for her in their journals. Students also predict how many drops will fit on the head of a nickel. (15 minutes)	12. Teacher asks students to explain surface tension to a friend in their journals. They end their entries by considering two things: How many drops of water will fit on the head of a nickel? What investigation would they like to try next with surface tension? (10 minutes)

of facilitator or intellectual coach in the inquiry lesson. Which format appeals most to you? Your answer says something about your stance toward education. Keep reading. Subsequent chapters will provide you with other strategies and planning formats consistent with your views of teaching and learning.

PARTING WORDS

One of the reasons that teaching is more difficult than the uninitiated might expect is that so much time is spent outside of instructional hours preparing effective learning experiences. There are no short cuts to good planning. Even teachers who are handed scripted materials and are asked to follow the text closely need to bring students and content together through careful planning. The more time and thought you devote to considering what your particular students need to learn and how you can help them learn it, the more likely they are to succeed.

Teaching is directed toward the goal of fostering change. This chapter was intended to help you think about structuring experiences likely to result in learning, and Chapter 5 gives advice on breathing life into your plans through your instruction.

LINKS TO RESEARCH, THEORY, AND PRACTICE

Allen, D. D. (1995). *Developing thematic units: Process and product.* Albany, NY: Delmar.

Anderson, L. W. (1994). Research on teaching and teacher education. In L. W. Anderson & L. A. Sosniak (Eds.) *Bloom's taxonomy: A forty-year retrospective* (pp. 103–145). Chicago: National Society for the Study of Education.

Apple, M. W., & Christian-Smith, L. K., (Eds.) (1991). *The politics of the textbook.* New York: Routledge.

Banks, J. A. (1997). *Teaching strategies for ethnic studies* (6th ed.). Boston: Allyn & Bacon.

Benzel, K. N. (Ed.). (1997). *Western landscaping book.* Menlo Park, CA: Sunset Books.

Berson, M. J., Cruz, B. C., Duplass, J. A., & Johnston, J. H. (2001). *Social studies on the Internet.* Upper Saddle River, NJ: Merrill/Prentice Hall.

Bloom, B., Englehart, M., Hill, W., Furst, E., & Krathwohl, D. (1956). *Taxonomy of educational objectives: The classification of education goals. Handbook I: Cognitive domain.* New York: Longman Green.

Ebenezer, J. V., & Lau, E. (2003). *Science on the Internet: A resource for K–12 teachers* (2nd ed.). Upper Saddle River, NJ: Merrill/Prentice Hall.

Ellis, A. K. (1998). *Teaching and learning elementary social studies* (6th ed.). Boston: Allyn & Bacon.

Gega, P. C., & Peters, J. M. (2002). *Science in elementary education* (9th ed.). Upper Saddle River, NJ: Merrill/Prentice Hall.

Goleman, D. (1995). *Emotional intelligence.* New York: Bantam Books.

Goleman, D. (1998). *Working with emotional intelligence.* New York: Bantam Books.

Green, T. D., & Brown, A. (2002). *Multimedia projects in the classroom: A guide to development and evaluation.* Thousand Oaks, CA: Corwin.

Harrow, A. (1969). *A taxonomy of the psychomotor domain: A guide for developing behavioral objectives.* New York: David McKay.

Hunter, M. (1982). *Mastery teaching.* El Segundo, CA: Instructional Dynamics.

Kovalik, S. (1993). *ITI: The model. Integrated Thematic Instruction* (2nd ed.). Village of Oak Creek, AZ: Books for Educators.

Krathwohl, D., Bloom, B., & Masia, B. (1964). *Taxonomy of educational objectives: The classification of educational goals. Handbook II: Affective domain.* New York: David McKay.

Marlowe, B. A., & Page, M. L. (1998). *Creating and sustaining the constructivist classroom.* Thousand Oaks, CA: Corwin Press.

Monson, M. P., & Monson, R. J. (1993). Who creates curriculum? New roles for teachers. *Educational Leadership, 51*(2), 19–21.

Pappas, C. C., Kiefer, B. Z., & Levstik, L. S. (1998). *An integrated language perspective in the elementary schools: An action approach* (3rd ed.). New York: Longman.

Popham, W. J., & Baker, E. (1970). *Establishing instructional goals.* Upper Saddle River, NJ: Prentice Hall.

Savage, T. V., & Armstrong, D. (2000). *Effective teaching in elementary social studies* (4th ed.). Upper Saddle River, NJ: Merrill/Prentice Hall.

Suchman, J. R. (1962). *The elementary school training program in scientific inquiry.* Report to the U.S. Office of Education, Project Title VII, Project 216. Urbana: University of Illinois.

Tiedt, P. L., & Tiedt, I. M. (1999). *Multicultural teaching: A handbook of activities, information, and resources* (5th ed.). Boston: Allyn & Bacon.

Tyler, R. (1949). *Basic principles of curriculum and instruction.* Chicago: University of Chicago Press.

Wiggins, G., & McTighe, J. (1998). *Understanding by design.* Alexandria, VA: Association for Curriculum and Supervision.

Wisconsin Model Academic Standards (1998). Retrieved May 21, 2003 from http://www.dpi.state.wi.us/dpi/standards/claa12.html

WEB SITES

http://www.statestandards.com
This web site includes links to lesson plans and content standards for each state

http://www.teachnet.com/resource.html
Teachnet.com/Web Links: Teacher2Teacher lesson ideas, resources, and links

http://www.kued.org/medsol/indes
Instructional Design: Works with reader to plan based on audience, objectives, constraints, and resources

http://www.funderstanding.com/learning_theory_instruct4.html
Funderstanding: Thematic instruction

http://www.awesomelibrary.org/lesson.html
Awesome Library, K–12 lesson plans (across the subject areas)

http://ericir.syr.edu/Virtual/Lesson
AskERIC lesson plans

http://faldo.atmos.uiuc.edu/CLA
Collaborative Lesson Archive

http://www.coe.uh.edu/archive
Archive.edu: A storehouse of instructional materials on a variety of topics

Use search terms to search the Internet for specific information:

backwards planning (sample units are found on many sites)
thematic instruction
lesson plans (you can list grade level and topic in an advanced search)

OPPORTUNITIES TO PRACTICE

1. Write behavioral objectives for some of the following skills and concepts or choose some concepts from your upcoming lessons.

   - Composing a five-sentence paragraph
   - Identifying plot structure in a narrative story
   - Preparing a persuasive speech
   - Forming letters in cursive
   - Explaining causes and effects of an important historical event
   - Solving challenging story problems in mathematics
   - Creating a device that throws marbles at least five feet
   - Serving a volleyball
   - Responding to a piece of music
   - Analyzing the use of color in a painting
   - Balancing chemical equations
   - Doing a cartwheel

   Analyze your objectives to be certain that each has

   - An observable verb (an action the students will take to demonstrate mastery). Underline the verb.
   - Conditions for performance of the observable action. Circle the conditions.
   - Criteria for acceptable performance. [Bracket] the criteria.

   Explain your work to a devoted friend.

2. Practice Bloom's taxonomy by identifying the level of each of the following general teacher statements. Then try writing your own statement at each of the levels.

   a. Did the main character make a good choice? Why or why not?

   b. Organize the story into parts and give a good title for each part.

   c. Tell about some people in real life who have the same problems as the person in the story.

   d. Name the characters in the story.

   e. Tell the story in your own words.

   f. Make a painting or construction to represent the main characters in the story.

   Key: a: evaluation, b: analysis, c: application, d: knowledge, e: comprehension, f: synthesis.

3. The taxonomies of educational objectives (cognitive, affective, and psychomotor domains) are useful in helping teachers to broaden their scope during planning. However, the domains have been criticized in their application to classrooms. Think about a classroom instance where you learned something that you value greatly. Analyze that experience in terms of the domains of objectives:

   - Which domain or domains were primarily involved?
   - Which levels of understanding or performance were required?

- What, if anything, can you conclude about the classroom use of educational taxonomies?
4. Plan a lesson using the open-body-close format. You will find a form in Figure 4.13. Choose an objective for your own students or rewrite one of the plans presented in this chapter. Use this format for other plans that you teach in your own classroom as well.

FIGURE 4.13 *Lesson plan form.*

Lesson Plan		
Students: Time:		
Materials: Concepts/skills: Objectives:		
Open:	(Time:	)
Body:	(Time:	)
Close:	(Time:	)
Assessment:		
Differentiation:		

5. Examine an existing unit that is touted as having a multicultural emphasis. Use Banks's (1997) levels of planning (from Figure 4.14) to determine the extent to which the unit can help students develop a knowledge base and view issues meaningfully from multiple perspectives. In terms of its depth of treatment, how representative is the unit you selected of other approaches that claim to be multicultural? Which level of multicultural curricular planning do you see at your site? Is that good or bad?

FIGURE 4.14 *Banks's (1997) levels of integration for multicultural content.*

Level 1: The Contributions Approach

- The mainstream perspective remains unchallenged.
- Study focuses on discrete elements that various cultures have contributed to the mainstream culture: their heroes and holidays.

Level 2: The Additive Approach

- Deeper content is introduced to the curriculum, but the structure of the curriculum remains unchanged.
- Books, readings, or lessons are added to existing materials.

Level 3: The Transformative Approach

- This approach shifts the assumption that there is one mainstream perspective and infuses the perspectives of several groups to enable students to view themes and issues from several perspectives.
- The structure of the curriculum is changed.

Level 4: The Social Action Approach

- Learning activities not only allow students to analyze issues from many perspectives but also require them to commit to personal social action related to those issues.

Before you begin reading Chapter 5

Take your pick of Exercise A or B . . . or, if you like, do both.

Warm-Up Exercise A

Think back to Chapter 1, which presented six propositions for the nature of teaching. How many propositions can you remember? Write as many as you can; then refer back to Chapter 1 to complete the list and check your work.

The Nature of Teaching

1. Teaching looks

2.

3.

4.

5.

6.

Good for you for taking the time to review and write! The six points you just reviewed provide the foundation for the advice you will find in this chapter. For instance, because teaching is goal directed, I suggest that you be organized when you teach. As you read, think about how these six propositions about teaching are reflected in the chapter's suggestions.

Warm-Up Exercise B

Think back to an instance when you, with the help of a coach or mentor, learned a new physical skill. Examples include sports and crafts. Make a list of the things that your coach or mentor did that were helpful. What made the coaching successful or unsuccessful?

Physical skill:

Things that helped me to learn the skill:

Things that interfered with my success:

Now generalize. Mark the points on your list that seem to provide advice for classroom teaching. Keep them in mind as you read this chapter's advice on instruction. (Thanks to Charlotte Danielson at Educational Testing Service for this exercise.)

CHAPTER *Five*

Advice on Instruction: COME IN

> "You have brains in your head.
> You have feet in your shoes.
> You can steer yourself
> any direction you choose.
> You're on your own. And you know what you know.
> And YOU are the guy who'll decide where to go."
>
> —Dr. Seuss, *Oh, the Places You'll Go!*

Dr. Seuss reminds us teachers that we are in the wonderful position of making important decisions. He also reminds us that our decisions need to be smart. We need to know what we know and use the brains in our heads as we choose how to teach. As you decide where to go in the classroom, you need to consider the stance toward education you developed through Chapter 2. Keep your stance in mind as you select strategies that are appropriate for you, for your learners, and for your setting. Always be on the lookout for opportunities to improve your stance and to add to your repertoire of teaching strategies.

This chapter is devoted to exploring six pieces of advice for instruction. Each guideline is supported by research and practice, but be warned: the presentation of each piece of advice is brief; you will probably need to re-read and rehearse them in order to use them effectively. Together, these six pieces of advice invite you to . . . COME IN.

1. **C**onnect to the life of the learner.
2. **O**rganize your instruction.
3. **M**odel.
4. **E**nrich.
5. **I**nteract.
6. Consider human **N**ature and developmental **N**eeds.

CONNECT TO THE LIFE OF THE LEARNER

One central aspect of good teaching is forging connections. If teachers fail to help students to connect with information, then it fails to become a lasting part of them. In fact, John Dewey, considered the father of American education, held that connection—intellectual integration—was the key to learning. According to Marlowe and Page (1998), Dewey "described the mind as roaming far and wide but returning with what it found and constantly making judgments as to relationships, relevancies, and bearings upon a central theme" (p. 17).

Thus, helping students to draw connections is more than "selling" students on the relevance of our content. It is instead a necessity based on how the brain works (Caine & Caine, 1994, 2001; Cole, 1995). Let's test this with an exercise. The next sentence will be one written in English with common words; be ready to explain it in your own words:

The cross from the midfielder was headed by the sweeper. At the far end of their pitch, the keeper caught it.[1]

What happened? Where were these people? What were they doing? And how do you know? The terms "cross," "headed," and "keeper" have many common meanings, depending on their context. Used together as they were in this sentence, they indicate that a soccer player kicked the ball, which bounced off the head of a defensive player on his team to be caught by their goalie. Phew. Only by connecting your background knowledge, gained through years of experience in the world, with the words you read could you correctly interpret the sentence. If you do not know soccer, how close did you come? What clues in the sentence connected with your knowledge?

Instruction needs to connect to—to become integrated with—students' prior experiences, to the real world and its important ideas, and to action, and it must connect classroom participants to each other. The rationale for each of these connections is made here. To help you assist students in making these varied connections, Figure 5.1 points you forward to specific tips found in later figures.

FIGURE 5.1   *Tips for connecting to the life of the learner.*

Connecting to . . .	
Prior Knowledge and Experience	Try Figure 5.7, Ideas for Encouraging Interaction and Active Participation, numbers 4, 5, 6, 12, 18, 19, 20, 22, 24, 28, and 29.
The Real World and Its Important Ideas	Try some Ideas for Enriching the Learning Environment (Figure 5.6). Use strategies (like analyzing newspaper articles) that place the content in a real context and show how it has been important to real people in different times and in different ways.
Action	Encourage action projects that allow students to apply their learning. Examples include fund-raising projects for charitable causes, letter writing campaigns, conservation efforts, and community improvement projects. Provide students with opportunities to share what they know with other audiences, like parents or other children at the school. Try simulation exercises and role play. Use guest speakers who apply in their lives the content you are studying.
Classroom Participants	See Ideas for Encouraging Interaction and Active Participation (in Figure 5.7), numbers 2, 5, 18, 19–24, 29, and 31. Also try learning students' names the first day you meet them. Encourage them to learn each others' names. Give students a space in the room to display items that are important to them. Share appropriate information about yourself that reveals your love of learning, your willingness to make mistakes, and your eagerness to apply the content. Laugh—and cry—with your students. Tell your own stories and listen to theirs.

Connecting to Prior Knowledge and Experience

Learners have experiences and ways of thinking that will influence what they will learn and how they will learn it. Your job as a teacher is to find out what students bring to the current learning situation and link it to your instruction. Re-

[1] Thanks to Tim Green for his help with this soccer sentence example.

search indicates clearly that students hold misconceptions (or "growing conceptions") which can be difficult to change (Marzano, Pickering, & Pollock, 2001). In fact, some suggest that the largest determinant of what students will learn in a given situation is what they *already know.* Surface their conceptions, challenge their misconceptions, and help them build richer, more useful ways of thinking. Strategies such as knowledge charts and clinical interviews can help you learn what students know. Chapter 7, Assessment, gives additional strategies that can be of use to you as you make it a point to include **pre-assessment** as a regular and important feature of your lesson and unit plans.

 QUESTION FOR THOUGHT

"Teaching exceptional and culturally different students involves building **bridges to the curriculum** that enable students to succeed. . . . In some cases, these bridges are temporary; in other cases, building these bridges entails broadening a teacher's repertoire of what counts as 'normal' ways of teaching and learning." (Grant & Sleeter, 1998, p. 12)

It is your responsibility to ensure that all students form meaningful connections. How are you helping students build bridges?

Connecting to the Real World and Its Important Ideas

In connecting to the real world, teachers provide students with authentic settings for using and developing their academic content. Reality-based approaches also provide students with opportunities to enhance their skills at analyzing problems, gathering and summarizing important information, solving problems, and reflecting on their solutions (Cole, 1995). Approaches such as these present real-world or realistic problems that are solved by using the content under study. This helps students to perceive the relevance or importance of what they are studying and enhances motivation to learn. Examples of real-world connections include reading primary sources such as historical documents and the newspaper, beginning lessons by presenting photographs or realistic problems, and inviting guest speakers such as scientists, writers, or elected representatives into the classroom. Authentic experiences are linked most closely to the settings in which students will use their new understanding. Important ideas are the ones worth having. For Duckworth (1996): the essence of intellectual development is the formation of connections or, in her terms, "the having of wonderful ideas." Wonderful ideas

> "need not necessarily look wonderful to the outside world. I see no difference in kind between wonderful ideas that many other people have already had, and wonderful ideas that nobody has yet happened upon. That is, the nature of creative intellectual acts remains the same, whether it is an infant who for the first time marks the connection between seeing things and reaching for them . . . or a musician who invents a harmonic sequence. . . . In each case, *new connections are being made among things already mastered.* The more we help children to have their wonderful ideas and to feel good about themselves for having them, the more likely it is that they will some day happen upon wonderful ideas that no one else has happened upon before." (p. 14; emphasis mine)

Connecting to Action

Your long view of learners is probably related to students' future behavior patterns and decision-making abilities. What we teach children, from kindergarten on, should connect to the ways we want them to act now and as adults. They deserve immediate opportunities to act on what they learn. Social action projects can serve as a powerful mechanism to shape schools and communities into more humane and inclusive institutions (e.g., Banks, 1997; Bomer & Bomer, 2001; Nieto, 1996). Another chance for students to take action is through service learning, wherein they test and apply their content learning by serving the community (Stephens, 1995). Examples include encouraging voter registration, teaching or tutoring younger students, and planning community gardens.

Connecting Classroom Participants

Classroom learning occurs in a social setting, so students are required to take learning risks in public. Kohn (1999, p. 21) powerfully states the human need for connection to others when he says, "All of us yearn for a sense of relatedness or belonging, a feeling of being connected to others . . . And all of us seek opportunities to feel effective, to learn new things that matter to us and find (or create) answers to personally meaningful questions." Helping students to form a cohesive group can encourage a safe environment, and it can help students learn important lessons about working as members of a group. Additionally, learning strategies that require students to work together are effective in supporting academic achievement (Marzano, Pickering, & Pollock, 2001), language development (Faltis, 2001), and social and emotional growth (Goleman, 1998).

There are plenty of strategies for building a sense of community in a classroom. Most importantly, teachers must model respect, revealing genuine interest in students as people, and they need to encourage students to do the same for each other. If one student ridicules another, the teacher's lesson of the day must necessarily shift to address expectations for how community members are to treat each other. Several entertaining techniques can foster a sense of community, as follows:

1. *Share expectations:* Hold a discussion, perhaps preceded by a journal writing session, of what class members expect from each other. What can students expect from their teacher? How do they expect to be treated by their peers?
2. *Use activities that help students get to know each other:* Choose from among many published activities that allow students to learn about each

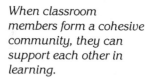

When classroom members form a cohesive community, they can support each other in learning.

other. In an activity called "Trading Places" (Silberman, 1996), students write a favorite (e.g., book, place, song) on a sticky note, place the note on their shirts, and circulate to discuss each others' ideas. They negotiate trades of sticky notes based on self-selected criteria.

Kagan (2000) similarly gives many games that can help build a sense of team spirit in noncompetitive and enjoyable ways. In "Smile if You Love Me," one student (Cupid) stands in the center of the circle, makes faces, and uses motions, words, and sounds to make another person smile. When people on the circle smile, they join the center of the circle as Cupids.

3. *Develop an outward symbol or sign to signify a sense of group identity:* Create a work of art, a name, a handshake, a logo, or other identification that signals your cohesion as a class. For instance, based on student Jodi's advice from her great-grandmother, my class recently decided on its motto: "Be good. And if you can't be good . . . be careful."[2]

ORGANIZE YOUR INSTRUCTION

Teaching is intentional. Professional educators do things *on purpose.* When you step into your classroom each day, you need to have goals in mind. Arrange your learning activities so that they allow you and your students to reach your goals. Actively encourage them to set and reach for goals as well. This is a terrific way to start with the student, and it is effective in helping them learn (Marzano et al., 2001).

You need to be organized on more than one level: You need to organize content within and across individual lessons, and you need to organize times and tasks within the larger teaching environment.

Organizing Content

Think back to Exercise B at the beginning of this chapter, where you were invited to think about what a good coach does well. One often-cited coaching skill is the ability to break a complicated task (for instance, sailing, golfing, or driving a manual transmission car) down into smaller, more easily mastered skills. As does a coach, you need to analyze the content you are teaching. It needs to be broken into chunks before it can be presented in your classroom. What size should the chunks be? What shape? In which order should you present them?

The manner in which you organize the content depends on your knowledge of the students, the amount of time you have with them, and your knowledge of the content itself. Before you teach, ensure that you have a firm grasp of the major concepts you will be teaching and that you understand the relationship among these ideas. Check your understanding by constructing a diagram or other visual representation of your knowledge. One example is a **concept map,** which relates ideas in a hierarchical structure. Figure 5.9, found in Exercise 3 at the close of this chapter, is a concept map of this entire text.

Being able to organize your ideas into a one-page diagram helps you discover the main points and supporting details so you can structure instruction and arrange your time appropriately. Additionally, using **graphic organizers,** or diagrams, and other nonlinguistic representations of the text supports student achievement (Marzano et al., 2001).

By presenting information in particular ways, your curriculum materials will also provide clues for content organization. Often textbooks follow predictable structures in presenting content. Some typical patterns for the structure of text are suggested in Figure 5.2.

As you organize your content, though, remember that textbook authors do not know your particular students when they write. Think about the organiza-

---

[2] Used with the permission of Jodi Elmore.

FIGURE 5.2   *Some organizational patterns of content.*

Organizational Pattern	Example
Time sequence	Historical events presented chronologically
General principles to specific examples	Scientific laws and then real-world examples of them
Specific examples to general principles	Letters of the alphabet as examples of vowels or consonants
Topical	Aspects of family life within a culture: recreation, food, and work
Cause and effect	Historical events and new laws they inspired
Compare and contrast	Plants and animals
Problem and solution	Present an enigma and work toward the solution

tion that would best suit your purposes, even if it differs from the organization used in your curricular materials. Your learners' developmental level provides one clue in organizing instruction. A general rule of thumb is that the less experience learners have with the content, the smaller the chunks of content need to be. For example, kindergartners, who tend to have fewer background experiences from which to draw, need consistently smaller pieces of content. Similarly, teenagers who have never heard the German language will probably not begin learning the language by reading entire essays in German. Age and other elements such as the students' capacity to learn and language proficiency affect the amount of experience students have with the content and hence the size of the chunks of information their teachers present.

The most common mistake novice teachers make when organizing content is to include too much information (too many chunks) in a single lesson. I also made that mistake when I taught a reading and science lesson to second graders, as I described in Chapter 4. You read my plan (Figure 4.8) for the 1½-hour lesson. I planned to guide the children through some reading experiences and then have them make their own fossils to build an understanding of how fossils are made. Upon reflection, I overestimated second graders' experience with text and could improve the lesson by breaking the reading portion of the lesson into even smaller chunks spread over more time. Similarly, the children's fine motor skills were not as well developed as I had anticipated, so shaping the clay molds took longer than expected.

My unreasonable expectations for students' motor development also reflects another common mistake that new teachers make: developing unrealistic expectations for their learners. Although it is critical to maintain high learning expectations for every student, it is equally important to recall that not all learners are college students. Although this point seems obvious, recall that one of the most recent and therefore potent instructional models new teachers witness is the college instructor. What works with a set of adult learners will usually not work well with less mature students.

Organizing Times and Tasks

After you arrange the content within individual lessons, place it into a framework of how activities will flow over the course of the day. When you are ready to teach, make certain that the class understands and accepts the organizational scheme you have devised. Even if you teach from great lesson plans, your learners may leave dazed unless you provide clues about the organization of content and activities—or they may leave indifferent if they perceive that they had no input into the agenda. Teaching is interactional. Students matter. Learners deserve both an overall sense of where the day is headed and clues to let them know where they are on the day's map. Figure 5.3 provides some techniques for building and sharing your organizational plan.

FIGURE 5.3 *Techniques for building and sharing your organizational plan.*

- Ask students for their expectations at the beginning of a class (e.g., "What do you hope to learn this year?" or "What do you hope to learn in this unit?").
- Write a daily agenda on the board. To the extent possible, allow learners to provide input about adding, deleting, or rearranging items.
- Provide a graphic organizer—a visual display such as a chart or diagram—on the overhead projector, chalkboard, or chart paper that shows how your instruction will be organized.
- Briefly tell students what will happen during the lesson.
- Preview the lesson's major points.
- If you intend to lecture, provide a note-taking form that helps student organize the information.
- During the lesson, use internal summaries and transition sentences so that students see when you are switching to a different point or activity.
- Refer back to your agenda or chart as the lesson progresses.
- Draw each lesson to closure. Try summarizing by asking students to share an important point or ask for input for the next agenda.

As you teach, events will conspire to encourage stalls and side trips. Because classrooms are crowded, busy places, it is easy for plans to be forestalled. Students, for instance, may raise interesting questions or bring up points that warrant exploration. Experienced teachers call such an instance a **teachable moment.** A teachable moment is not found explicitly listed in the daily plan book, but it presents a wonderful opportunity for learning. One difficult aspect of your job will be to decide which moments to pursue because of their rich promise and which opportunities may not be worth the time invested. That decision is not always easy, and not all students will perceive your adherence to or diversion from the plan with the same optimism. When the situation arises in my classroom, I often tell students "You are raising important issues! We can certainly explore them now. We will need to modify our agenda to make room for it by deleting *X*. Shall we?" Use your professional judgment, and refer back to your stance toward education and its important goals, as you decide which paths to pursue. The point is to remain intentional. Keep your goals in mind.

Teaching Tips

GIVING CLEAR DIRECTIONS
Ensuring that your directions to students are crystal clear will help you and your students remain organized and productive. When giving directions, remember the following:

1. Limit your directions to no more than three steps.
2. Use more than one form of input: Say your directions aloud, post them on the board, and model them. For older students, using just two forms of input may suffice.
3. Hold up your fingers to count steps as you state your directions: "The *first* thing you will do is . . . " Be certain that, for older students, you use natural phrasing and do not overemphasize the gesture.
4. Check for understanding of the directions before you release students to work: "What is the first thing you will do?" Reteach if students do not demonstrate understanding.
5. No matter the age of the learner, give your directions immediately before you want students to follow them. Students may forget what to do if you give directions and then talk about something else before releasing them.

It is also easy to lose track of time. If we were to list Murphy's Laws of Classroom Teaching, at the head of the list might be "Things always take longer than expected." Keep one eye on the clock and remember your agenda to ensure that you are spending your students' time wisely.

MODEL

According to the fable, a young crab was chastised by her mother because she walked sideways, not straight ahead. Her mother, as do all crabs of her variety, also walked sideways. After trying unsuccessfully to follow her mother's admonitions to walk forward, the young crab implored her mother: "Show me!" The moral? Giving advice *through words* is easy. Demonstrating that advice *through actions* is harder . . . and is almost always more helpful for learners.

In life outside the classroom walls, we often learn by example, by being shown how to conduct ourselves. Modeling, or showing students how to carry out a skill, is a powerful instructional strategy (Cole, 1995). Think about what you want students to learn and then show them how to do it. Modeling is effective for learners of all ages, and it is appropriate in every subject area. It is important for helping students learn behaviors, such as using manners and showing consideration, as well as for helping them master content area outcomes. Figure 5.4 provides four examples of modeling. When you model, try some of the suggestions in Figure 5.5.

FIGURE 5.4 *Four examples of teacher modeling.*

Concepts and Skills	Modeling
Tying shoelaces	Mr. Alvarez positions himself on the rug, where his circle of six kindergartners can all see clearly. He demonstrates each step of tying a bow, exaggerating and slowing his motions to make the steps obvious to the students. He asks the students to verbalize the procedure with him as he ties several times before handing each student a shoe to tie while he watches.
Writing a persuasive essay	On a monitor display of her computer screen in her seventh-grade class, Ms. Simon shows and reads aloud two examples of good persuasive essays. She shares the criteria for effective persuasive writing and then states that she will use those criteria to write her own essay. She talks through her decisions about selecting a topic and its supporting points. As she expresses her decisions, she writes a couple of drafts on the projected computer screen. Together, she and the students check to see whether the essays meet the criteria for good persuasive writing.
Solving a challenging word problem in math	Miss Thompson reads the problem aloud to her ninth graders, varying her intonation as she reads critical components of the problem. She summarizes her understanding of the problem, discusses what she needs to know, and reacts to the problem to show her stance as a problem solver: "This one looks tough, but I have solved similar problems!" She attacks the problem on the white board, sharing her decisions for trying certain strategies. When her strategies do not bring immediate success, she shows students how to move forward by trying new approaches. When she reaches a solution, she shares the joy she finds in persisting and solving a challenging problem.
Cooperating with peers when working with partners	Having assigned his fourth graders to work in pairs, Mr. Pease reviews his expectations for partner work: "Partners support each other by reaching decisions together. Partners help each other when they get stuck." He invites a student to the front of the room to play the role of his work partner. The partners show the class how to compromise to reach decisions and how to use helpful words to get unstuck. Mr. Pease reminds the class: "Here's what cooperation *looks like*, and here is what it *sounds like*." As a result, his students have some specific advice and behaviors to help them work together.

FIGURE 5.5 *Suggestions for modeling.*

Suggestions for Modeling

1. As you plan, think about the most important elements of the skill or process you will model. List them. This will help you to draw students' attention to *critical attributes* and will remind you that in many cases students' performances need not match yours. Their efforts may be both different from yours *and* good.

2. Verbalize your decisions; talk about what you are thinking and doing. When we talk about our thought processes, we model *metacognition;* we show that we understand and have control over our thinking.

3. Provide plenty of good examples, including student models. Point out when the examples are different from each other and say what they have in common that makes them good. Showing different examples—**multiple embodiments**—will help students focus on the criteria for a successful performance or good example.

4. If the behavior is complex, model sections of it and slow down your performance.

5. Model desired behaviors more than once. The less familiar students are with the skill you are modeling, the more careful repetitions they may need to see.

6. Model regularly, even if you are short on time.

Finally, through their modeling, teachers teach more than content area skills, behaviors, and knowledge. Good and Brophy (1987) make the important point that, through their modeling, teachers shape a healthy group climate, convey an interest in the students as people, and teach ideas about good listening and communication habits. Through teacher modeling, students learn to socialize as members of groups, to gain rational control over their own behaviors, and to respect others. Teacher modeling, then, is an important socializing force that helps teachers induce students toward the good.

ENRICH

Because teachers are responsible for presenting a great deal of information to large groups of students in relatively brief periods of time, classrooms tend to ring with auditory input, or teacher talk. Listening is an efficient learning strategy for many students much of the time, but it does have at least six drawbacks:

1. People process information at different rates.
2. Because speech comes in a stream, listeners may not be able to separate main points and discern the supporting points.
3. It can be difficult for students to contribute to a lecture, change its pace, or connect with its content.
4. People learn differently (Gardner, 1993).
5. Students may have insufficient experience with the language of instruction or with the content to comprehend it solely by hearing it. Meaningful instruction for students acquiring English is most often embedded in realistic and rich contexts (Echevarria & Graves, 1998).
6. Recent work in human learning suggests that varied stimulation is essential for brain development. The more varied and frequent the stimulation the brain receives, the more complex its development (e.g., Caine & Caine, 1994, 2001).

For all of these reasons, teachers need to enrich the learning environment by providing rich input.

Think about powerful learning experiences you have in life. Potent learning experiences tend to be full of sensations: new sights and sounds, textures and smells. We hear beautiful words and ideas that make us reconsider what we know. We try new things that just the day before seemed beyond our capabilities.

Rich environments foster deeper learning.

> *L*ife is amazing, and a teacher had better prepare himself to be a medium for that amazement.
>
> —Edward Blishen

Classroom learning should mirror the most powerful kinds of learning from our outside lives. How well do our lectures, worksheets, spelling lists, and pages of math exercises live up to that challenge? As you teach, remember to fill students' lives with authentic—rich and real—opportunities to learn. Focus on meaning. Give students the chance to see and try new things, to hear the music and speech of faraway places, to experience the struggles of those fighting for independence, to touch the moist skin of the amphibians they study, to read or hear the words of people who have shaped history. Figure 5.6 gives some ideas for enriching the learning environment.

Will providing enriched experiences take more of your preparation time than would photocopying a worksheet page? Almost certainly so. You can minimize your time investment by saving your collections and by utilizing the expertise of community members and colleagues. On the other hand, do worksheets and book activities have their place in the classroom? Almost certainly so. You will need to balance the kinds of activities and input you provide, checking to see that you select a variety of activities that promote meaningful learning. Your efforts to provide rich input will pay off. Remember that you are a window to the world for your students.

INTERACT

"Too often, 'teaching as usual' in American classrooms consists of children sitting still and listening to the teacher or filling in a series of worksheets; these time-honored practices have proved to be ineffective and actually damaging for students—particularly those at risk of academic failure," intones Cole (1995, p. 2). Perhaps one of the reasons that such practices are harmful is that they are absent of the *interaction* between teacher and students—or students and students—that so forcefully fuels learning.

Learning is personal, and students' reactions matter. As a result, teaching must be interactional. Teaching is more than telling. Accomplished teachers listen, and they diligently search the faces and reactions of their learners to modify their instruction. If you gather ongoing information about how students are learning and responding to the lesson, you will be better equipped to adjust

FIGURE 5.6 *Ideas for enriching the learning environment.*

Look for a variety of ways to present your content and for varied representations of it.

- *Meaning:* Focus on conceptual understanding, not just rote learning. Help students build sophisticated understanding of the world and its people. Provide authentic experiences in the content areas.

- *Many kinds of print:* Fill your room with books of different genres. Include, too, other kinds of print such as posters, recipes, student-generated work, letters, and signs (Schifini, 1994).

- *Picture files:* Start clipping and saving pictures to support your instruction. Pictures can be used for concept sorts or to encourage small-group discussion. Old magazines and calendars are a good place to start. Many images can be downloaded and printed as well.

- *Realia:* Find real objects to provide examples of what you read and study.

- *Works of art:* Reproductions of great works are available in teaching materials and at libraries. They can set the stage for the study of concepts from the content areas.

- *Newspapers and current periodicals:* Look in the news for examples of what you are studying. Encourage your students to do the same. Or, allow current issues to suggest topics for study.

- *Technology:* Help your students access information around the world through the Internet. Use Internet video clips or video disks to study phenomena that are difficult to observe directly. Books on disk are often recorded in multiple languages. At the New York Art Line (http://www.kids.ccit.duq.edu) students can download, among other things, pictures drawn by students in other countries. World Wide Web Virtual Library (http://syy.oulu.fi/music.html) is one of the most extensive music catalogs on the Internet. See the websites at the close of this chapter for resources that can bring the world into your room.

- *Living things:* Instead of assigning only worksheets to study insects, bring in mealworms from the pet store. Create a worm garden in an aquarium. Grow mold.

- *Music:* Many students love to sing, and nearly all love to listen. Find recordings to support your study of history and culture. Try compact discs. Make instruments in science to study sound. Dance.

- *Food:* Try foods from different places or that illustrate different scientific or mathematical applications. Make butter as an example of a physical change. When students study about George Washington, bring in George's favorite breakfast: hoe cakes and tea.

- *Real tools:* Have your students *seen* the simple tools they read about in science? Bring in wedges, screws, and pulleys. Encourage students to hunt for them also. Bring in a typewriter or toaster beyond repair, cut off the plug, and let the students take it apart.

- *Models:* Use physical models to provide opportunities to study hard-to-reach phenomena such as atoms, planets, rockets, or the human heart.

- *Graphic organizers:* Provide visual displays of your information to support auditory input (Bromley, Irwin-De Vitis, & Modlo, 1995). Try Venn diagrams to compare and contrast. Make an outline that students view before they read. Allow students to make their own organizers.

- *Guest speakers and visitors:* Bring in family members and other guests who have lived through important events or have honed special skills. Do you know someone who has seen war? Volunteered? Marched in a protest? Named a star? Escaped persecution? Written a book? Played professional sports? Learners' lives are enriched when they meet people with great accomplishments.

- *Field trips:* Few classroom learning experiences can substitute for a good field trip. Be certain to prepare your students for the trip by building connections between their studies and what they will be experiencing in the field. List their questions before you go. Consider whether it would be appropriate for your students to record information during the trip. When you return, process the field trip by focusing on what students saw, heard, and learned. Find out if they have answered their questions. Connect questions to past and future study. Even a 10-minute walk can provide abundant learning experiences (Russell, 1990).

your activities. Gathering and using feedback from students can help you modify your teaching and will foster learning.

Some teachers rely on informal student feedback during their lessons: Are there dazed looks? Attentive gazes? Nods of approval? Nonverbal signals can be useful for adjusting instruction, but they are not always valid. Teachers may

Teaching Tips

SHARING THE WEALTH

When you feel obliged to ask a question, try this: Ask the question. Then say, "No matter what the first answer is, I'm going to call on four more hands." Wait a few seconds, then call on five in a row. This strategy can increase student participation for both convergent and divergent questions.

misinterpret students' cues—which may be culturally bound—or they may base their instructional decisions on a few unrepresentative students' responses. In addition to relying on nonverbal feedback, teachers often ask questions to check students' understanding: "Does everyone understand?" There are some drawbacks to using questions as a sole guide for encouraging interaction. One drawback is that the use of persistent questions from the teacher can serve to reinforce the power differential between teacher and students: Teacher asks, and students answer, and then await the next question. Additionally, students do not need to be very old before they learn that admitting ignorance is not always perceived as a good thing to do.

Fortunately, many strategies can encourage each student to overtly engage in the lesson and provide feedback on teaching. As you gather information about students' learning, experiences, and preferences, your interactions will vary by both participants and format. Sometimes you will interact directly with the students, and sometimes they will interact with each other. Sometimes your exchanges will be verbal, and sometimes they will be through actions, writings, or drawings.

Figure 5.7 gives a list of 31 ideas for encouraging active participation. Some strategies are best for checking content mastery and others for sharing students' perspectives. Mastery strategies are listed first in each section. As you select ideas, remember that you need to use a variety of strategies, and the strategies you select should be consistent with your learners' needs and with your personal stance toward teaching.

Two themes run through these suggestions for active participation. First, the strategies provide tasks for students to complete so that you, the teacher, can determine whether and what students understand. These strategies promise to be more productive than asking "Does anyone have a question? Anyone *not* get it?" Second, active strategies can break the traditional pattern of the teacher doing most of the talking while students either listen quietly or respond, one at a time, to the teacher's numerous questions. The bottom line: Do something that allows you to elicit all students' perspectives and understandings and then do something with what you find out.

Because teaching is interactional, students also deserve explicit and specific feedback. Give students clear and immediate information about their learning. If you use praise, precisely name students' appropriate efforts, and gently redirect efforts that are less than successful. Vary the form of your feedback to include oral, written, and nonverbal messages. Include both informal and formal messages to your students and their families.

The classroom belongs to all of you. Help students chart their own growth by sharing information about their progress and adjust your teaching based on what you learn from the students. What will you teach tomorrow? Your answer depends partly on your long-range plans, but it also depends on what happens in your classroom *today*. Teaching is more than telling.

FIGURE 5.7 *Active participation strategies: 31 ideas for encouraging interaction and active participation.*

Give prompts to discover what students know, think, feel, have experienced, and wonder.

	Teacher–Student Interactions
"Tell Me"	1. Choral response: When questions have convergent, brief answers, all students respond at once instead of one at a time. Teacher records and discusses items with muddy responses.
	2. Whip: Everyone shares a brief response (word, phrase, or sentence) to a topic or question. Contributions move from one student to the next with no teacher intervention. Students are allowed to "pass."
	3. Stand to share: All stand when they have developed a response to a question such as, "What was an important point in the chapter?" One person shares aloud, and all with the same or similar responses sit. Sharing continues until all are sitting (Kagan, 1994).
	4. Opinionnaire: All respond privately to a set of statements related to the current topic, such as, "Efforts to clone humans are wrong." Responses can be formed as agree or disagree or as numbers that indicate degrees of agreement. Teacher leads a discussion to elicit students' responses.
	5. Share a story: Teacher elicits students' stories related to the topic. If there are many stories, students can tell their stories to smaller groups or to partners. For instance, "I have told you a story about crickets in my apartment. I would like to hear a true cricket story that you may have."
	6. Student questions (Dillon, 1988): Teacher provides time for students to formulate their questions about a topic. He might record them for discussion and study. For example, "We will be studying space. I have always wondered why stars twinkle. What do you wonder about space?"
"Show Me"	7. Flash cards: Individually or in groups students hold up color-coded or other flash cards in response to teacher's or peers' mastery questions. For example, teacher asks questions about the federal government, and students hold up red for legislative, yellow for executive, or blue for judicial. Students can also ask the questions.
	8. Finger signals: Students hold up numbers of fingers to respond to mastery questions (e.g., "How many sides on a triangle?"). Other gestures can also be used. For instance, "I will watch while you draw a triangle in the air."
	9. Chalkboards or wipe boards: Students record responses on individual boards, then show teacher or peers. Some examples include spelling words, cursive letter formation, French vocabulary, and brief math exercises. Chalkboards can be purchased or made. One inexpensive technique is to cut strips of dark tag board; students cover the surface with chalk and then erase. Individual wipe boards can be constructed or purchased.
	10. Letter and number tiles: Students have sets of ceramic, magnetic, or tag board tiles displaying letters of the alphabet or digits 0 through 9. They display their tiles in response to tasks from the teacher or peers. For instance, "Build an even number that is greater than 50." Or: "Round 5,723.86 to the tenths place. I will come around and check your tiles."
	11. Comprehension check: Students complete brief quizzes, written by teacher or pulled from existing materials, at the beginning or end of class. Students check their own work and analyze what they need help with before passing their papers to teacher.
	12. Quick write: Students respond in writing to a prompt. For example, "Before we read this chapter, please take a minute and write about a time when you felt powerless." Quick writes can spur discussion and allow all students to express feelings or experiences in writing, even if they choose not to share aloud. Quick writes are not graded.

continued

FIGURE 5.7   *Continued*

	13. Fuzzy points: Near the end of a lesson, students anonymously record their fuzzy points, the concepts about which they are still unsure. Teacher collects and analyzes them for the next time. This activity differs from comprehension checks because in fuzzy points, students report on their learning without demonstrating their understanding directly.

Student–Student Interactions

"Tell Each Other" (Be sure to process these activities. Come together as a class and briefly share. Discuss findings.)	14. Peer coach: In pairs, students take turns serving as coach and coachee. Coach observes coachee solve a problem and provides praise and suggestions. Roles switch. Teacher circulates to check for accuracy and social skills (Kagan, 1994).
	15. Student-led recitation: Students prepare written comprehension and challenge questions over course and reading material. They sit in a circle and take turns asking, answering, and evaluating each others' questions and responses (Dillon, 1988).
	16. Numbered heads together: In small groups, students number off. Teacher (or a peer) asks a question, and group members put their heads together to discuss. Teacher calls on one number to respond for each group; for example, "Number Fours, let's hear from you" (Kagan, 1994).
	17. Toss the ball: Students give a response to a factual or opinion question and toss a soft ball, Koosh ball, or Nerf ball to a peer, who becomes the next to answer or question.
	18. Talk to your partner: Students turn and discuss with a nearby partner. For instance, "Tell your partner about an animal you know with protective coloration." Or, for older students, "Tell your partner what you know about the word *secession*."
	19. Peer interview: Students ask their partners questions about their experiences with a certain topic. For example, "Ask questions about your partner's travels. You may try these questions on the board if you like. Be ready to share with another group."
	20. Values line up: Present a prompt that is likely to elicit a wide range of responses. For instance, "To help the environment, families should own only one car." Have students numerically rate their agreement with the statement and then line up in order of their numerical ratings, 1 to 10. Split the line in half and pair students with extreme scores (1 goes to 10). Instruct them to give their responses and rationales and then to paraphrase each other's points of view. Draw conclusions as a class once students are again seated.
	21. Scavenger hunt: Prepare a scavenger hunt form that encourages discussion of students' varied backgrounds and knowledge. Allow students to circulate and record the names of peers who fit certain criteria. For instance, "Find someone who has seen a famous monument" or "Find someone who has lived a million seconds." You can also make the prompts content oriented. Students might be required to find the match for their chemical symbol, for instance.
"Show Each Other" (Process these activities, too.)	22. Group chart: In groups, students draw diagrams or charts to illustrate their understanding of the content. Charts are displayed for class review and comparison.
	23. Group problem: Each member of a small group is given a vital piece of information necessary to solve a problem. Only when students share their information can they solve the problem together.
	24. Snowballs: Invite students to record their questions or perceptions on a sheet of paper. Then have them crumple the sheets into wads and, on your signal, toss them across the room. After the chaos subsides, students open the wad nearest them and respond to the question or add their own perspective in writing. Toss and respond a few times so that students can read a variety of perspectives. Process by asking for themes or questions that need to be addressed. For example, "Write one thing you learned and one thing you still wonder about the world's great religions." Then, "Who is holding a question that is still unanswered? Let's hear it."

FIGURE 5.7   *Continued*

25. Student quiz: Students develop written quizzes to check their peers' mastery. They check the content before handing papers to teacher. As an option, students can complete quizzes in groups.

26. Follow the leader: One partner gives oral directions as the other partner tries to draw, make, or build a construction that fits the leader's description. Roles switch. Teacher leads discussion about effective communication.

27. Sorts: In small groups, students sort objects (such as leaves or small tools) or ideas (recorded on cards such as elements on the periodic table). In open sorts, students choose but do not reveal their criteria for sorting. Peers discern the criteria by observing groups. In closed sorts, students follow the grouping criteria given by the teacher or a peer. Older students can use multistage classifications; younger students may group by one attribute only.

28. Brainstorming and fact-storming: Students in groups record as many ideas as they can generate related to a topic or solutions to a problem. Praise is given for fluency (number of ideas) and flexibility (variety of ideas). For example, "What are some uses for a toothpick?" In fact-storming, students record as many relevant facts as they can. For instance, "List products yielded by the rain forest." Facts can be grouped and labeled, or they can be placed on a chart for future revisions and additions.

29. Partner journals: Students can be paired anonymously or with friends. They respond to classroom activities and content by writing to each other. Teacher chooses whether to collect and review journals.

30. Blackboard blitz: During small-group work, representatives from each group simultaneously record their group's best ideas on the board. All students can view each others' ideas, and work continues while students write on the board (Kagan, 1994).

31. Gallery tour: Upon completion of individual or group projects, students place their projects on desks and tour the room to view other works. Students can respond to each other's works on sticky notes or on a response sheet for the author.

CONSIDER HUMAN NATURE AND DEVELOPMENTAL NEEDS

Finally, when we start with the students, our instruction reflects students' current physical and emotional states, and it should reflect an understanding of human nature. What you know about how humans learn and behave should be reflected in your teaching. For instance, we know that people have limited ability to take in new information and that they need opportunities to process—to think about—what they hear. As a result, you will need to vary your activities within a single lesson. As another example, people tend to protect themselves from public displays of ignorance; they tend to avoid intellectual risks in large groups. For that reason, you will probably want to create a comfortable environment where students are free to express their questions and wonderful ideas. Using strategies such as partner discussion instead of whole-class discussion can lower students' perceptions of personal risk. Another critical human need is the need to be treated as an individual deserving dignity and respect. Every student you face will come to you with a unique constellation of characteristics, with an idiosyncratic set of strengths and issues. You must value all students and the contributions they will make to your life and work. When asked what you teach, perhaps your first response will be, "I teach *people.*"

Although we can consider human needs and nature overall, we must also recognize that, at different times in their lives, humans vary predictably: They change, or develop, over time. Development refers to "the orderly, durable changes in a learner resulting from a combination of learning, experience, and maturation" (Eggen & Kauchak, 1999, p. 27). You will need to carefully observe your students to observe their current levels of physical, emotional, and cognitive development. Watch their physical skills, the ways they interpret problems, the ways they play or talk together on the school grounds, and listen to the issues they consider important. From your readings, observations, and conversations, your understanding of your students will become richer and more reliable explanations of human development.

Your instruction will not only need to take into account students' current levels of functioning, but it will also need to propel students' growth toward sophisticated ways of thinking, moving, and acting. To encourage development, teachers can provide varied experiences in rich physical and social environments and encourage students' to confront their current understandings and ways of thinking and acting.

PARTING WORDS

In his quote at the beginning of this chapter, Dr. Seuss celebrated the "brains in your head." If you are reading this text's chapters straight through, you are at the halfway point. Where have the "brains in your head" taken you in your journey thus far? Through Chapter 1 you considered teaching as a complex activity influenced by context and aimed at promoting learner growth. In Chapter 2, you developed a stance toward education to serve as your guide in managing the complexity of teaching and keeping your priorities clear. Chapter 3 provided a rationale and some strategies for placing your students at the center of your instructional decisions, and Chapter 4 helped you to plan instruction at different levels to address students' needs.

This chapter, Chapter 5, attempted to put "feet in your shoes" (thanks again, Dr. Seuss) by providing instructional principles that can give you a push on your journey. Its advice provides mechanisms to bring your growing professional knowledge base to life every day in the classroom. You COME IN as a teacher when you . . .

Connect
Organize
Model
Enrich
Interact
Consider Nature and Needs

You provide instruction that emphasizes the centrality of the student and the thoughtfulness required in good teaching and careful decision making. Chapter 6 provides another nudge forward by presenting a variety of instructional models that can enhance students learning in meaningful ways. Let's go.

LINKS TO RESEARCH, THEORY, AND PRACTICE

Banks, J. (1997). *Teaching strategies for ethnic studies* (6th ed.). Needham Heights, MA: Allyn & Bacon.

Bomer, R. & Bomer, K. (2001). *For a better world: Reading and writing for social action*. Portsmouth, NH: Heinemann.

Bromley, K., Irwin-De Vitis, L., & Modlo, M. (1995). *Graphic organizers: Visual strategies for active learning*. New York: Scholastic.

Bruner, J. (1960). *The process of education*. Boston: Harvard University Press.

Caine, R. N., & Caine, G. (1994). *Making connections: Teaching and the human brain*. Menlo Park, CA: Addison-Wesley.

Caine, G. & Caine, R. N. (2001). *The brain, education, and the competitive edge*. Lantham, MD: Scarecrow Press.

Campbell, L., Campbell, B., & Dickinson, D. (1996). *Teaching and learning through multiple intelligences*. Needham Heights, MA: Allyn & Bacon.

Cole, R. W., Ed. (1995). *Educating everybody's children: Diverse teaching strategies for diverse learners. What research and practice say about improving achievement.* Alexandria, VA: Association for Supervision and Curriculum Development.

Dillon, J. T. (1988). *Questioning and teaching: A manual of practice.* New York: Teachers College Press.

Duckworth, E. R. (1996). *The having of wonderful ideas and other essays on teaching and learning* (2nd ed.). New York: Teachers College Press.

Echevarria, J., & Graves, A. (1998). *Sheltered content instruction: Teaching English-language learners with diverse abilities.* Boston: Allyn & Bacon.

Eggen, P., & Kauchak, D. (1999). *Educational psychology: Windows on classrooms* (4th ed.). Upper Saddle River, NJ: Merrill/Prentice Hall.

Elkind, D. (1994). *A sympathetic understanding of the child: Birth to sixteen* (3rd ed.). Needham Heights, MA: Allyn & Bacon.

Erikson, E. (1968). *Identity: Youth and crisis.* New York: W. W. Norton.

Faltis, C. (2001). *Joinfostering: Teaching and learning in multilingual classrooms* (3rd ed.). Upper Saddle River, NJ: Merrill/Prentice Hall.

Gardner, H. (1983). *Frames of mind: The theory of multiple intelligences.* New York: Basic Books.

Gardner, H. (1993). *Multiple intelligences: The theory in practice.* New York: Basic books.

Goleman, D. (1998). *Working with emotional intelligence.* New York: Bantam Books.

Good, T. L., & Brophy, J. E. (1987). *Looking in classrooms* (4th ed.). New York: Harper & Row.

Grant, C. A., & Sleeter, C. E. (1998). *Turning on learning: Five approaches for multicultural teaching plans for race, class, gender, and disability* (2nd ed.). Upper Saddle River, NJ: Merrill/Prentice Hall.

Hoffman, M. (1979). Development of moral thought, feeling, and behavior. *American Psychologist, 34,* 958–968.

Kagan, S. (1994). *Cooperative learning.* San Juan Capistrano, CA: Kagan Cooperative Learning.

Kagan, S. (2000). *Silly sports & goofy games.* San Clemente, CA: Kagan Publishing.

Kohlberg, L. (1963). *Essays on moral development.* San Francisco, CA: Harper & Row.

Kohn, A. (1999, September). Constant frustration and occasional violence. *American School Board Journal, 186*(9), 20–24.

Marlowe, B. A., & Page, M. L. (1998). *Creating and sustaining the constructivist classroom.* Thousand Oaks, CA: Corwin Press.

Marzano, R. J., Pickering, D. J., & Pollock, J. E. (2001). *Classroom instruction that works: Research-based strategies for increasing student achievement.* Alexandria, VA: Association for Supervision and Curriculum Development.

Nieto, S. (1996). *Affirming diversity: The sociopolitical context of multicultural education* (2nd ed.). White Plains, NY: Longman.

Piaget, J. (1952). *Origins of intelligence in children.* New York: W. W. Norton.

Russell, H. R. (1990). *Ten-minute field trips* (2nd ed.). Washington, DC: National Science Teachers Association.

Schifini, A. (1994). Language, literacy, and content instruction: Strategies for teachers. In K. Spangenberg-Urbschat & R. Pritchard (Eds.), *Kids come in all languages: Reading instruction for ESL students* (pp. 158–179). Newark, DE: International Reading Association.

Silberman, M. (1996). *Active learning: 101 strategies to teach any subject.* Boston: Allyn & Bacon.

Slavin, R. (1997). *Educational psychology: Theory and practice* (5th ed.). Boston: Allyn & Bacon.

Stephens, L. S. (1995). *The complete guide to learning through community service: Grades K–9.* Needham Heights, MA: Allyn & Bacon.

Vygotsky, L. S. (1978). *Mind in society: The development of higher psychological processes* (M. Cole, V. John-Steiner, S. Scribner, & E. Souberman, Eds.). Cambridge, MA: Harvard University Press.

Yopp, H. K., & Yopp, R. H. (1996). *Literature based reading activities* (2nd ed.). Boston: Allyn & Bacon.

WEB SITES

http://www.nationalgeographic.com
National Geographic. Go to the site index for a listing of resources. Good geography resources

http://nga.gov
National Gallery of Art. Take a look at the online education programs, NGA Kids, and the loan programs. The gallery will send you loan materials through the U.S. mail. I have tried it; it works!

http://www.si.edu
Smithsonian Institute

www.exploratorium.edu
Museum of Science, Art, and Human Perception. Students will enjoy the science information and activities

http://www.loc.gov
Library of Congress. An incredible source for American and world history and culture

www.historychannel.com
The History Channel. Listen to historic speeches such as Martin Luther King's "I have a dream" speech and Amelia Earhart's discussion of the future of women in flying

www.nytimes.com/learning
New York Times *for learning. Try out the Learning Network Web Explorer online tours*

Also visit newspapers and magazines online. Examples include http://Newsweek.com or Time.com

FIGURE 5.8 Lession analysis: COME IN.

Advice	Evidence
Connect	To prior knowledge: To important ideas or the real world: To action: Participants:
Organize	Content: Time and activities:
Model	Draw attention to critical attributes: Use appropriate number and pace of repetitions:
Enrich	Provide rich experiences:
Interact	Strategies for active participation (verbal? written?):
Nature and **N**eeds	Human nature: Developmental needs:

OPPORTUNITIES TO PRACTICE

1. Take another look at the fossil lesson in Figure 4.8. Use the Lesson Analysis in Figure 5.8 to analyze whether, during the lesson, I followed my own advice. Record any evidence you find and then draw a conclusion for each of the six pieces of advice.

2. Use the form in Figure 5.8 to analyze the plan you developed as an exercise for Chapter 4, or analyze plans or lessons you prepare or observe.

3. Implement and practice one or more aspects of COME IN through mini-lessons. Try the following examples to get you started:

FIGURE 5.9 *Concept map of* K–12 Classroom Teaching *textbook.*

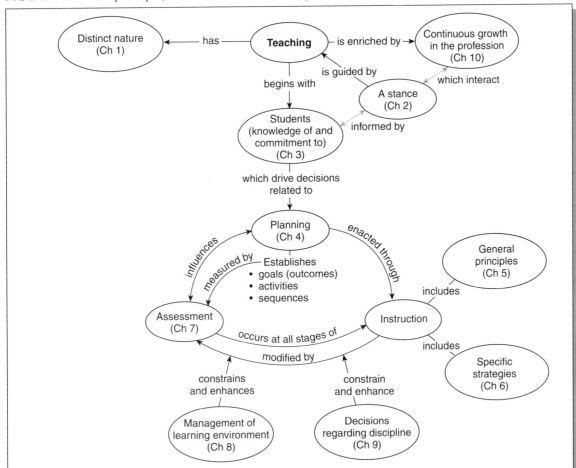

- Draw a semantic map or some other graphic organizer for a piece of text that either you or your students will read in the coming days. A concept map of this text, found in Figure 5.9, offers an example.

- Write a daily agenda and share it with your class. Invite students' reactions and modifications.

- Write and give a set of directions for how you want students to spend the first 5 minutes in your classroom each day. Use the advice for directions given in the teaching tips on p. 81.

- Model a new behavior, either for your students or for a willing friend. Select a skill or technique that is unfamiliar to your audience and, after modeling the skill, ask for feedback on which elements of your modeling were most successful.

- Plan to use one active participation strategy (Figure 5.7) in an upcoming lesson. If you are not currently teaching, select a strategy from Figure 5.7 that could have been used during a lesson you recently experienced as a student.

- Add one resource to your classroom materials. Consider adding to your picture file or find or construct a model for a concept that is difficult to learn.

- Commit to opening an upcoming lesson with an activity that accesses students' prior knowledge. Seek to value different cultural experiences that students share. If you are not teaching now, have a conversation with a friend about an aspect of your friend's life with which you are unfamiliar. Remember to protect your friend's dignity and to appreciate what you learn.

- Watch young students play either at recess or during unstructured class time. What is the range of differences you note in their physical development? Their social development? Their reasoning? How could you improve your instruction by using this specific information? If you are not teaching, try observing people at a playground or other public place. What conclusions can you reach about physical, social, and moral functioning?

4. Write a letter or presentation for families that describes your principles of instruction. How will you teach their children? Why have you chosen those principles? Share your letter or notes with a colleague and then, if appropriate, with the families of your students.

Before you begin reading Chapter 6

Your prior experience with instructional strategies will influence what you learn from this chapter. Before you read, check your familiarity with some of Chapter 6's teaching strategies by completing the following chart. Use your results to focus your efforts as you read, and check your ideas against those presented in the chapter.

Warm-Up Exercise for Instructional Strategies

Strategy	Rate your level of familiarity*	List bulleted phrases that come to mind when you think of this strategy.
1. Classroom questions	1 2 3 4	
2. Direct instruction	1 2 3 4	
3. Inquiry	1 2 3 4	
4. Cooperative learning	1 2 3 4	

*1 = I have no idea; 4 = I am a pro at using this strategy

CHAPTER *Six*

Instructional Strategies

"The difficulty in life is the choice."

—George Moore

Teaching is intended to foster change, and teaching is more than telling. Given these two propositions on teaching, how will you teach? Selecting the strategies you will employ for your lessons may be difficult. You will need to consider the needs and characteristics of your students, the demands of the content and context, and your personal stance as you choose instructional strategies. However, it can also be a great pleasure and give you a sense of power to select from a number of well-honed strategies those that you will use to respond to students' learning needs. The greater the number of instructional strategies that you master, the better able you will be to select strategies that encourage student growth. This chapter presents seven instructional strategies or approaches that can serve as the basis for your instructional repertoire. But first it addresses another essential element of your instructional repertoire: the use of questions in the classroom.

QUESTIONS IN THE CLASSROOM

One way to know for certain that you are standing in a classroom is to listen for questions. Hundreds of questions can be heard each day in the typical classroom. Regardless of the instructional strategy you select, then, questions will no doubt play a role in each of your lessons. How can you ensure that you harness the power of these potential learning tools in a way that helps you enact your stance and encourages student growth?

Figure 6.1 shares some conclusions from research on classroom questioning, reminding us again that classroom teaching looks easy . . . from the outside. Findings indicate that current researchers continue to focus on the number and types of questions teachers ask (e.g., Koufetta-Menicou & Scaife, 2000). Teachers tend to ask many questions, and those questions are often not used to their best instructional advantage (e.g., Becker, 2000; Wimer, Ridenour, Thomas, & Place, 2001). Just as you need to be intentional about selecting your instructional strategies, you need to be thoughtful about your use of questions.

Research indicates some promising practices for classroom questioning. First, carefully planned questions can enhance students' opportunities to learn (e.g., Lenski, 2002; Marzano, Pickering, & Pollock, 2001). Second, current research supports the power of *student questions* as mechanisms that help students

FIGURE 6.1   *What we know from the research on questioning.*

- *Teachers ask many, many questions.* Research reviewed by Borich (1992) finds that questions and answers account for 80% of classroom talk, with elementary and secondary teachers asking between 100 and 150 questions *per hour.*

- *Students ask very few questions.* Dillon (1990) reviewed elementary and secondary school studies and found that each pupil asks an average of only *one question per month.*

- *Teachers' questions serve many purposes.* Teachers use questions for:
  1. Checking for understanding
  2. Encouraging further thinking
  3. Fostering discussion
  4. Maintaining lesson flow
  5. Maintaining student attention
  6. Punishing misbehavior

- *Classroom questioning exchanges are typically rapid and follow a predictable pattern* (Borich, 1992; Dillon, 1990; Good & Brophy, 1987). The typical sequence is:
  1. Teacher asks a question.
  2. One student answers the question.
  3. Teacher evaluates the answer and asks a new question.

We also know that . . .

- *Expectations for conversational flow vary by culture and often run contrary to expectations for discourse in American classrooms.* This can cause misunderstandings about students' behavior, knowledge, and willingness to participate (Eggen & Kauchak, 1999).

- *Teachers' use of questions varies some by their perceptions of students' gender, ethnicity, and socioeconomic status.* Unwittingly, teachers sometimes use their questions to reinforce stereotypes and limit learning opportunities (Horgan, 1995).

- *Research has not clearly linked the type or level of a question to the type or level of the response* (Good & Brophy, 1987; Eggen & Kauchak, 1999; Slavin, 1997). Therefore, teachers cannot assume that asking higher-level questions will necessarily prompt higher-level responses, or the reverse.

read with a purpose, pursue meaningful investigations, and learn in deep and connected ways (Becker, 2000; Chin & Brown, 2000; Costa, Caldeira, Gallastegui, & Otero, 2000; Middlecamp & Nickel, 2000; vanZee, Iwasyk, Kurose, Simpson, & Wild, 2001). Teachers can encourage students' questions by providing time and opportunities to ask them and by using specific strategies to support students' question formation and pursuit. Figure 6.2 gives some specific promising practices for questioning. As you think carefully about questions, you will also make judicious decisions about the strategies you will use to teach your students.

SELECTING INSTRUCTIONAL STRATEGIES

Look back to your work in the Before You Begin section of this chapter. How many strategies were familiar to you? Teachers tend to teach the way they were taught. It is tempting to select strategies that feel comfortable and familiar, but part of good teaching involves taking risks and trying ideas that may, at least initially, fall beyond the realm of comfort. Several factors weigh into the choice of instructional strategy, including your stance, your students, the research, and the context.

One of the primary guides you can use in deciding how to teach your students is your stance toward education. Your hopes for students' futures, your

FIGURE 6.2 *Promising practices in classroom questioning.*

Promising Questioning Practices

(Dillon, 1988; 1990, except as noted)

1. *Plan your questions carefully.*
   - Consider the purpose of the questions you will ask.
   - Think about what you will do with the answer.

2. *Listen to students' responses.*
   - Take time to appreciate students' thinking. Slow down the pace of interaction.
   - Use wait time (Rowe, 1986). Wait 3 to 5 seconds before selecting a student to respond to a question, and wait again before responding to the student's reply.

3. *Ask fewer questions. Encourage children to ask more* (Sternberg, 1994).

Try Dillon's (1988) four S's as alternatives to questions:

   - **Statements**: Say what you think, or reflect on what the student thinks.
   - **Student questions**: Encourage a single student to ask a question about a puzzling circumstance, or invite the class to phrase the question in the air.
   - **Signals**: Use gestures or brief utterances ("mmm!") to refrain from taking control of the discourse.
   - **Silence**: Say nothing for a few seconds to allow others to join in.

knowledge of how people learn, and your convictions about what it means to teach well will all have direct implications for the methods you select. If you are convinced, for instance, that people learn through working together and through experience, you will necessarily choose strategies that provide for social interaction and firsthand experience. If you believe the purpose of education is the transmission of a core body of knowledge, you will select strategies that help you share information effectively. You may wish to again pull out the stance you developed through Chapter 2 and take some brief notes on what your convictions tell you about how you need to teach. (If you completed Figure 2.5, your work here is easy.)

Students' characteristics and developmental levels should also inform your selection of strategies. For instance, there is some support in the research to indicate that students with learning disabilities can benefit from **direct instruction** (a strategy presented later in the chapter; Swanson, 2001; Swanson & Sachse-Lee, 2000). Rather than relying on generalizations about groups, though, it is important to gather systematic information about your own students (Grant & Sleeter, 1998; Horgan, 1995). Chapter 3 provided some strategies to learn about your students. These included, for instance, attitude surveys, informal interviews, drawings, and journal writings.

The content and learning goals can also suggest potentially useful instructional strategies. Some of the strategies presented in this chapter focus, for example, on information mastery, and others focus on the processes by which knowledge is created, or the processes of inquiry. Though all subject matters can benefit from a discovery approach, inquiry is a special focus of science educators.

Another criterion for selecting instructional strategies is empirical research: How well does the strategy work? Although the effectiveness of many strategies is documented through research that links the teaching strategy with student outcomes such as increased academic achievement (e.g., Marzano et al., 2001), in general, research does not point to any one "best" instructional strategy. Research is clearer in providing information related to questions such as "Under what conditions is this strategy useful? For whom?"

Your selection of instructional strategies, then, will be guided by your stance, your knowledge of your students, and your knowledge of each strategy's potential for accomplishing certain purposes. Each strategy places distinct demands on the teacher and learner. As you make decisions about the ways you will teach your students, consider how well a strategy will encourage the intended growth of your students.

DEDUCTIVE AND INDUCTIVE STRATEGIES

One useful distinction among strategies is the point at which the major concept, skill, or understanding is stated during the lesson. Lessons that state the concept or understanding early in the lesson are deemed *deductive*. Using **deductive strategies,** the teacher states the concept of major learning promptly and then provides practice on that concept throughout the remainder of the lesson. Deductive strategies reason from the general to the specific: They present general rules, then specific examples. **Inductive strategies** do the reverse. In an inductive, or discovery, lesson the teacher provides specific data and guides students toward discerning a general rule or rules from those data. The major concept, skill, or understanding in an inductive lesson is not explicitly stated until later in the lesson. The contrasts between inductive strategies and direct instruction can be found by examining the two sample lesson plans on surface tension found in Figure 4.12.

You will want to master both deductive and inductive strategies because each can address different needs and foster different kinds of student skills and attitudes. Both have been found to be effective in increasing student achievement (Marzano et al., 2001). How often you use each of the contrasting strategies will depend on your own convictions about education, your learners, and the particular setting within which you find yourself.

> **Deductive Strategies:**
>
> general rule →
> specific examples
>
> **Inductive Strategies:**
>
> specific examples →
> general rule

A SAMPLING OF INSTRUCTIONAL STRATEGIES

The remainder of this chapter presents seven instructional approaches:

1. Direct instruction
2. Inquiry training
3. Concept attainment
4. Learning cycle
5. Concept formation
6. Unguided inquiry
7. Cooperative learning

Each is presented first through a description, then a listing of stages using the open-body-close format, next an example, and finally a discussion of strengths and criticisms.

Direct Instruction

The direct instruction model is one of the most widely used, helpful deductive strategies. Direct instruction allows teachers to impart information or skills straightforwardly to their students. The direct instruction format is flexible, and because one of the teachers' primary responsibilities is to present information, it fills a vital need in most classrooms.

Description of the Direct Instruction Model   In a directed lesson, the teacher systematically presents information related to an objective and carefully guides students' participation to ensure mastery. The emphasis is on efficient teacher presentation and eventual student command of a convergent set of objectives. Control over information or skills initially resides with the teacher, who relinquishes control as students first practice under the teacher's supervision and then eventually demonstrate independent mastery.

Stages of the Direct Instruction Model   There are a few versions of direct instruction. In the seven-step model (Hunter, 1982), the directed lesson begins with the teacher's statement of his expectations for student behavior throughout the lesson. For example, the teacher may remind his students: "I need to see you sitting up straight and staying in your seat throughout this lesson." That statement of expectations is missing from the five-step version of the direct instruction model, but its reduced number of steps may make the five-step model easier to integrate into daily planning.

In the direct instruction lesson, the teacher provides a *set* for learning, gives focused input, helps the students practice, ensures that they mastered the objective, and then encourages them to practice on their own. As you read through the five stages of the model, found in Figure 6.3, remember that it provides a mere blueprint for structuring lessons. Some teachers think of the stages as options from which they can choose, so not every lesson contains all five (or seven) steps. The length of a lesson can vary so that it may take a number of sessions to complete all of the stages. Also, through a teacher's ongoing assessment of student performance, he may decide to employ some back-and-forth movement between the lesson stages. For instance, students' performance during guided practice may indicate the need for further input rather than

FIGURE 6.3   *Stages of the direct instruction model.*

Open	1. *Anticipatory set*
	   a. Focus: Briefly gain the students' attention.
	   b. Objective: State the lesson's objective in student-friendly language.
	   c. Purpose: Tell students why this objective is important.

Body	2. *Input* Provide clear information related to the objective. One or more of the following may be appropriate: • Present definitions. • Share critical attributes. • Give examples and nonexamples. • Model. • Check for understanding, usually through active participation devices. 3. *Guided practice* Allow students to practice the objective under your supervision. Circulate to provide feedback to all learners. Employ praise–prompt–leave, wherein you give specific praise related to a student's effort, provide directions about what to improve, and then leave to check another student.
Close	4. *Closure* Observe all students performing the objective without your assistance. A performance, a brief test, or an active participation device can help you check mastery. 5. *Independent practice* Students practice the newly acquired objective on their own, often as homework or during individual work time. (Note: Some versions of the direct instruction model place independent practice before closure; however, that arrangement does not allow teachers to assess mastery before students practice alone.)

Immediate and specific feedback is an important part of guided practice.

a move forward to closure. Because the steps of the direct instruction model are generic, this lesson format is used by many teachers regardless of the strategy they choose to employ for a particular lesson.

A Sample Directed Lesson   One of the two lessons on surface tension presented in Figure 4.12 is a directed (or direct instruction) lesson that teaches a concept, surface tension. Figure 6.4 presents another brief example that presents a skill, cursive letter formation.

Strengths and Criticisms of Direct Instruction   Some forms of direct instruction have been shown effective in teaching basic skills, primarily in elementary-grade reading and mathematics (Slavin, 1997). Direct, explicit teaching is now highly prevalent across the nation, given current interests in students' acquisition of basic literacy and mathematics skills. The strength of direct instruction lies in the fact that it is carefully sequenced to provide key information, to lead the students in supervised practice, and then to finally release them for independent work after they demonstrate mastery of the content. Direct instruction provides an efficient mechanism to address one central purpose of education: to pass information and skills from one generation to the next. Direct instruction shows that, even when a teacher is primarily sharing information, she can do so much more than by just telling. She can carefully steer students toward control over new information or skills.

Direct instruction is comfortable for many new teachers because most directed lessons follow a predictable path, and the teacher retains control over most decisions during the lesson. Further, direct instruction exemplifies some of the principles of instruction from Chapter 5: It is highly organized, it makes use of modeling, and it is interactive.

One criticism of direct instruction offered by some (e.g., Coles, 2000) is that direct instruction's focus on the transmission of information or skills is too

FIGURE 6.4   *A sample direct instruction lesson.*

Objective: Third-grade students will correctly form the lowercase letter *t* in cursive.	
Anticipatory Set (Open)	1. Focus: "Watch me write a few words in cursive on the board and see if you can determine what they all have in common." "You are right! They all have the cursive letter *t*." 2. Objective: "By the time you leave for lunch, each of you will be able to write *t* in cursive." 3. Purpose: "*T* is important because it will help with lots of other letters we will be learning to write in cursive. Learning to write *t* will make your cursive job easier. Besides, we cannot spell *Natalie* or *Xochitl* without *t*!"
Input (Body)	4. Model: "Watch me as I form the letter *t* on the board." (Teacher describes his actions as he forms five *t*s on the board.) 5. Critical attribute:"Notice that the vertical part of *t* is closed, not like *l*. Also notice that I cross the *t* from left to right." 6. Check for understanding: Teacher draws incorrect *t*s and correct ones. He allows students to exclaim, "No! No!" or "Yes!" as he models, checking whether students are aware of the critical characteristics of the letter. "You seem ready to try your own *t*s! Let's go!"
Guided Practice	7. Teacher circulates and checks each student's progress. "Raymond, you are holding your pencil just right! Remember that *t* doesn't have a loop. Close it up. I will be back to check on you soon."
Closure (Close)	8. "I have seen many excellent *t*s! We will do one more for the record. Please take out a piece of scratch paper. Write your name at the top and then form your best *t* for me. Make three or four *t*s if you like!" (Teacher can collect and check the slips later or circulate now and mark them as correct.)
Independent Practice	9. If the students do not demonstrate mastery during closure, teacher will provide additional instruction. If the objective is mastered, teacher tells students "Aha! Remarkable *t*s! Please practice your *t*s on the white board or in the salt box during center time today."

narrow. Because it is fully deductive, with the teacher presenting important concepts and students then practicing them, direct instruction is sometimes criticized as encouraging student passivity. The teacher retains primary control over the content, over the pace of delivery, and over selection of learning activities. Students have limited choices and control in a directed lesson. Also, direct instruction may not connect to the life of the learner or use enriched resources as readily as other instructional strategies might. It may also decrease student motivation to learn (as described by Flowers, Hancock, & Joyner, 2000).

Finally, despite its potential power, some of the research documenting the effects of direct instruction offers mixed results. This is the case in the use of directed teaching in literacy instruction today. Although some recent studies support the effectiveness of direct instruction (e.g., Din, 2000; Yu & Rachor, 2000), others (e.g., MacIver & Kemper, 2002; St. John, Manset, Chung, & Worthington, 2001) find no significant effects of direct instruction.

Given its strengths and weaknesses, when, if at all, will you use direct instruction? Direct instruction may be helpful when (1) it is important that all students master the same objectives to a similar degree, (2) you are interested in efficient use of time, (3) it may not be safe for students to discover concepts, and (4) students start from similar background experiences.

As a practical indicator of when it may be appropriate to use direct instruction, watch for telltale signs. When you have the urge to begin a lesson with the words "Please open to page 42" and then march your students straight through some exercises, please think *direct instruction.* Your students will almost certainly have a higher chance of success if you teach to the text's objective but structure your lesson using stages of the directed lesson.

INDUCTIVE TEACHING

Inductive teaching presents a stark contrast to direct instruction. Through inductive methods, students create or discover important ideas by interacting with concrete materials or other data sources and their peers. When students analyze a poem, look for patterns in population distributions, or discover the identity of a mystery powder, they inquire.

> *T*he art of teaching is the art of assisting discovery.
>
> —*Mark Van Doren*

Instead of stating the learning explicitly at the beginning of the lesson, during inductive lessons, the teacher guides students to interact with data, materials, and each other so that they discover the ideas. Additionally, whereas direct instruction focuses primarily on the *product,* or outcome, to be gained, inductive strategies also focus on the *processes* by which knowledge is formed. Reviewing state and national student content standards in science and social studies demonstrates that students literate in these subject matters not only have mastery of a body of information, they also can use the methods by which scientists and social scientists build knowledge. They can formulate questions, address their questions through appropriate methodologies, collect information, analyze it, and draw appropriate conclusions. Students learn these processes by using them, and inductive instruction provides an appropriate vehicle.

Inductive methods can be convergent or divergent in nature. In convergent, or guided, approaches students are expected to discover or infer a single concept or generalization. In divergent, or unguided, approaches the number of concepts or generalizations to be formed is greater.

Although many inductive approaches exist, unfortunately, most of us have had limited experience with inductive instruction as students. This chapter

Students analyze data and draw conclusions through inductive instruction.

presents a variety of inductive strategies. The first three are convergent, and the last two are more divergent.

Inquiry Training

Suchman's (1962) inquiry training assists students in asking questions that help them move from the observation of facts to the development of theories. This strategy's power resides both in the way that it capitalizes on students' natural curiosity—the need to know—and in the fact that it puts students in the questioner's seat. Usually students in classrooms are expected to *answer* the questions, not to *ask* them. Asking a question can propel learning.

Description of the Inquiry Training Model   In an inquiry training lesson, the teacher presents a phenomenon, called a discrepant event, that piques curiosity. In a *discrepant event,* there is a mismatch between what students expect to happen, based on prior experience, and what actually does happen. For instance, a teacher may drop two full, unopened cans of soda into an aquarium. Students look puzzled when one floats and the other sinks (the floater is a diet drink, lacking sugar, which adds to the other can's density). For a discrepant event, I once filled a half-liter clear water bottle with water and baby oil. Although both liquids were clear, when students dropped food color into the bottle, the dye fell through the oil and dispersed in the water that rested in the bottom half of the bottle. A sample discrepant event in language arts might be a poem with no capitalization or punctuation. In social studies, it might be an unusual cultural artifact.

After presenting the discrepant event or stimulus, the teacher invites students to ask yes–no questions to develop explanations for what they observe. Through their questions, students develop and test causal connections to explain the discrepant event.

Suchman developed his model for science instruction, but as long as a teacher can locate relevant discrepant events or stimuli, inquiry training can be used across subject areas. It is useful for students of many ages, though younger children and English learners need extra support in formulating yes–no questions.

An unusual artifact can spark students' curiosity and provide a discrepant event to begin a lesson.

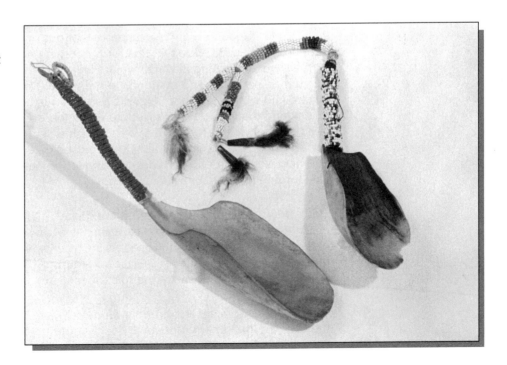

FIGURE 6.5 *Stages of the inquiry training model.*

Open	1. Present a discrepant event or puzzling situation.
	2. Describe the procedure: Students are to form explanations for what they see by asking questions that you can answer with yes or no.
Body	3. Allow for questions that *verify* what events and conditions students observe. Forestall causal questions until the next stage.
	4. Allow for questions that allow children to *identify relevant variables* and *test their hypotheses.*
Close	5. Guide students to state the explanations they have formulated.
	6. Prompt students to analyze their inquiry strategy.

Note: Inquiry training is more than a guessing game. If a student states the correct explanation early on, resist the temptation to scold the student for "giving away" the answer. Treat the student's proposed explanation as yet another tentative explanation that needs to be verified through empirical testing. The social atmosphere is important; encourage students to listen to each other.

Stages of the Inquiry Training Model   Figure 6.5 lists the stages of Suchman's inquiry training, moving through the presentation of the discrepant event through two stages of questioning: verification and hypothesis-testing questioning.

A Sample Inquiry Training Lesson   Figure 6.6 relates an inquiry training lesson I have used with enthusiastic students of a variety of ages.

Concept Attainment

Recall that inductive teaching methods foster students' ability to discern patterns, impose structure, and discover important ideas by working with concrete data. The ability to categorize information is central to these processes of discovery. Categorization, or grouping items into classes, serves a number of important functions: It reduces the complexity of our environments, it helps us identify individual objects, it makes learning more efficient, it helps us make decisions without the need for testing every object's properties, and it allows us to relate and order classes of events (Bruner, Goodnow, & Austin, 1960). Further, Bruner, Goodnow, and Austin note that our understanding of the world is not purely objective. Our systems for processing new information are shaped by the ways of thinking in which we are immersed: "The categories in terms of which man sorts out and responds to the world around him reflect deeply the culture into which he is born. . . . His personal history comes to reflect the traditions and thought-ways of his culture, for the events that make it up are filtered through the categorical systems he has learned" (p. 10). The concept attainment model (Bruner et al., 1960) makes categorization schemes explicit and guides students to consider information conceptually toward the aim of categorizing information meaningfully.

Description of the Concept Attainment Model   One object at a time, students observe a set of objects or examples, each deemed by their teacher as belonging— or not belonging—to a particular set. As the teacher presents more examples, students make hypotheses about the rule for grouping. They test their hypotheses on additional objects, and, finally, the rule (or concept) for grouping is induced.

Stages of the Concept Attainment Model   Figure 6.7 delineates the stages of the concept attainment model. Notice that the teacher presents one item at a time. It may be necessary to change the order of presentation or to gather new

FIGURE 6.6 *A sample inquiry training lesson.*

Objectives:	Fifth-grade students will state the necessary components of an electric circuit.
	Students will demonstrate the ability to test cause–effect relationships by asking relevant yes–no questions (Guillaume, Yopp, & Yopp, 1996.)
Open	1. Teacher presents a toy chick that chirps only when its circuit is completed by simultaneously touching both terminals to an electrical conductor, such as skin or metal. The terminals are two metal rings embedded in the toy's feet. Students chatter and express curiosity about the toy.
	2. Teacher states the task: "Your job is to ask me questions that I can answer with *yes* or *no* so that you can determine what makes the chick chirp."
Body	3. Students ask questions to verify what they see and interpret as the problem. Sample questions include "Is there a battery in the chick?" and "Are you flipping a switch to make it chirp?" When students ask questions that test causal relationships ("Are you completing an electric circuit?"), teacher asks them to save those questions for a few minutes. When children ask questions that cannot be answered with yes or no, teacher asks them to rephrase, enlisting help from peers as necessary.
	4. Teacher asks for questions that move into the phase of identifying relevant variables and exploring hypotheses about cause–effect relationships. For instance, "Does it have anything to do with the heat in your hand?" When students hypothesize about the materials necessary to complete the circuit, teacher responds with actions: She places the chick on metal, then wood, and finally glass so that students can see the answers to their questions.
Close	5. Teacher directs students to talk in groups about their explanations. She entertains new questions that arise from group discussions.
	6. In their groups on sentence strips (long, 2-inch high strips of tag board), students write an explanation for the chirping chick. They post and examine the explanations: An electrical circuit requires a power source, a conductor, and in this case a load (the chirping mechanism).
	7. The class analyzes its inquiry strategy and then applies its knowledge by exploring electrical circuits with batteries, foil, and lightbulbs.

FIGURE 6.7 *Stages of the concept attainment model.*

	Before the lesson, select a concept or rule and collect a wide variety of examples and nonexamples of your concept.
Open	1. To build interest, briefly display some of the items. (Items can vary. Examples include words, objects, pictures, and places on a map.)
	2. Introduce the students' task: to discover your rule for grouping.
Body	3. One at a time, present the items that serve as examples or counterexamples of your grouping. State whether each item belongs or does not belong to your group, perhaps by calling each a *yes* or a *no*.
	4. Continue presenting examples and counterexamples, providing opportunities for students to share their hypothesized rules and discuss them with their peers. Guide students' discussion to be certain that their proposed rules conform with all the data you have presented. Provide examples that challenge students' erroneous rules.
Close	5. When most students have induced the rule, furnish a final chance for consensus. Allow the rule to be stated aloud for the class.
	6. Invite students to explore further examples or to group the data according to a criterion they select.
	7. Process the activity by making observations about the process and content as appropriate.

Note: Occasionally students discover a rule that is accurate given the data they observe but is not the rule you meant to illustrate. Be certain to provide many different-looking or different-sounding examples of your concept so that students can focus on the critical attributes of the rule. If students induce a rule other than the one you planned, you may need to provide additional examples that contradict their rules.

FIGURE 6.8   *Where should this angle be placed? Is it a flop or a flump?*

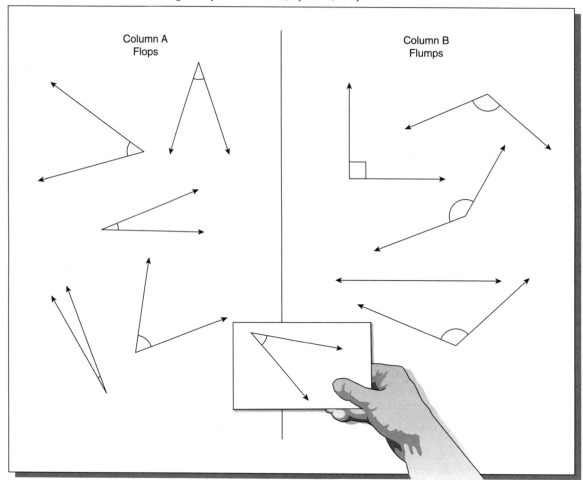

items to challenge the students' emerging hypotheses. Figure 6.8 shows some angles a teacher just presented to his geometry students. Column A has angles he calls "flops." Column B has "flumps." Is the angle in the student's hand a flop or a flump? What is the rule?

A Sample Concept Attainment Lesson   Figure 6.9 presents a sample lesson using the concept attainment format.

Learning Cycle

The learning cycle approach is inductive in that it moves from firsthand experiences to well-formulated understanding of the content and real-world application. It is based on constructivist learning theory that defines learning as both the process and the result of questioning and interpreting, the application of thought processes and information to build and improve our understandings, and the integration of current experiences with past experiences (Marlowe & Page, 1998). The learning cycle model differs from other inductive approaches in that the first and last stages of the lesson must be based in real-world or realistic experiences. The learning cycle approach can level the playing field by ensuring that all students have firsthand experiences to build background knowledge and deepen content knowledge. This is especially important for English learners and for students whose background experiences may be limited (Guillaume, Yopp, & Yopp, 1996).

FIGURE 6.9 *A sample concept attainment lesson.*

Objectives:	Kindergarten students will distinguish between examples and nonexamples of a triangle. Students will group items based on relevant attributes.
Open	1. "Come sit with me here on the rug and have a look at some of the things I brought today." (Students are allowed to handle and comment on a few of the items.) 2. "Some of these items are members of my club, and some are not. Your job today is to discover the name of my club. Then we will know which items can join and which cannot." 3. "I will place the members of my club in this hoop of yarn. Items that are not members will go outside the hoop. Ready?"
Body	4. Teacher shows one item at a time, placing it in the hoop if it is a triangle and outside if it is not. He provides plenty of examples and nonexamples that vary not only in the number of sides and angles but also in color, size, and texture. 5. After presenting five or six items, teacher encourages the children to guess where he will place subsequent items and guides them to explicitly state their hypotheses: "Whisper to your neighbor what you think is the name of my club." Teacher helps students test their hypotheses by examining the present examples and by adding others.
Close	6. When most students have demonstrated knowledge of the "triangle club" rule, teacher invites students to state it aloud: "Okay, club experts, what is the name of my club? Everyone, say it aloud on three. One . . . two . . . three!" 7. "Who can look around the room to find a member of my club? Who can find a nonmember?" 8. "Let me see if I understand the rules about triangles, then. Does size matter? Does color? Texture?" (All: "No!") "What matters about a triangle is that it has exactly three sides and exactly three angles." 9. "After recess maybe you would like to think of your own club using these objects."

Description of the Learning Cycle Model A learning cycle begins with a real-world problem or event that piques students' interests. A personal story, discrepant event, a current event, a toy, a poem, or a thoughtful question from a student or the teacher can all serve to engage the students. Next, students interact with data sources and concrete materials to explore the problem or event. Exploration builds background knowledge, from which more abstract understandings arise. After students have firsthand experiences the teacher begins to formally help students to systematize their knowledge, label concepts, and generate explanations. Finally, students apply their newly formulated knowledge to a similar real-world problem or event.

Stages of the Learning Cycle Model Different versions of the learning cycle approach to planning and instruction vary only slightly in the number of stages they propose, typically between three and five. Figure 6.11 depicts the phases of the learning cycle using one popular version of the model. This version of the learning cycle embeds assessment in each phase of the lesson. Another useful version of the learning cycle model is the 5E approach: engage, explore, explain, extend, and evaluate.

A Sample Learning Cycle Lesson The lesson in Figure 6.12 is a visual arts lesson for high school students that follows the learning cycle model. Notice that a single lesson can last more than one day and that it can make use of many kinds of resources. In following the learning cycle model, the lesson begins with a real-world phenomenon to engage the students (discussion of a painting), explores ideas related to that phenomenon (examination of the use of color in many other paintings), develops concepts surfaced through the exploration

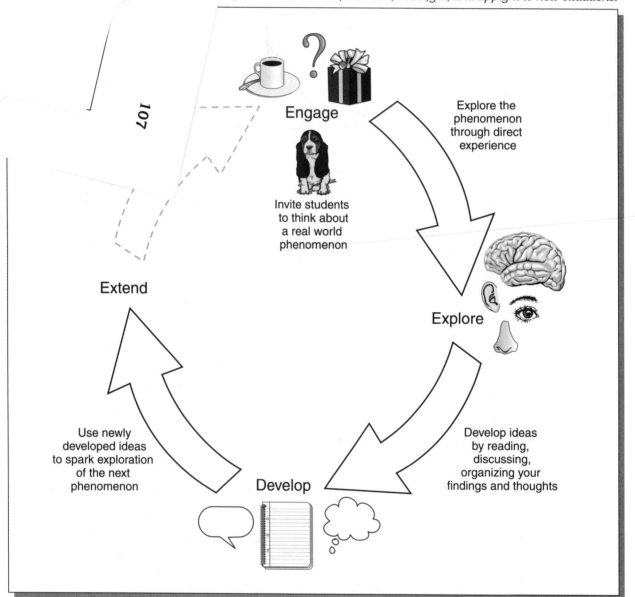

FIGURE 6.11 *Stages of the learning cycle.*

Open	1. *Engage:* Provide a brief real-world phenomenon, an object, or an issue that engages students' interest in the topic. Listen carefully to determine students' prior knowledge related to the topic and to expose their questions. Do not provide explanations of phenomena yet.
Body	2. *Explore:* Provide materials so that students engage in firsthand experience with the issue under study. During the explore phase, students begin to address their questions from the prior phase. They begin to generate new concepts and questions. Observe students carefully to determine emerging concepts and vocabulary.
	3. *Develop:* Systematically develop the concepts that arise during the exploration phase. Supply vocabulary terms appropriate given students' experiences. Provide direct presentations of the information and reading experiences as necessary so that students refine their understanding.
Close	4. *Apply:* Present a new problem or situation that can be addressed given students' newly formed understandings. Connect to the real world.

FIGURE 6.12 A sample learning cycle lesson.

Objectives:	Tenth-grade students will analyze works of art to determine principles of color use.
	Students will create their own work of art that uses color to convey a message.
Engage (Open)	1. With Zydeco, Cajun, or jazz music playing in the background, the teacher shares a brightly rendered watercolor painting from New Orleans.
	2. "I recently traveled and bought this painting. Look at this painting, where do you think I went?" She supports the students' guesses by asking for their evidence. "What about the picture makes you say, 'Europe?' " They discuss, among other student-generated topics, the architecture portrayed in the painting.
	3. Once the students conclude that the painting depicts a courtyard in New Orleans, teacher asks students to examine how the artist used color to capture the sense of energy, cultural fusion, and joy that many people associate with the city.
	4. To set the stage for exploration, teacher states that artists throughout time and all over the world use color to convey or enhance the message or mood of their works.
Explore (Body)	5. Teacher sets the task: "We have the computer lab tomorrow. Your job is to go on a virtual tour of museums around the world and download examples of visual art that use color in a variety of ways. You will share your examples with the class."
	6. In the lab, the tour launches with a visit to the National Gallery of Art (www.nga.gov). The teacher supplies addresses of other museum sites, and in pairs, students find examples of art that vary in their use of color to convey mood and message. When permitted, students print out copies of the art and create a class gallery of the varied works. Teacher and students add reproductions such as posters of famous works and their own works to the gallery as well.
Develop (Body)	7. The following day, teacher commends the students on their diligent searching: "We have created quite the collection of works in our class gallery. Very impressive! Your next task is to study all the works to determine themes in how color is used."
	8. Students tour the class gallery, grouping works that create similar moods or convey similar messages. They test the hypotheses they formed in viewing works they found with their partner on the virtual tour by studying the larger set of works found by their classmates.
	9. The day ends with the students writing and submitting journal entries on their tentative conclusions about the use of color. One student writes, for example, "When artists use a subdued palette, it expresses a calmer message. Mixing black with the colors adds an air of sadness to the work."
	10. That night, the teacher studies the students' entries and reproduces some of their most telling findings on overhead transparencies.
	11. The next day, the teacher lectures on the use of color, drawing from the concepts and tentative generalizations about color students recorded in their journals. She introduces terms such as "hue," "value," and "saturation" to formalize what the students stated informally in their entries. For homework, students read from their text a chapter on the use of color.
Apply (Close)	12. Students select a life event that evoked strong emotions from them. They create a work using a medium of their choice and use color to convey their intended emotions. Students plan a gallery showing, including background music related to their works. Families attend the lively showing.

phase (color concepts), and ends with a connection back to the real world (creation of students' own works that make use of what they learned through the lesson, principles of color use).

Concept Formation

Hilda Taba's (1967) strategy allows learners to build new ideas by categorizing specific pieces of data and forging new connections among those data.

FIGURE 6.13 *Stages of the concept formation model.*

Open	1. Challenge the students with a question about the topic that will encourage them to generate an extensive list.
Body	2. *List:* In full view, record students' contributions in the form of a list. Some teachers use sentence strips or large cards.
	3. *Group:* Invite the students to place like objects together. Questions such as "What goes together?" can elicit grouping.
	4. *Label:* Ask students to label their new groups: "What can we call this group?"
Close	5. Call students' attention to new concepts that arise from their groupings.
	6. Categorize new pieces of information according to the students' system and invite them to regroup and label the information.
	7. You may require students to use the information in some way, such as through a writing or retelling assignment.

Description of the Concept Formation Model   Often deemed "list–group–label," concept formation should increase students' ability to process information. Students begin by developing extensive lists of data related to a topic or question. Next, they group the data based on criteria they select, and they develop labels for their groups. The labels of the groups convey a concept or generalization. Oftentimes students are asked to re-sort data in different ways. Lessons often conclude with students using the information in a new way, such as by composing an explanatory paragraph.

Concept formation can be used to induce one particular concept or can be used in a divergent manner so that a number of accurate concepts or generalizations result. It has a wide range of applications.

Stages of the Concept Formation Model   Figure 6.13 lists the stages employed in the concept formation lesson.

A Sample Concept Formation Lesson   Figure 6.14 gives a concept formation lesson I used with second graders. In this lesson, students generated many words related to the topic *water.* They sorted the words into groups that shared certain characteristics. I was surprised that students initially grouped the words according to **linguistic** clues rather than by **semantic** clues. With prompting, students regrouped words in a few different ways to discover that water can be both helpful and harmful to humans. Finally, they wrote books about how we interact with water.

Unguided Inquiry

Through unguided inquiry, students address a problem or issue through first-hand experience with plentiful materials and information sources. The teacher serves as a facilitator instead of as a presenter. Many possible answers or solutions may be generated. Glasgow (1997) touts the contemporary relevance of unguided inquiry, which he calls problem-based learning:

> In most professions, knowledge is dynamic and requires current understanding for optimal success with contemporary problem solving. Information, concepts, and skills learned by the students are put into memory associated with the problem. This improves recall and retention when the students face another problem. . . . Problems actively integrate information into a cognitive framework or system that can be applied to new problems. (p. 42)

FIGURE 6.14   *A sample concept formation lesson.*

Objectives:	Second-grade students will form two accurate statements about the interrelationship of humans and water. Students will group data in rule-governed ways.
Open	1. "Class, come sit with me and listen to my rain stick." Students join teacher and listen intently as she turns the column once, then twice. They chat briefly about their experiences with similar instruments. "I brought my rain stick in today because we are beginning to study weather." 2. "Let's begin today by writing down as many water words as we know. I will write the words here on our board." As teacher writes, the instructional assistant copies each word onto a large index card for later.
Body	3. *List:* The class creates an extensive list of water words. Examples include *evaporation, puddle,* and *mud slide.* When the students' listing slows down, the teacher prods their thinking. 4. *Group:* Teacher calls the class of 20 to the carpet, and in their circle they lay out all the index cards that list their words. "That's quite a list, my friends! Now let's think about putting some of the cards together in groups. Who sees some cards that go together?" Teacher jokes with students, suggesting that they sit on their hands, because each is so eager to group the cards. She makes a note to herself that making individual or partner cards may work even better than class cards for grouping. Students group words into those that include *-ation* within them and those that do not. Teacher praises the ingenuity of their grouping and then asks students to regroup them another way. Students continue grouping until each card is with others. Teacher encourages students to collapse groups and to consider cross-groupings. *Label:* Students dictate the names of the groups they have generated, and the teacher writes group names on new cards, which she places near the three groups: *Ways water helps us, Ways water can be dangerous,* and *Other water words.*
Close	5. Teacher leads students to draw conclusions about the groups they have generated. Students conclude that humans interact with water in many ways, both helpful and harmful. 6. Teacher provides materials and instructions for students to make water pop-up books that contain two accurate sentences of ways that humans interact with water. Later, students read their books aloud to their sixth-grade buddies.

Description of the Unguided Inquiry Model   Unguided inquiry can be used in any subject matter through which students can personally experience a problem and then work firsthand with data to address (and perhaps solve) that problem. In social studies, for example, students may frame the problem of homelessness in the local community, either by experiencing homelessness themselves or by observing others who are homeless. They work to define the problem by formulating a question, to investigate the issue through reading and interviewing, and then to generate possible solutions. Their efforts may lead them to fund-raising or other social action opportunities. In mathematics, students may design survey studies that allow them to collect, analyze, and present data and then act on their findings.

Although unguided inquiry leads students to gain understanding of disciplinary content, the teacher may not be able to determine in advance which understandings will be developed. Rather than presenting information directly, the teacher provides for a rich environment and gently guides students' efforts to discover relevant information and address the problem productively.

Stages of the Unguided Inquiry Model   Figure 6.15 gives stages of the unguided inquiry model.

FIGURE 6.15   *Stages of the unguided inquiry model.*

Open	1. Present or capitalize on a problem that has multiple solutions and that captures the interests of students.
Body	2. Guide students in clearly stating the problem, perhaps by formulating a question.
	3. Lead a discussion of methods that may allow students to address the problem. Set the guidelines for study. Provide access to a variety of appropriate resources, including concrete materials and information sources.
	4. Monitor students as they employ their methods, helping students to revise and refine their methods as appropriate.
	5. Encourage students to take action based on findings, when appropriate.
Close	6. Direct students to draw conclusions regarding (a) the problem and (b) the processes of investigation.

FIGURE 6.16   *A sample unguided inquiry lesson.*

Objectives:	Seventh-grade students will describe useful techniques for cleaning oil spills and state at least one possible drawback of each technique.
	Through a closing discussion, students will demonstrate the ability to clearly define a problem, to employ an appropriate method, and to analyze their efforts.
Open	1. Teacher shows a news magazine photo of an oil-soaked sea bird and leads students to conclude that an oil spill at sea was responsible for the bird's condition.
	2. The class creates a semantic map (a chart with related concepts) on oil spills. Teacher focuses students' attention on the portion of the newly created map that lists a few cleanup methods: "Let's think about this part of the map. You already know some ways that specialists attempt to clean up spills at sea."
	3. Teacher shows a clear container with water and vegetable oil meant to simulate an oil spill. "Here I have my own oil spill."
Body	4. Teacher directs pairs of students to phrase the problem for investigation as a question. Students share their questions aloud and revise based on peers' ideas.
	5. Students spend one period reviewing encyclopedias, newspapers, and Internet materials to study cleanup methods. The next day, they bring in some cleanup materials and place them with those gathered by the teacher. Materials include coffee filters, detergents, soaps, sponges, eyedroppers, and paper towels.
	6. In pairs, students devise and record a plan for cleaning up the vegetable oil spill.
	7. With plans in hand, each pair creates its own oil spill using one tablespoon of vegetable oil in a pan of water. Students implement their plan to clean up the slick. Teacher monitors, prompting students to work carefully and to record their efforts in specific detail. She attempts to enrich their thinking through strategies such as visits to other student groups for observation.
Close	8. As testing concludes, teacher guides students in constructing a class chart of cleanup methods and their potential usefulness. The class also discusses drawbacks of its methods and reflects on how its future tests may be improved by the strategies the students attempted in this inquiry. Teacher challenges students to devise a method for cleaning up oil spills on land.

A Sample Unguided Inquiry Lesson   Figure 6.16 recounts an unguided inquiry lesson, inspired by Project WILD's (2000) lesson, "No Water Off a Duck's Back." Students of all ages participate merrily in the lesson, creating and cleaning up the **simulation** of oil spills.

Strengths and Criticisms of Inductive Strategies

Each of us probably has a story that illustrates the old saying "Experience is the best teacher." Experience allows us to form rules that can be useful in guiding our behavior and solving related problems in the future. Most of us report that, when we generate the rules by distilling experience rather than simply by reciting the rules we have heard stated for us, learning is more potent and tends to be longer lasting. Inductive strategies capitalize on the tremendous power of discovery learning.

Additionally, one widely professed purpose of education is to foster students' ability to think independently, to find order and patterns in the huge amount of information that confronts us daily. Inductive approaches are useful for that purpose because they provide students with opportunities to frame problems, to select appropriate methodologies, and to analyze their reasoning. To expand students' ability to face problems and complicated issues, inductive strategies focus on the processes of questioning, gathering information, and learning, in addition to content mastery.

Finally, inductive strategies make use of many principles from Chapter 5: They connect easily with the lives of the learners by using student interest and allowing for some student choice in the methods of study and the pacing of the lesson. Inductive approaches address human nature and needs by sparking and sustaining curiosity and by encouraging students to be puzzlers and problem solvers. Further, inductive strategies often make use of a wide range of information sources and real-world materials, which results in an enriched learning environment. When students engage in unguided inquiry into problems they themselves experience, they have the important opportunity to question existing conditions and to work on improving one piece of the world.

Inductive strategies can be criticized for a number of reasons. First, because student input can so dramatically shape the direction of the lesson—not only its pacing but in many cases its content as well—it can be difficult for the teacher to predict a lesson's content outcomes. Releasing partial control to students can be unsettling to teachers because they must approach content and time decisions with greater flexibility, especially in divergent lessons. Whereas the outcomes in a directed lesson are clear at the outset, divergent inductive lessons such as unguided inquiry result in multiple generalizations. Some teachers feel that this divergence places heavy demands on their own stores of knowledge.

The divergent, somewhat unpredictable nature of certain inductive methods also worries some teachers because of the pressure they feel to systematically treat a large body of content information in short periods of time. Focusing study on relevant, real-life problems may not allow for orderly treatment of some of the more mundane topics teachers are expected to address.

Finally, inductive lessons require resources and time. Whereas it takes very little time for a teacher to directly *state* a generalization, *inducing* a generalization requires repeated and varied experiences. Although they can produce lasting and memorable learning, inductive strategies can be less time efficient than direct instruction.

When will you use inductive methods? Check your stance toward education to gain a sense of what you want students to be able to do as adults. If you include outcomes such as the ability to analyze information sources, to think critically and creatively, or to solve complex problems, you need to master and employ inductive strategies. Because of their potential to address both content and thought-process goals, I hope you will use inductive strategies frequently. As a general rule, when you plan your lessons, ask yourself: "Could the students effectively discover these points for themselves if I arranged conditions appropriately?" If your answer is yes, use an inductive strategy. My own stance toward education reminds me not to tell students that which they could discover on their

Through cooperative learning, students work together to meet goals and build social skills.

own. The last strategy addressed in this chapter, cooperative learning, can include both inductive and deductive approaches.

Cooperative Learning

Popularized in the 1970s and 1980s, cooperative learning was formulated as an attempt to move classroom practices away from the highly individualistic and often competitive emphases of the typical American classroom. Cooperative learning includes a family of methods and structures designed to capitalize on every classroom's diversity and to enrich students' cognitive learning and social behaviors (Jacob, 1999; Johnson & Johnson, 1999).

Research indicates that cooperative learning is effective for encouraging content learning, social interaction, and students' attitudes toward learning and the subject matter. Recent examples of its effectiveness include a meta-analysis of the research by Marzano et al. (2001) and a study of sixth graders by Maheady, Michielli-Pendl, Mallette, and Harper (2002). Even very young children can use cooperative learning in its simple forms.

Description of the Cooperative Learning Model   In cooperative learning lessons, students are expected to help each other learn as they work together in small groups. Groups can be temporary or year-long. Frequently cooperative groups include four members, but other configurations are also prevalent. Cooperative learning is more than simply assigning students to work together and then issuing group grades. According to proponents (Kagan, 1994; Slavin, 1995) cooperative learning needs to accomplish three basic principles:

1. *Positive interdependence.*   Conditions must be arranged so that students are dependent on each other for success. This interdependence can be facilitated by providing group awards or by structuring tasks so that individual students cannot complete them alone.
2. *Individual accountability.*   Each student must remain accountable for exhibiting mastery of the content.
3. *Simultaneous interaction.*   Lessons should keep a maximum number of students overtly active at once. This is in contrast to traditional lessons in which only one student in the entire class speaks at a time.

FIGURE 6.17   *Cooperative learning includes both individual accountability and positive interdependence.*

A fourth principle is *equal participation* (Kagan 1994). Students need to make balanced contributions to the group's work (see Figure 6.17). Kagan argues that, to accomplish these principles, teachers must:

- Structure teams so that they are heterogeneous. Ability, language, gender, and ethnicity may be criteria teachers use to sort students into teams where members differ.
- Use team-building and class-building activities to create the will to cooperate.
- Use management techniques specifically suited for group work. Examples include a quiet signal to regain students' attention and the use of assigned roles within teams.
- Explicitly teach social skills such as listening and conflict resolution techniques.

In sum, cooperative learning lessons structure resources and activities so that students remain responsible for their own learning and become responsible for assisting their teammates in learning.

Stages of the Cooperative Learning Model   Although for many teachers cooperative learning has come to mean simply allowing students to help each other, there are scores of formal cooperative learning structures that breathe life into the principles of cooperative learning. The stages listed in Figure 6.18 do not represent a single lesson. Instead, they suggest a sequence of events that take place over an extended period of time as a teacher works to establish a cooperative learning classroom. Individual cooperative learning lessons that make use of a variety of structures can be embedded within this sequence.

FIGURE 6.18 *Stages of the cooperative learning model.*

Form teams and set the stage	1. Select the dimensions along which students will be heterogeneously grouped. 2. Use assessment results and demographic information to place students into groups of four that include members who differ according to the selected dimensions. For example, each group may have two high achievers, two lower achievers, and be balanced in terms of girls and boys and English and Spanish speakers. (Note: Random teams, interest teams, or skill teams may also be used.) 3. Teach a defined and explicit set of social behaviors. Examples include active listening and responding in positive ways to peers' contributions.
Implement cooperative management system	4. Select and teach a quiet signal. Examples include a raised hand, a flick of the lights, a noise maker, and patterned hand claps. 5. Teach students to distribute and collect materials within their teams.
Build teams	6. Encourage students to rely on each other by using team-building activities. Examples include team interviews and developing team names or hats.
Teach social skills	7. Directly teach students to interact in positive ways. Post a list of the behaviors you expect to see and model those behaviors for the students. Consider assigning roles such as encourager and task master to help students learn skills. 8. Monitor social skills. Reinforce appropriate social behaviors. Allow students to evaluate their own use of social skills regularly.
Use cooperative learning strategies throughout instruction	9. Select from a variety of structures to embed cooperative learning within your regular instruction. Some samples for different purposes include the following: • Jigsaw II (Slavin, 1995): Students in heterogeneous teams read the same chapter of material, with each member focusing on particular "expert" topics in the chapter. Students meet in groups with other experts to discuss the material and decide how to present it to group members. Back in their home teams, members teach each other their expert topics, ensuring that each member has mastered all topics. Students are assessed on the material, and the teacher records both individual scores and team scores that are based on the improvement gains of each individual student. (Content mastery) • Inside–outside circle (Kagan, 1994): Two concentric circles form, and students face each other. Partnered with the outside circle person directly across from him or her, each inside circle student shares and then listens as the outside circle person shares. The outside circle rotates so new partners can converse. (Information sharing) • Student-Teams Academic Divisions (STAD) (Slavin, 1995): Based on the lesson objective, the teacher presents new information in a manner that closely relates to quizzes students will take later. Then team members practice the information together, using worksheets or other materials. Team members' responsibility is to ensure that all members have mastered the content. Next every student takes a quiz on the material. Individuals receive scores based on their improvement over time. Team scores are determined by combining individual improvement scores. Recognition is given to teams based on their team scores. (Content mastery) • Team statements (Kagan, 1994): Each person writes an individual statement about a topic. Students share their statements and then develop a team statement that synthesizes each of the individual statements. (Thinking skills)
Analyze and revise	10. Monitor students' growth in social skills and encourage them to self-monitor through self-assessments. Reorganize teams as appropriate. Set new goals for yourself and your students based on their current work.

FIGURE 6.19 *A sample cooperative learning lesson.*

Objectives:	Second-grade students will synthesize information from their aquarium field trip as evidenced by their descriptions of the murals they create.
	Students will exhibit two social skills: listening to each other and asking the teacher a question only when no group member can answer it.
Open	1. Class is seated on the floor in a misshapen circle. Teacher states, "Here are some plastic animals like the animals we saw on our aquarium field trip. I have plenty. Choose one, talk to your partner about what you remember about the animal on the trip, and then return it to the center and choose another animal."
	2. Teacher compliments the students: "Do you know what I noticed as you were talking? When your partner spoke to you, you really listened. I could tell because you were looking at your partner, nodding and sometimes smiling. You didn't interrupt either. Careful listening is the social skill we'll practice today and tomorrow. What does it *look like* to listen carefully? What does it *sound like*?" A brief discussion ensues.
	3. "I can tell from your conversations that you learned many things from our field trip. Today you will have a chance to share what you learned by creating a team mural. Tomorrow we will describe our murals to each other."
Body	4. At their team tables, students fact-storm on their trip: Using a strategy called roundtable, one student writes a memory from the aquarium trip on a large sheet of paper, then passes the paper to the next member. Students continue writing for about 10 minutes, until the paper is full. "Now that you have so many animals and plants recorded, see if your team can group them in some logical way. Write on the chart."
	5. "Use your groupings to create a mural. Look toward the back of our room and you will see many materials you may use." Students: "Cool! Glitter!" Teacher continues: "Here's the rule for making your mural. I have made a sign that describes your job. See? Member One, you are in control of the scissors. Only you may cut. Member Two, you are the magazine monitor. Any pictures selected from the magazine are your responsibility. You see that you may need One to cut for you, right? Member Three, your job is fancy material captain. Glitter and crepe paper belong only to you. Member Four, markers are your job." He checks for understanding on directions. Satisfied, teacher states, "Use your charts and get to work."
	6. Children work until lunch on their murals. Teacher monitors to be certain that members are making their unique contributions based on their roles. When individuals ask him questions, he asks, "Have you asked each person in your group that question yet?" He applies some time pressures to keep groups productive, and he reinforces the listening skills students demonstrate.
Close	7. The next day: to share their murals and allow the teacher to assess the first objective, students use the "one stay, three stray" structure. All Number Ones stand by their group mural and describe it to three visitors. Next, Number Twos stay and describe while the others stray to see other groups' murals. Teacher takes anecdotal notes on students' presentations. Back in their home groups, groups write one statement about what they saw and heard about other groups' murals. Statements are posted near the murals.
	8. Students talk briefly in their groups to evaluate their social skills. They focus on the chosen skill, careful listening. They discuss the questions "What did we do well as a group today?" and "What will we work on for next time?"

A Sample Cooperative Learning Lesson Figure 6.19 shares a sample lesson for second graders that uses three of Kagan's cooperative learning structures.

Strengths and Criticisms of the Cooperative Learning Model Cooperative learning offers refreshing changes to traditional classroom practice. First, it breaks the typical discourse pattern where teachers do most of the talking. It can enliven a classroom because it allows a far greater number of people to talk—to develop oral communication skills—at once. Second, cooperative learning changes the typical expectation that students need to succeed only as individuals and instead builds as norms social interaction and interdependence. Third, whereas student differences are sometimes seen as problematic, cooperative learning suggests that the more diverse the group, the richer the potential outcomes. Fourth, cooperative learning meets many of the principles addressed in Chapter 5. It is highly interactive, it capitalizes on human nature by allowing students to be actively involved throughout the lesson, and it allows students to form connections to the subject matter and with other students.

Still, cooperative learning brings some difficulties. Cooperative learning lessons can take more time than traditional presentations because students are simultaneously learning social skills. Cooperative classrooms require diligence from the teacher in terms of classroom management. It takes skill to harness students' energy and ensure that students are working productively. It can also be a challenge to guide students in solving their social difficulties when a teacher's temptation is to quickly solve the problem and move on. Finally, it is the teacher's responsibility to structure lessons that require every student to contribute to the group's work. One of the greatest challenges of cooperative learning is to bar the possibility that students can freeload.

When will you use cooperative learning? Informal techniques such as partner sharing are easily integrated into traditional instruction. Individual lessons that employ cooperative structures are also possible. Structuring your entire classroom around the principles of cooperative learning will probably require you to receive additional training or to study some of the excellent resources that describe cooperative learning methods. As you consider cooperative learning, remember the power of your role as instructional leader. You must arrange events so that you can manage students' behavior, monitor their social skills, and ensure that they truly are helping each other succeed. Think through your activities, anticipate trouble spots, and plan some alternative responses to keep your cooperative lessons productive.

PARTING WORDS

Classroom teaching is so demanding that it is easy to retreat to instructional methods that do not require us to consider best practice, to enact our stances toward education, to stretch as professionals, or to stray from the ways we were taught as children. However, teaching is more than telling. Skilled teachers can use a number of instructional strategies to suit their purposes and encourage different kinds of growth for their learners. Make learning and using a number of instructional strategies a priority, perhaps selecting one or two based on your work from the Before you Begin exercise in this chapter. When you try any new strategy, think very carefully about what you will say at each point, what you will expect from the students, and what you will do if things do not go as planned. Expect that you will need repeated opportunities to practice new strategies; in fact, research on staff development suggests that a strategy may not feel natural until you try it about a dozen times. A dozen times! Further, be vigilant in thinking about how using a variety of instructional strategies can help you differentiate your instruction so that it pushes each of your students to their learning potential. The harder you work to build your instructional repertoire, the better able you will be to help your students grow and develop.

LINKS TO RESEARCH, THEORY, AND PRACTICE

Baloche, L. A. (1998). *The cooperative classroom: Empowering learning.* Upper Saddle River, NJ: Merrill/Prentice Hall.

Becker, R. R. (2000). The critical role of students' questions in literacy development. *Educational Forum, 64,* 261–71.

Borich, G. D. (1992). *Effective teaching methods* (2nd ed.). Upper Saddle River, NJ: Merrill/Prentice Hall.

Bruner, J. B., Goodnow, J. J., & Austin, G. A. (1960). *A study of thinking.* New York: John Wiley & Sons.

Chin, C., & Brown, D. E. (2000). Learning in science: A comparison of deep and surface approaches. *Journal of Research in Science Teaching, 37*(2), 109–38.

Coles, G. (July 2000). "Direct, explicit, and systematic"—Bad reading science. *Language Arts, 77,* 543–45.

Costa, J., Caldeira, H., Gallastegui, J. R., & Otero, J. (2000). An analysis of question asking on scientific texts explaining natural phenomena. *Journal of Research in Science Teaching, 37,* 602–14.

Dillon, J. T. (1988). *Questioning and teaching: A manual of practice.* New York: Teachers College Press.

Dillon, J. T. (1990). *The practice of questioning.* London: Routledge.

Din, F. S. (2000). Use direct instruction to improve reading skills quickly. *Rural Educator, 21*(3), 1–4.

Eggen, P., & Kauchak, D. (1999). *Educational psychology: Windows on classrooms.* Upper Saddle River, NJ: Merrill/Prentice Hall.

Flowers, C. P., Hancock, D. R., & Joyner, R. E. (2000). Effects of instructional strategies and conceptual levels on students' motivation and achievement in a technology course. *Journal of Research and Development in Education, 33*(3), 187–94.

Glasgow, N. A. (1997). *New curriculum for new times: A guide to student-centered, problem-based learning.* Thousand Oaks, CA: Corwin Press.

Good, T. L., & Brophy, J. E. (1987). *Looking in classrooms* (4th ed.). New York: Harper & Row.

Grant, C. A., & Sleeter, C. E. (1998). *Turning on learning: Five approaches for multicultural teaching plans for race, class, gender, and disability* (2nd ed.). Upper Saddle River, NJ: Merrill/Prentice Hall.

Guillaume, A. M., Yopp, R. H., & Yopp, H. K. (1996). Accessible science. *Journal of Educational Issues for Language Minority Students, 17,* 67–85.

Horgan, D. D. (1995). *Achieving gender equity: Strategies for the classroom.* Boston: Allyn & Bacon.

Hunter, M. (1982). *Mastery teaching.* El Segundo, CA: Instructional Dynamics.

Jacob, E. (1999). *Cooperative learning in context: An educational innovation in everyday classrooms.* Albany, NY: State University of New York Press.

Jacobs, G. M., Power, M. A., & Inn, L. W. (2002). *The teacher's sourcebook for cooperative learning: Practical techniques, basic principles, and frequently asked questions.* Thousand Oaks, CA: Corwin Press.

Johnson, D. W., & Johnson, R. T. (1999). *Learning together and alone: Cooperative, competitive, and individualistic learning* (5th ed.). Boston: Allyn & Bacon.

Kagan, S. (1994). *Cooperative learning.* San Juan Capistrano, CA: Kagan Cooperative Learning.

Koufetta-Menicou, C., & Scaife, J. (2000). Teachers' questions—Types and significance in science education. *School Science Review, 81*(296), 79–84.

Lenski, S. D. (2001). Intertextual connections during discussions about literature. *Reading Psychology, 22*(4), 313–35.

MacIver, M. A., & Kemper, E. (2002). The impact of direct instruction on elementary students' reading achievement in an urban school district. *Journal of Education for Students Placed at Risk, 7*(2), 197–220.

Maheady, L., Michielli-Pendl, J., Mallette, B., & Harper, G. F. (2002). A collaborative research project to improve the academic performance of a diverse sixth grade science class. *Teacher Education and Special Education, 25*(1), 55–70.

Marlowe, B. A., & Page, M. L. (1998). *Creating and sustaining the constructivist classroom.* Thousand Oaks, CA: Corwin Press.

Marzano, R. J., Pickering, D. J., & Pollock, J. E. (2001). *Classroom instruction that works: Research-based strategies for increasing student achievement.* Alexandria, VA: Association for Supervision and Curriculum Development.

Middlecamp, C. H., & Nickel, A. L. (2000). Doing science and asking questions: An interactive exercise. *Journal of Chemical Education, 77*(1) 50–52.

Nieto, S. (1996). *Affirming diversity: The sociopolitical context of multicultural education* (2nd ed.). White Plains, NY: Longman.

Project WILD. (2000). *Project WILD: K–12 activity guide.* Houston, TX: Council for Environmental Education.

Rowe, M. (1986). Wait-time: Slowing down may be a way of speeding up. *Journal of Teacher Education, 37*(1), 43–50.

Slavin, R. E. (1995). *Cooperative learning* (2nd ed.). Boston: Allyn & Bacon.

Slavin, R. E. (1997). *Educational psychology: Theory and practice* (5th ed.). Boston: Allyn & Bacon.

St. John, E. P., Manset, G., Chung, C. G., & Worthington, K. (2001). *Assessing the rationales for educational reforms: A test of the professional development, comprehensive reform, and direct instruction hypotheses.* Policy Research Report. Indiana University, Bloomington. Education Policy Center. (ERIC Document Reproduction Service No. ED458 641)

Sternberg, R. J. (1994). Answering questions and questioning answers: Guiding children to intellectual excellence. *Phi Delta Kappan, 76*(2), 136–138.

Suchman, J. R. (1962). *The elementary school training program in scientific inquiry.* Report to the U.S. Office of Education, Project Title VII, Project 216. Urbana, IL: University of Illinois.

Swanson, H. L. (2001). Searching for the best model for instructing students with learning disabilities. *Focus on Exceptional Children, 34*(2), 1–15.

Swanson, H. L., & Sachse-Lee, C. (March/April 2000). A meta-analysis of single-subject-design intervention research for students with LD. *Journal of Learning Disabilities, 33*(2), 114–36.

Taba, H. (1967). *Teacher's handbook for elementary social studies.* Reading, MA: Addison-Wesley.

van Zee, E. H., Iwasyk, M., Kurose, A., Simpson, D., & Wild, J. (2001). Student and teacher questioning during conversations about science. *Journal of Research in Science Teaching, 38*(2), 59–90.

Wimer, J. W., Ridenour, C. S., Thomas, K., & Place, A. W. (2001). Higher order teacher questioning of boys and girls in elementary mathematics classrooms. *Journal of Educational Research, 95*(2), 84–92.

Yu, L., & Rachor, R. (2000). *The two-year evaluation of the three-year direct instruction program in an urban public school system.* (ERIC Document Reproduction Service No. ED 441 831)

WEB SITES

Use the names of strategies given in this chapter to conduct your Internet search for teaching techniques. Examples include the following:

http://www.nifdi.org/
National Institute for Direct Instruction

http://www.imsa.edu/team/cpbl/cpbl.html
Center for Problem-Based Learning by Illinois Mathematics and Science Academy

http://ilf.crlt.indiana.edu/
The Inquiry Learning Forum: Supporting Student Learning & Teacher Growth Through Inquiry. Housed at the Center for Research on Learning and Technology at Indiana University

http://www.clcrc.com/
The Cooperative Learning Center of University of Minnesota

Note that many individuals, including university faculty and groups of practicing teachers, maintain their own web sites related to specific instructional strategies. These sites can be unstable, so conduct your own search using the name of the strategy itself or in conjunction with the term "lesson plans."

The instructional strategies presented in this chapter are just a subset of the myriad strategies you can try. Others, such as *virtual field trips* and *simulations*, are also readily available. To get started, try these sites:

http://www.uen.org/utahlink/tours/
Virtual Field Trips by Utah Education Network

http://www.theteachersguide.com/virtualtours.html
Virtual Field Trips by the Teachers' Guide

http://www.awesomelibrary.org/
Awesome Library. Search for the word "simulation" within the site and locate many activities that allow students to experience content through memorable, role-play type activities.

OPPORTUNITIES TO PRACTICE

1. Tape yourself teaching or ask for permission to observe another teacher. Tally the number of questions the teacher asks and how many the students ask. Analyze your data of question–answer patterns according to some of the topics given in Figure 6.1. Compare your findings to those reported in Figure 6.1. What is your evaluation of the questioning you observed?

2. Observe another teacher lead a lesson. Afterward, discuss with the teacher the choices he made about instructional strategies. Ask him how many of the strategies from Chapter 6 he knows and which he prefers. If an observation is not possible, try analyzing teachers' editions from a published curriculum series. How many of the strategies are suggested? What is your evaluation of the use of instructional strategies? What changes might you suggest?

3. Bruner's work (Bruner et al., 1960) on concept attainment purports that the ways we group objects are culturally bound. They list a grouping used by the Navajo: *witch* versus *nonwitch*. Make a list of grouping systems that you find in your own culture and through your experiences with other cultures. For instance, is it true that Eskimos have words for 16 kinds of snow? What power do those grouping systems provide for the people who use the knowledge?

4. Make a prioritized list (Figure 6.20) for yourself of the strategies you will work to master. Busy? I suggest you choose, for a start, direct instruction and one other strategy. Study the stages of the models as if you are studying for an exam. Commit them to memory and then bring them to life through intense effort to model them each a couple times. Work with a colleague and discuss your experience.

5. Write two contrasting lessons using strategies from Chapter 6. Use an objective from your classroom or the following one: "Students will retell three major events from a story [name one] in the correct sequence." Blank lesson plan forms are included in Figure 6.21.

6. Figure 6.21 includes lesson plan formats for each of the instructional strategies in Chapter 6. Use them as you plan lessons that incorporate different strategies. Remember to include cognitive, affective, and psychomotor objectives as appropriate. Also, include assessment to match each of your objectives.

FIGURE 6.20 *A list of strategies to master.*

To Do
Instructional Strategies to Master
1.
2.
3.

FIGURE 6.21 *Lesson plan formats.*

Direct Instruction Lesson

Objective(s):   Materials:

Expectations for behavior:

Open	1. Anticipatory set:
	
	  • Focus:
	
	  • Objective:
	
	  • Purpose:

Body	2. Input:
	
	  • Provide input:
	
	  • Check for understanding:
	
	3. Guided practice:

Close	4. Closure: 5. Independent practice:

FIGURE 6.21   *Continued*

Inquiry Training Lesson		
Objective(s):		Materials:

Open	1. Discrepant event: 2. State students' task:
Body	3. Elicit questions that verify conditions and events of the discrepant event • Sample acceptable questions: • Sample prompts to encourage appropriate questions: 4. Elicit questions that test hypotheses • Sample acceptable questions: • Sample prompts to encourage appropriate questions:
Close	5. Guide students to formally state their explanations:

continued

FIGURE 6.21 *Continued*

Concept Attainment Lesson

Concept or rule to be discovered:

Objective(s):

Materials (list examples and counterexamples of your concept to be used):

Open	1. Briefly display objects: 2. State students' task:
Body	3. Present examples and counterexamples of the concept or rule (list the order in which examples will be presented): 4. Allow students to test their hypothesized rules by (a) citing their own examples and nonexamples and/or (b) talking with peers. Prompts:
Close	5. Allow the rule to be stated for the class: 6. Allow for observations of the content and process of the lesson: 7. Invite further exploration (e.g., allow students to create their own groups):

FIGURE 6.21   *Continued*

Learning Cycle Lesson

Concept or rule to be discovered:

Objective(s):   Materials:

Open	1. Engage (hook the students; elicit questions; determine background knowledge):
Body	2. Explore (work with concrete materials; determine emerging concepts and terms): 3. Develop (formally develop concepts and terms from the explore phase; use readings, direct presentations, and other methods to ensure mastery of the objective):
Close	4. Apply (provide a novel problem to which new knowledge can be applied or make some other real-world connection):

continued

FIGURE 6.21   *Continued*

Concept Formation Lesson

If specified, concepts or generalizations to be discovered:

Objective(s):   Materials:

Open	1. Introduce the topic and ask a question that will generate a list:
Body	2. List (prompt students to generate an extensive list related to the topic):
	3. Group (prompt students to group items from the list):
	4. Label (prompt students to name their groups):
	5. Optional: Regroup (prompt students to find other ways items can be grouped):
Close	6. Call students' attention to the concepts or generalizations that arise from their groupings. Prompt:
	7. Extend learning through an additional assignment, such as a drawing, writing, or speaking opportunity:

FIGURE 6.21 *Continued*

Unguided Inquiry Lesson

If specified, concepts or generalizations to be discovered:

Objective(s) (consider both content and research skill or process objectives):

Materials (list concrete materials and information sources):

Open	1. Present stimulus material that suggests a problem or issue for study:
	2. Guide students to state the problem in clear terms. Prompts:
	3. Decide on appropriate methods to address the problem. Prompts:
	4. Set the guidelines for study. Prompts:
Body	5. Monitor students as they employ their methods. Prompts to encourage careful study:
Close	6. Encourage students to draw conclusions regarding (a) the problem and (b) the processes of investigation. Prompts:

continued

FIGURE 6.21 *Continued*

Cooperative Learning Lesson

Content objective(s):   Materials:

Social skill objective(s):

Prelesson questions	a. How are teams formed? b. What quiet signal will you use? c. What team-building and class-building efforts have you taken or will you take?
Open	1. Focus students' attention and allude to the lesson's content and activities: 2. State expectations for cooperative work and teach social skills:
Body	3. Use a cooperative learning structure to present information or encourage discovery learning. Samples from Chapters 5 and 6 include the following: blackboard blitz inside–outside circle round table brainstorming jigsaw roving review four corners numbered heads together stand to share gallery walk one stay, three stray values lineups group problems peer interviews 4. Monitor students' use of social skills. Sample prompts:
Close	5. Summarize the learning. Prompts or cooperative strategy: 6. Process students' use of social skills:

Before you begin reading Chapter 7

Warm-Up Exercise for Assessment

Think back to your years as a student. How did your teachers know whether and what you learned? What kinds of feedback did you receive? Take three minutes to jot down as many different assessment strategies as you can recall experiencing.

Now mark each of these statements with *agree* or *disagree:*

1. Teachers knew me as a multifaceted person with varied strengths and skills.
2. Teachers were interested in my own assessments of my work.
3. Teachers encouraged me to set my own learning goals.
4. The feedback I received from tests and other assessments helped me learn.
5. Teachers changed what they did in the classroom based on student assessment data.

Finally, evaluate your answers for statements one through five. Were your experiences with assessment as a student positive? Would it have been better if teachers had assessed your learning differently?

Here is a chance for you to use effective practices from both the past and present to make a difference for today's students. Use your conclusions to help make sense of the following chapter and to build your own system for assessing student progress.

CHAPTER *Seven*

Assessment

> *"Open your mouth and say, 'Ahhh'."*
>
> —Anonymous Physician

Physicians are fortunate. They can evaluate patients' well-being with physical signs and tests using well established protocols. The teachers' task of assessing their clients' progress is a bit more elusive. Teachers need to gather information that is more varied and that can be less direct. Careful assessment of student progress is challenging—and essential. A solid understanding of what your students currently know and can do allows you to plan appropriate instruction and nudge each student forward. Thus, planning, instruction, and assessment are all integrally linked.

This chapter presents six guiding principles for assessing student learning. Then it provides examples of different assessment strategies, each useful for different purposes.

 READER'S TIP

If you have limited experience with student assessment and would benefit by seeing descriptions of some assessment strategies, glance at the section "Assessment Strategies" on page 145 before reading these general guidelines.

GENERAL GUIDELINES FOR STUDENT ASSESSMENT

Effective teachers gather information of different kinds over time to ensure that their pupils are learning and that they themselves are providing appropriate instruction. An assessment instrument is not inherently good or bad. Rather, its worth depends on whether it is effective for particular purposes in specific settings. The following six guidelines can help you to select and develop instruments that are useful elements of your own system for student assessment. Assessment needs to be:

1. Tied to your stance on education
2. Driven by learning goals
3. Systematic
4. Tied to instruction
5. Inclusive of the learner
6. Integrated into a manageable system

Assessment Needs to Be Tied to Your Stance on Education

As a nation, we test what we value, for better or worse. As a professional, your views about the good society, about the purposes of education, and about teaching and learning should be reflected in the ways you assess student progress. For example, if it is important to you that students master a large body of factual knowledge, then it is essential that you use assessment strategies that carefully tap into students' mastery of facts. Likewise, if one of your goals is for students to become independent thinkers, then you need to provide opportunities for them to evaluate their own work and to show that they are growing in their capacity for autonomous thought. Check the tests and other assessment tools you use. Make sure they send a message that is consistent with the way you are convinced life should be.

Assessment Needs to Be Driven by Learning Goals

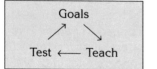

You are entering the profession of education when **accountability** is a sharply prominent issue facing families, schools, and the public. This means that schools are held responsible for student performance in very discrete and public ways. Student achievement results are published, and many schools offer rewards and punishments based on students' growth or lack of growth as measured by standardized test scores. Additionally, students are increasingly held accountable for learning, with many states requiring students to pass examinations in order to complete a certain grade level or to graduate from high school.

Central to the accountability effort is that student performance is assessed in line with our instructional goals. We select our goals based on priorities for student learning. The planning and instruction chapters of this book (Chapters 4, 5, and 6) argue that we should teach to our goals. Then we test what we have taught. As the accountability movement emphasizes, goals, instruction, and assessment all need to be aligned.

Most of us have at least one college horror story about course goals and class activities that had no apparent relation to the class's final examination. Remember your horror and save your students. Select or write goals that address important points and teach what is important. Then test (or more broadly, assess) what you have taught. Remember, too, that if a concept, generalization, skill, attitude, or ability was important enough for you to include in your list of instructional goals, it is important enough to include in your list of items to assess as well. Using goals to drive assessment requires that we address different levels, time schedules, and domains.

 READER'S TIP

Check back to your work in Figure 2.4. Your chart should show how teachers' conceptions of education result in very different strategies for assessment.

Assessment Occurs on Different Levels   Recall the bull's-eye from Chapter 1 that placed you and your students within a system. Because your classroom is embedded in concentric societal layers, you and your students will participate in different levels of assessment. Figure 7.1 lists many current test-related terms.

One of our national goals is general literacy. As a result, the federal No Child Left Behind Act (introduced in Chapter 1) requires all students in grades 3

FIGURE 7.1   *Test talk.*

Alternative (or authentic) assessment: strategies that assess student learning in realistic contexts and input from the learner.

Assessment versus evaluation: Many use the terms synonymously. Some draw a distinction: *assessment* is the process of gathering information; *evaluation* is the act of judging that information, assigning a value to it.

Norm-referenced tests: Students' achievement is based upon a comparison of their scores with other students' scores; grading on a curve. Similarly, schools can be compared with other schools using norm-referenced procedures to examine schoolwide achievement.

Criterion-referenced tests: Students' achievement is based upon a comparison of their work with an external criterion. Student performance on criterion-referenced measures is often determined by comparing their performance to a proficiency level (e.g., "highly proficient" or "below basic"). In contrast to norm-referenced measures, all students are awarded the highest level if they demonstrate that level of achievement.

High-stakes evaluation: Assessment results that have real consequences for the participants or other stakeholders. Examples include tests that determine eligibility for special services for individuals, or the withholding of funding for entire schools.

Low-stakes evaluation: Assessment results that are useful primarily in local and informal ways. An example is a classroom attitude survey that measures students' interests in reading.

through 8 to take annual statewide achievement tests in reading and mathematics by the year 2005. These examinations must match state content standards, the learning goals. Additionally, a sample of fourth and eighth graders across America must take the National Assessment of Educational Progress examination to allow for achievement comparisons across states. (Visit the Web sites at this chapter's close if you would like to learn more about these issues.)

Standardized tests typically provide **norm-referenced** information, which means that your students' achievement will be compared with the achievement of students in a norming group. Your school's overall achievement may also be compared with that of other schools. How well your students (or your school) score depends on the relation of their scores to those of the norming group. Additionally, standardized tests can provide **criterion-referenced** information, which deems certain outcomes as "mastered" or compares performance to various levels of mastery.

The public maintains an eager interest in standardized test scores because standardized tests give general information about students' progress at the school, district, state, and national levels. The public interprets standardized test scores as one measure of the health of America's schools. Heated debates arise about the validity of standardized tests as a measure of important outcomes. Proponents argue that well educated students should be able to communicate their knowledge via mechanisms such as carefully constructed, broad-based measures. Some vocal critics (e.g., Kohn, 1999) condemn standardized tests as incapable of measuring important outcomes, of limiting our vision of what is important, and of being biased against students of color. Some seriously doubt the ability of standardized tests to measure the types of learning and intelligence that relate to success in the real world. Sternberg (1997a, 1997b), for instance, argues that successful intelligence—the ability to adapt to one's environment to accomplish goals—is not measured by standardized tests. Sternberg also asserts that standardized tests emphasize conformity in thought instead of valuing diverse approaches to learning.

Because of the great interest—and increasingly the tangible rewards and punishments—attached to standardized tests, such measures are considered high-stakes evaluations. However, Reineke (1998) notes that the purpose, development, and relevance of standardized tests tend to fall outside the

READER'S TIP

Talk about high-stakes testing with an experienced teacher you admire. What benefits does she see stemming from standardized tests? How does she manage the tension of preparing students for standardized tests and remaining true to aspects of her stance that may run contrary to high-stakes testing?

classroom. For this reason, large-scale tests have limited utility for guiding classroom instruction. For instance, content measured on national examinations may not be a good match with the content selected for your locale. Also, your students' scores may remain relatively stable, but their standing can change radically based on changes of the norming group's scores. **Local assessments,** on the other hand, provide information more directly related to your instruction. Classroom assessments serve the primary purpose of immediately fostering student learning and improving instruction.

Local instructional goals are more specific and dictate the use of classroom-based assessments. Many classroom assessments are *criterion referenced* instead of norm referenced. Through criterion-referenced tests, students' achievement is measured by comparing their scores to predetermined criteria instead of to other students' scores. For example, you may set the criterion of 85% accuracy as demonstrating satisfactory mastery of particular mathematics concepts. Local assessments are often considered lower-stakes measures (though perhaps not to the students).

Both levels of assessment—large-scale and local—can contribute unique information to our understanding of students' progress. The trick is to be smart in considering the kind of information that each level of assessment can provide. Keep in mind the purpose of particular assessments as you interpret your students' progress and speak with students, families, and professionals about that progress. The kinds of assessments we select also depend on the time frames of our goals.

Different Time Spans Require Different Assessments   You have both long- and short-term goals for your students, so you need measures to assess students in both the long and short ranges. At the most immediate level, you will conduct assessments related to your daily lesson objectives. Assessment for every lesson needs to determine students' progress toward the lessons' objectives. With the crush of classroom events, it is tempting to restrict assessments to those that measure quick, discrete skills and ideas. But don't. Beyond single, discrete objectives, you will assess mastery of a certain standard or generalization that consists of work with several objectives. Then, for documenting students' long-range growth, you will need to gather information that allows you to track students' progress over time. Pardon my use of an illustration to draw an analogy between assessment of a major learning goal in mathematics and the various objectives that comprise that goal. Assessing the quality of the necklace depends on assessment of each individual gem, of sections of gems together set in metal, and of the piece overall (see Figure 7.2).

Assessment Needs to Be More Than Cognitive   Based on your stance toward education and on grade-level recommendations, you probably have goals for your students in the cognitive, psychomotor, and affective (the thinking, doing, and feeling) domains. School assessments in the past have focused heavily on the cognitive domain, and as a result, teachers may have glimpsed only a seg-

FIGURE 7.2 *Assessing the quality of complex performance usually requires assessment of individual components and of the work overall.*

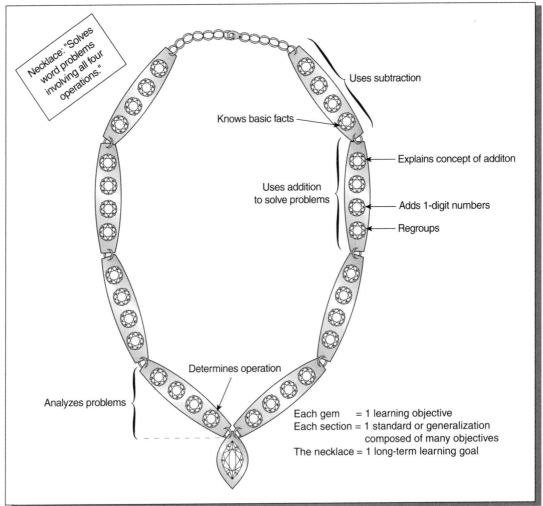

ment of students' progress. A multiple-choice test, for instance, tells very little about students' attitudes toward the subject matter.

Recent development of state standards may help address this shortcoming. Some national standards have. The National Science Education Standards (National Research Council, 1996), for instance, require students to master the *abilities* necessary to do scientific inquiry, which include, for instance, *employing equipment and tools* to gather data. Those abilities include psychomotor skills. The National Service Standards also emphasize *appreciation* for science as a way of knowing the world and the *dispositions* and *attitudes* associated with science.

Even if your state standards do not yet address domains outside of the cognitive realm, you as a teacher have the responsibility to assess student progress in *each area* you have deemed as important given your view of what it means to be educated, local planning efforts, and your knowledge of the discipline. Match your goals across domains with at least one way to check students' growth related to those goals. Stiggins (2001) suggests that teachers use assessments to measure a variety of targets including:

- Knowledge and understanding
- Reasoning
- Performance skills

- Proficiency in creating products
- Dispositions

You will need to think hard about ways to tap student learning for some of your goals, especially when multiple domains are addressed or when goals seem elusive. Strategies described later in the chapter, such as journal entries, observations, and attitude surveys, can help. Different kinds of goals and objectives often require different assessment strategies. Devise a plan that includes a number of ways to determine whether and what students are learning related to your varied goals.

In fact, Reineke (1998) and Walvoord and Anderson (1998) argue that even when teachers have no plans for assessing affect, assessment tends to involve a good deal of emotion for students. Walvoord and Anderson (1998, p. 13) intone

> Because grades [the results of assessments] are highly symbolic, because they reveal and complicate the bases of power in the classroom, because they so powerfully shape interrelationships among students and teacher, and because they often carry high stakes for learners, they will evoke strong emotions.

Teachers should therefore seize the opportunity to teach when students respond to evaluations with emotion: "Such moments of emotional intensity may be the most powerful teaching moments of the semester," Walvoord and Anderson suggest (1998, p. 14).

Teaching Tips

ASSESSING PROGRESS TOWARD LESSON OBJECTIVES

1. Assessment begins in the planning phase. As you write lesson objectives, check to see that they represent valuable outcomes that are measurable.
2. Consider including a brief assessment of the objectives in the closure portion of each lesson. You could give a quick quiz, use unison response, or some "show-me" technique to check each student's learning.
3. Think about what the results of your assessment tell you. Are your students ready to move on? Do you need to reteach? Provide enrichment?

Assessment Needs to Address Incidental Learnings, Too   Despite the fact that planning, instruction, and assessment must be logically linked (goals → teach → test), many things influence student learning; teaching is one. Learning can be highly individualistic. Students learn things related to our goals, but not only those things. Additionally, based on their idiosyncratic characteristics, students do not learn the same things, even given the same instruction. Therefore, you need to include in your assessment plan a means to determine, in ad-

Teaching Tips

Before you collect a major assignment or close a long-range unit of study, say to your students, "People learn different things. You may have learned something about yourself, about your peers, or something about the content that you did not expect." Invite students to share via discussion or a quick write the things they learned.

dition to your goals for student learning, *what else* students have learned. A journal prompt such as, "What surprises did you encounter during our unit of Ancient Rome? What did you learn from your peers? What questions do you still have?" may tap into these serendipitous outcomes.

Assessment Needs to Be Systematic

No matter your stance toward education, you need to gather information about your students' learning in ways that are accurate, fair, and systematic. Because teachers busily engage in many activities at once, their conclusions about students are sometimes based on recollections of informal and fleeting observations. Unfortunately, human perception tends to be selective, and teacher memory is faulty. Reineke (1998, p. 7) reminds us that assessment involves *people:* "Assessments, formal or informal, considered or casual, intentional or not, powerfully affect people, particularly students. . . . Students' assessment experiences remain with them for a lifetime and substantially affect their capacity for future learning." Therefore, you need to develop a plan that will allow you to gather information about student learning in ways that are logical and equitable. Make a plan for collecting information in a fair manner that gives students ample opportunity to display the breadth and depth of their growth and understanding.

Being systematic will increase the chances that the measures (tests and other assessments) you use are **valid** and **reliable.** A *valid* instrument measures what it was intended to measure. Does it tap into students' understanding of the intended content? Whether an instrument measures what it should is based partly on its reliability. A *reliable* measure gives consistent results under different conditions and with different raters. A measure may be valid in one setting and completely inappropriate in another. When you work on being systematic with your assessments, you will guard instruments' reliability and validity (see Figure 7.3).

Although the criteria of validity and reliability seem obvious, they are regularly trampled in classroom practice. One example is the sixth-grade class in which a group of English learners took their social studies instruction in Spanish (as was consistent with the school's policies for bilingual education). When it was time for the Spanish-speaking students to share what they had learned, however, they were given the same written exam—in English—as other members of the class. Their teacher probably received inaccurate information about the students' knowledge of social studies, and the experience may have eroded students' dignity, which was probably not in keeping with the teacher's stance toward education.

Another example of invalid assessment also concerns the use of language in assessment. In many classes, students who read at lower levels of proficiency are given written tests with no modifications. For low-proficiency readers, written tests can be more tests of reading ability than they are of content knowledge. If teachers' intent is to gain a valid picture of students' content knowledge, teachers may need to consider altering the testing format to sidestep reading issues. For instance, it may be appropriate for struggling readers to hear written tests read aloud.

One of the best ways you can ensure that you are developing a thorough and valid understanding of students' progress is by using **multiple measures,** or varied formats. This approach will help you to provide a number of chances and avenues for students to show what they know, to account for student differences, and to ensure that you are sampling different kinds of information about students' knowledge, attitudes, and development. Be sensitive, thorough, and careful—be fair—so that you can determine whether and what every one of your students is learning.

FIGURE 7.3   *Multiple measures help ensure valid results.*

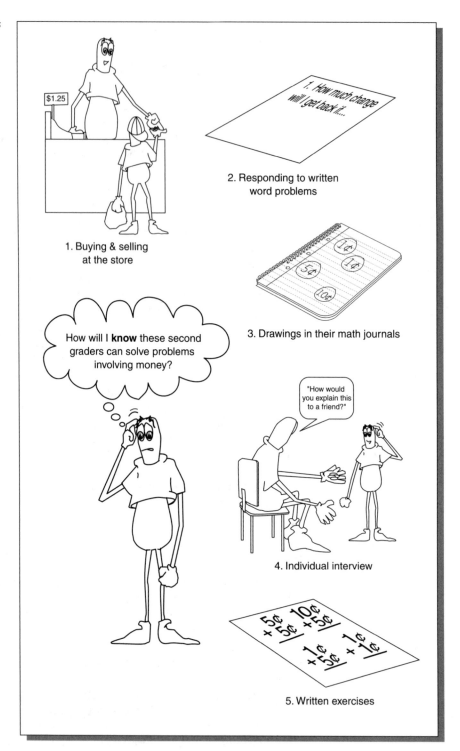

Assessment Needs to Be Tied to Instruction

The goals → teach → test cycle is indeed a cycle. Assessment results should both drive instruction and guide the selection of future learning goals. Tying assessment to instruction means that you assess *before, during,* and *after instruction* to enhance student learning and spend your planning and instructional efforts wisely.

Assessing Prior to Instruction By assessing students' prior knowledge, teachers' lessons have a greater chance of connecting to what students know. Results on **preinstructional assessments** may tell you, for instance, that students do not have the background knowledge necessary for success in the unit you were planning or that they have already mastered the standards you intended to teach. In either case, had you not preassessed students, you would have wasted valuable instructional time and effort. Preassessments are also important in helping you to determine special interests and needs students may have so that you can differentiate your instruction to provide all students with access to the core curriculum.

 TEACHER TALK

Three practicing teachers reflect on the power of prior-knowledge interviews, where they talked with individual students to discover what the students knew about specific science content:

1. "My [middle school] student felt privileged to share her knowledge with me one-on-one. I don't often take the time to sit with one student and listen carefully to her view of the world."
2. "I taught my same students last year, so I know what they were exposed to in science. I couldn't believe that my prior knowledge interview student didn't have the concepts I thought I taught so well last year. He could repeat definitions that we memorized, but he hadn't glued those definitions to real ideas or explanations of the world. It was a humbling experience."
3. "I interviewed a small group of kindergartners to discover what they knew about sinking and floating. I know people learn things at home, but I was amazed at all the connections these five-year olds made with their outside lives. They talked about going fishing, about throwing pennies into a fountain, and about playing with bathtub toys. I learned vividly that even my very young students are working hard to make sense of things."

Assessing During Instruction Use a variety of strategies to find out what students are learning as you teach. Active participation strategies where each student responds during your lesson allow you to make mid-lesson adjustments. As an example, in a graduate research course, I was teaching the concept of hypothesis testing. My students became suspiciously enamored of the papers on their desks when I asked a question to check comprehension. There, apparently, *was* no comprehension. They just sat and stared at their papers. I modified my assessment strategy: "Okay, turn to your partner. Tell him one thing you know about hypothesis testing and one thing that makes absolutely no sense. You have two minutes, then be ready to report." The use of partner talk as an active participation strategy allowed each person to safely express his fragile, newly forming knowledge, and their questions allowed me to attack the concept in another way.

Teaching Tips

For an inexpensive class set of wipe boards, place card stock into a plastic page protector and hand it, a dry erase marker, and a tissue to each student. Every student can now "do the problem on the board" and hold up work for you to quickly assess. I have found, to date, 84 uses for these boards.

Assessing After Instruction   Ensure that your post-lesson assessments will allow you to determine the level at which students mastered your objective. Some checks on objectives will be brief and informal, and some will be much more complex and formal. One "quick check" strategy is to collect and analyze short student work samples. For example, you may have had your chemistry students write brief responses to the prompt, "What is the difference between endothermic and exothermic reactions?" You collect their responses and sort them into two stacks: Those who stated a correct difference, and those who did not. You count how many are in each stack and determine whether to **reteach** or move on. If you need more detailed information, you could sort the incorrect examples into stacks based on students' apparent misconceptions. For example, one group may have understood something about energy entering and leaving reactions, whereas one group did not even mention energy. Based on your assessment information, you can differentiate your instruction to address students' ideas.

Figure 7.4 presents some strategies for assessing students before, during, and after instruction. Do some look familiar? They are active participation strategies drawn from a figure in Chapter 5; when assessment is ongoing, the line between it and instruction blurs nicely. Figure 7.4 also includes a few new strategies and descriptions. Additionally, the second part of this chapter describes a variety of assessment options that may be used during each phase of instruction (before, during, and after).

Although traditional tests can evoke anxiety, they have a place in an assessment system because their judicious use can provide important information. Most assessment opportunities, though, should feel low risk (low stakes) to students, undertaken with the trust that the teacher is interested in improving instruction and facilitating learning. Herman, Aschbacher, and Winters (1992) recommend the use of alternative (or authentic) assessment tools to more closely link instruction with assessment. Assessment tools such as clinical interviews, observations, portfolios, demonstrations, and journals share the common vision of alternative assessments in that they

- Ask students to perform, create, produce, or do something.
- Tap higher-level thinking and problem-solving skills.
- Use tasks that represent meaningful instructional activities.
- Invoke real-world applications.
- Are scored by people using human judgment rather than by machines.
- Require new instructional and assessment roles for teachers. (Herman, Aschbacher, & Winters, 1992, p. 6)

Teaching Tips

TYING ASSESSMENT TO INSTRUCTION
1. Assess before, during, and after instruction.
2. Use a mix of formal and informal assessments that keep student anxiety at bay.
3. Assess frequently as you teach and use results to guide your decisions.
4. Do not assess unless you have a plan for what to do with the results.

Assessment Needs to Be Inclusive of the Learner

Check back to your work from the exercise preceding this chapter and think about, as a student, the role you played in the assessment of your learning. How often did you have choices about the content to be assessed, about the form of assessment, or about selecting the testing conditions? Many adults state that, as

FIGURE 7.4 *Using active participation to assess student learning throughout all phases of instruction.*

Preinstruction Assessments	1. Quick writes 2. Brainstorming and fact-storming 3. Values lineup 4. Four corners 5. Peer interviews 6. Prior knowledge interviews: Teacher assesses students' prior knowledge by observing them complete a task and asking a few gentle questions. (Teacher: "Use these balls to show me how the solar system is arranged and how parts of it move.") 7. Drawings: Students draw current understandings of content under study and use drawings to describe their knowledge. (Teacher: "Draw a picture of someone wearing clothes from long ago.") 8. Storytelling sessions: Students tell stories in small groups or to the whole class about personal experiences with the content. (Teacher: "Tell me about a time when you watched the night sky.")
During-Instruction Assessments	9. Choral response 10. Whip 11. Flash cards 12. Chalkboards 13. Peer coaching 14. Letter and number tiles 15. Finger signals 16. Student-led recitation 17. Partner journals 18. Numbered heads together 19. Toss the ball 20. Talk to your partner 21. Sorts
Post-Instruction Assessments	22. Comprehension check 23. Fuzzy points 24. Gallery tour 25. Student quiz 26. Blackboard blitz 27. Charts and diagrams (individual, group, or whole class) 28. Graphic organizers: Alone or with assistance, students create visual displays of content information to illustrate their understanding of key concepts and relationships. (Teacher: "With your partner, please make a chart to show what we have learned about electricity this week.")

learners, their role in assessment was as passive participants. Their primary role seems to have been to study in preparation for tests and then to keep their eyes on their own paper. Assessment was done *to* them, not *with* them. Further, it appears that existing assessment procedures were accepted as normal and correct. No one questioned the red ink or percentages scrawled near the top of each test.

Every act of teaching—including assessment—conveys our professional convictions. If we wish to protect students' dignity, to encourage them to build responsibility for their own learning, and to foster their growth as self-assessors, then assessment must involve students' voices and choices. My son Alex

*Students need to be
active participants in
their own assessment.*

taught me this lesson during his kindergarten year. In the left-hand portion of Figure 7.5 is a self-portrait Alex drew near the beginning of the year. "Good detail," said his mother. "Lots of realistic subtleties! Smart kid!" In the right-hand portion is the self-portrait Alex completed near that year's close. "Yikes!" said his mother. "Less detail. No pupils, no digits, no feet, no hair! No growth in fine motor abilities!" I struggled with my interpretation of those portraits until a wise teacher suggested that I ask *Alex* to analyze the portraits. Alex easily explained to me the significance of the second portrait. There was less detail, yes, but, he held up both arms, made fists, and flexed his biceps, "Mom, look how *strong* I am!" Alex's most treasured change of his kindergarten year was that he had become physically more capable, much stronger: Superman strong! Had I not asked Alex to attach meaning to his work, to self-evaluate, I would have been left with an unnecessarily limited conclusion about his progress.

COMMUNICATING RESULTS OF INSTRUCTION

According to the National Board for Professional Teaching Standards (1998), accomplished teachers communicate assessment results to parents. Talk with an experienced teacher to determine how he shares assessment information with students and their families. How can you engage parents in an ongoing conversation about student progress?

This self-portrait experience humbled me as an instructor and assessor. It taught me not to overestimate my ability to judge learning based on the information I gather. It taught me that, to understand student learning in holistic terms, I need to ask the students. So that you can involve students in the process of assessment, provide opportunities for students to set goals, to have choices in assessment, to self-evaluate, and to evaluate your instruction. One way to

FIGURE 7.5 *Alexander's self-portraits.*

| Alex's Early Kindergarten Self-Portrait | Alex's Late Kindergarten Self-Portrait |

do so is to give **student-led conferences** (Bailey & Guskey, 2001; Benson & Barnett, 1999). Also, Figure 7.6 provides examples of how you can include your students' voices and choices in your assessment. Bear in mind that these options must be considered in conjunction with other principles of assessment. For instance, you need to remain systematic in assessing learning even as you allow for student choice.

Assessment Needs to Be Integrated Into a Manageable System

You have a tough job to do in your assessor role. You will assess progress every day, at many levels, and across many domains, all while remaining true to your stance on education and staying fair and respectful to your students. Stiggins (2001) suggests that lack of time is a significant barrier to effective assessment. He notes four issues: (1) the scope of the school curriculum continues to expand so that teachers are responsible for assessing a broadening variety of student achievement, (2) the expectations for instruction continue to expand, (3) current assessments tend to be labor intensive, and (4) teachers are often also expected to store large amounts of assessment information.

You can manage the weighty assessment role by developing an overall system of assessment that allows you to gather the information you need to be accountable and to encourage student progress. By *system* I mean a collection of assessment instruments that allows you to focus on student learning and enact the five principles of assessment in a way that is reasonable for your circumstances. Figure 7.7 lists some pointers for developing an assessment system. The section that follows provides specific examples of assessment strategies that may play a role in your system.

FIGURE 7.6 *Involving students in assessment.*

Goal Setting	• Students discuss previous years and create a chart at the beginning of the year of topics they would like to study. • Students provide input into the course content, choosing units and lessons based on assessment results and interests. • Students examine their records (portfolios, work samples, and report cards) to set class and personal goals. • Students keep individual records of their progress. They discuss progress and revise goals with their teacher. • Students end an examination by answering the question "What would you like to learn next?" • Students write a note to their teacher explaining what she should focus on as she assesses a piece of writing or a performance. • The teacher invites students to write long-term goals and seal them in envelopes. The teacher may mail these letters back to students when they reach a certain age.
Student Choice	• Students select some forms of assessment. Teachers who implement multiple intelligence theory often allow students to choose from among seven or eight assessment formats. • Students work in groups to list what they consider the key content to be assessed. • Students develop some questions or prompts for the assessment. • Students select writing prompts or test items from a larger bank. • Students respond to prompts that allow for a broad range of appropriate responses (for example, "Devise a method of sharing equally"). • Students have some say over the assessment conditions (for instance, students are allowed to move to the library if they need isolated conditions or are allowed to have a prompt read aloud to them).
Self-Reflection and Self-Evaluation	• In small groups or in their journals, students discuss their thinking or analyze a problem. • Before submitting work, students analyze their growth, in writing or in a conference. • Before submitting work, students turn the paper over and write to their teacher: "What would you like me to know as I read this paper?" • Students study good and poor examples of the product to be created and assessed. They develop rubrics for use in scoring their products. • Students use rubrics or a checklist from the teacher to assess their own work before submitting it. • Students grade their own papers and hold onto the grade. They compare their analysis with the teacher's analysis and discuss. • Students reflect on their progress over time by comparing work samples from different time periods.
Evaluation of Teaching and Assessment	• Students rate problems and exercises for appropriate level of difficulty (too easy, just right, or too difficult) and for appropriateness of content. • In their journals or on anonymous slips of paper, students tell the teacher what worked well in facilitating their learning and what may have worked even better during particular lessons or units. • Students periodically rate the teacher's instruction, giving specific praise and criticism. Using a specific format can help structure feedback into a format most useful for the teacher, but open-ended questions are important as well. • The teacher regularly provides students with choices for future activities based on the class's assessment of current activities. • The teacher shares his instructional goals with students and revises them based on ongoing assessment.

FIGURE 7.7 *Pointers for developing an assessment system.*

1. Determine which assessment strategies you are required to use. (Ask the principal.) Be certain you are prepared to use them well.

2. Talk with experienced teachers about assessment. Ask to see how they maintain student records and their assessment system. Ask about the time investments required. Determine whether those teachers' systems allow them to obtain important information about their students.

3. Select a variety of instruments that will allow you to gather information about all students, in every domain, over time, and across levels. Use the check sheet in Figure 7.8 to assess the potential of each instrument.

4. Review the guidelines for assessment from this chapter and think about specific assessment tools that will allow you to enact those guidelines. Is your system fair? Inclusive of the learner?

5. Streamline your list so that you use the minimum number of assessment strategies possible to obtain the variety and amount of information you and your students require. Drop an item from your list if you can gather the same information using another item you have already listed. Add items when you notice that certain goals or domains are missing.

6. Sit down with your school calendar or plan book and think about when and how often you should use each type of instrument.

7. Be realistic in estimating the time and effort required to implement your system.

8. Be certain that the system yields information that matches the time and energy investments it requires.

9. Monitor the effectiveness of your system. Is it accurately and humanely assessing the progress of each of your students? What modifications are you making to gain accurate information about your students with diverse cultural and linguistic backgrounds? Eggen and Kauchak (1999) suggest that you may need to consider whether your students are familiar with the structures and purposes of testing, whether you need to modify the format (including the language) of your assessments, and whether you need to modify the conditions under which information is gathered. For instance, you may need to include additional visual supports or examples, read directions aloud, or provide extra work time.

10. If you cannot manage your assessment system, change it.

ASSESSMENT STRATEGIES

This section of the chapter describes nine classroom assessment techniques. Figure 7.8 analyzes the potential usefulness of the instruments in terms of general guidelines for assessment. Although each can play a useful role in your assessment system, some fall within the realm of traditional assessments, and some are more often considered alternative or authentic assessments. Figure 7.9 explores a bit of the history and some of the differences between traditional and alternative assessment measures.

Traditional Tests

Traditional paper-pencil measures can be furnished through adopted textbook series or written by teachers (most typically alone, but students can contribute items). Some common types of questions on traditional tests include objective items such as true–false, multiple-choice, fill-in-the-blank, and matching items. Objective items tend to be time-consuming to write but quick to grade and are subject to little interpretation from the grader. Open-ended questions include short-answer items, essay questions, and less traditional variations such as graphic organizers and pictorial representations of students' knowledge. Teachers' time investment with open-ended items tends to be not in the writing phase but in the assessment phase. Open-ended items require more judgment from the grader than do objective items.

Attitude Surveys

Usually developed by teachers, attitude surveys are paper-pencil scales that assess students' preferences and feelings toward a topic or skill. Some

FIGURE 7.8 Assessing assessments.

	Goal-Directed	Systematic	Tied to Instruction	Includes the Student
Traditional Tests	Most often cognitive. Select items that match objectives and what was taught. Careful to dig deeper than facts for generalizations. Write special questions for incidental learnings.	Easy to collect for every student. Objective items are most reliable.	Usually used post-instruction. Reteach based on results. Brief, self-graded quizzes can be used during instruction.	Typically not, but is possible with teacher effort.
Attitude Surveys	Great for affective domain.	Validity may be affected by students' desire to please.	Good for pre-instruction to influence planning.	Special strength. However, if you won't use results, don't ask.
Products	Can tap all three domains. Can tap integrated, complex understandings. Can span longer time periods.	If students are allowed choice, can be difficult to assess uniformly across products. Reliability is affected if work was conducted outside of class.	Find an audience to appreciate products. Think specifically about what to do with results.	Can be a strength if students are allowed choice. Encourage self-evaluation of work.
Portfolios	Can tap all three domains. Good for measuring progress toward larger goals. Good for long-term growth.	Argued as being highly valid because entries are samples from many time periods and different conditions. Train raters for best reliability. May overestimate competence if work is completed collaboratively.	Can profoundly influence instruction. Time intensive.	Excellent potential—when author has ownership. Good for goal-setting.
Journals	A collection of entries over time can give indications of long-term development. Excellent for assessing incidental learning and affective domain.	Can be difficult to assess using a standard protocol unless prompts are very structured. Journals depend upon teachers' ability to interpret students' written words and symbols. Discussion can protect validity.	Can be used at all instructional stages. Must have an audience. Time-consuming if teacher is sole audience.	Open prompts include a great deal of student choice. Students need to be able to express themselves in writing. Students need to value the prompts for journals to be useful.

prompts are closed-ended. For instance, students can rank order lists of subjects in terms of their preferences or agree/disagree with a set of items. For young students, a survey item can be read aloud while the students circle one of a continuum of faces, very happy to very sad. Open-ended items allow for

FIGURE 7.8 *Continued*

Performance-Based Assessments	Use regularly throughout the year to collect evidence of long-term growth. Excellent for psychomotor (and other) domains.	Each student must be given the same opportunity to perform. Validity can be affected if the performance situation is uncomfortable for the child. Scoring procedures need to clearly specified.	Many teachers obtain baseline information through performances, and then assess again after instruction.	Allow students to self-assess their performance and to evaluate your instruction to suggest the next step.
Teacher Observations	Excellent for affective and psychomotor domains.	Structured observation guides and class lists can help focus teachers' attention on certain items for all students.	Individual lessons can include a period during which teacher observes to check for student progress.	Variable, depends upon structure of the observation
Interviews	Used primarily for cognitive and psychomotor items, but affect can naturally arise.	Allows for great depth for individual students. Tied to verbal skills.	Depth of information obtained can be very useful for instruction planning. Requires careful planning to interview all students.	Respectful questioning can allow children to share what they know, can do, and find important.
Drawings and Diagrams	Drawing uses psychomotor skills. Cognitive and affective domains can both be addressed.	Allow students to describe the meaning behind their works to ensure that you fully understand what the students are trying to convey.	Highly appropriate at all phases of the instructional cycle.	Presents tasks (drawing) that are atypical for school for many students; many students enjoy the novelty and the nonlinear, nonlinguistic opportunity. Some students do not feel comfortable drawing.

a broad range of student responses. An example is "What I would like you to know about me as an artist is . . . " Many teachers use attitude surveys near the beginning of the year to become acquainted with their students.

Products

Students submit items (written or constructed) to demonstrate their understanding or skill. Examples include student-composed newspapers, brochures, posters, works of art, and scientific or practical inventions. Products can be assessed through the use of rubrics, or scoring guides that specify the criteria against which an item will be assessed. Rubrics can be used for scoring many kinds of student works; for example, portfolio entries, performances, and products can all be assessed through rubrics. Teachers, or students and teachers together, can generate rubrics. If students do not help to develop rubrics, the criteria for grading should be made clear to students at the onset of the assignment. A **holistic rubric**

FIGURE 7.9   *What is the opposite of authentic assessment?*

A Bit of Assessment History

Early in the twentieth century, assessment procedures in American schools served primarily a sorting function: Teachers' assessments separated students who knew much from students who did not. With the advent of standardized testing in the 1930s, instruction was divorced from assessment: Teachers taught and ranked students; assessors checked learning. In the 1970s and 1980s society voiced two concerns: (1) Students sorted to the bottom of the stack had no means to contribute to the economic vitality of the nation and (2) businesspeople asked for influence over the quality of their potential workforce. Those two forces gave rise to an expanded set of outcomes to be measured through schools' assessment procedures (Stiggins, 1997). Traditional assessment can be contrasted with alternative or authentic assessment.

Traditional Assessment	Alternative or Authentic Assessment
Examples: Standardized tests and teacher-created paper-pencil tests.	Examples: Portfolios and performance-based assessments.
Designed to measure a narrow slice of student achievement for a brief period of time.	Designed to capture a complex range of outcomes (including cognitive, psychomotor, and affective ends) over longer periods of time.
The form of the test is not designed specifically to match the conditions under which the information will be used. As a result, traditional tests may measure primarily unintended capabilities such as reading or test-taking skills.	Assessment is to be measured in a form similar to the conditions of use (context embedded).
Assessment conditions are not necessarily expected to mirror the conditions under which knowledge is gained (context free or context reduced).	Assessment conditions are to mirror the conditions under which students learned the information.
The power resides with the teacher as evaluator.	The power for assessment and subsequent planning is shared by the teacher and student.
The focus is primarily summative, and results are not always used to inform instruction.	Assessment includes a focus on formative assessment, and results should directly inform instruction.
Evaluation is often norm referenced, which does not necessarily convey a clear picture of the outcomes mastered.	Evaluation is criterion referenced, which provides a picture of what students know and can do irrespective of their peers' achievements.
Tests have the benefits of efficiency and more objectivity in scoring.	Measures have the benefit of richness because information is collected over time and in a range of contexts.
Traditional standardized measures are criticized as focusing on student deficits instead of showing what students do know, as providing little valuable information related to realistic settings, and as being biased against students who come from a nondominant group (see, for example, Murphy, 1994).	Alternative assessments are criticized as failing to provide sufficient evidence of validity and reliability (Bateson, 1994). Authentic measures can lack meaningful standards, and biases against minority students also exist for alternative assessments (Howell et al., 1993).

(one that addresses the overall characteristics of the entry) is found in Figure 7.10. In contrast to the holistic rubric, an **analytical trait rubric** assesses individual traits, or components, of the performance separately (Arter & McTighe, 2001).

Portfolios

In developing portfolios, students collect and analyze work samples over time and from a variety of contexts (Hebert, 2001; Stefanakis, 2002). Some items

FIGURE 7.10 *A sample holistic rubric for scoring portfolio entries.*

Score 3	Score 2	Score 1
Entry briefly describes the item that follows but devotes more attention to careful analysis.	Entry describes the item that follows and reflects on it in brief ways.	Entry is solely a simple description of the item that follows. Description may be quite long.
Entry reflects on the author's thinking in meaningful ways.	Entry includes superficial or limited information about the author's thinking.	Entry does not include information about the author's thinking.
Entry addresses content area concepts accurately and in ways that enrich the reader's understanding of the item that follows the analysis.	Entry addresses content area concepts in limited, accurate ways.	Entry does not reveal content area knowledge or content information is inaccurate.

In preparing portfolio entries, teacher and student discuss the significance of particular student works.

are typically chosen by the teacher, and some are student selected. Students write reflections of the entries in order to discuss their learning.

Schipper and Rossi (1997) recommend five stages for incorporating portfolio assessment:

1. *Lay the groundwork.* Examine your own values and help students "name" their learning by writing explicit criteria for what constitutes high-quality performance.
2. *Collect baseline data.* Because portfolios assess long-term growth, collect samples to indicate students' initial knowledge and skills.
3. *Select and collect.* Choose artifacts for inclusion in the portfolio.

4. *Write self-assessments.*   Have students analyze their work.
5. *Conference.*   Meet with students to share and assess their portfolios.
6. *Celebrate.*   Reflect on the students' successes.

Rubrics are sometimes used for the formal assessment of student portfolios. A teacher might use the rubric in Figure 7.10 to assess students' literature portfolio entries. He would study an entry (which might be, for example, a student writing sample) and the writer's reflection sheet on that entry to attach a score of 1, 2, or 3 to the entry. As an alternative, the teacher might award scores to whole sections of the portfolio or to the portfolio as a complete document.

Journals

Used primarily for informal assessment, journals can be completed by children as young as kindergartners. Students can respond to prompts from the teacher in pictures, symbols, or written words. They may also write with no prompt from the teacher. One of the primary benefits of journals is that they have a broad range of applications. Students can use them to describe their thinking, to document their experiences, to ask questions, to converse with a peer or the teacher, and to analyze their growth. Sample journal prompts include "What is mathematics?" and "How do you use mathematics in your daily life?" (Newmann, 1994).

Performance-Based Assessments

Students demonstrate competence by performance. Discrete skills such as cutting, counting, shooting a basket, or focusing a microscope can be assessed through student performances, as can more complex behaviors such as reading and social problem solving. Rubrics and other formal scales can be used to assess student performances. For instance, many teachers assess students' oral reading by marking and categorizing students' errors (or miscues) as they read. Then teachers analyze students' error patterns (e.g., Ashlock, 2002) to devise instructional plans to address student difficulties.

Teacher Observations

In addition to formal, performance-based assessments, teachers also observe their students working and interacting under more typical conditions. Examples include students' use of science process skills, their play behavior, and their ability to work as part of a team. To be systematic in their observations, teachers keep anecdotal records that describe their students' behaviors. Some teachers take notes on individual students, date the observations, and then collect them into file folders. This system allows teachers to analyze individual students' performances over time.

Interviews

In clinical interviews, teachers work with one student, or just a few students, at a time. Students typically complete a task that allows the teacher to probe their reasoning. For instance, in an interview to assess a student's prior concepts in science, a teacher might sit with the student and display a house plant. The teacher may ask her pupil to describe the plant and to hypothesize about the functions of the plant's parts. In a reading interview, a teacher might ask her student to point out and discuss features of the text that help convey the text's message. In a history interview, a teacher might ask a student to examine a primary source and talk a bit about its context and significance.

Drawings and Diagrams

Drawings and diagrams allow you to tap into students' knowledge through visual means. Students can draw their understandings of specific terms, emotions, experiences, and objects throughout history. One example is provided in Figure 7.11. The left side shows Zachary's portrayal of a squid when he was 4 years old. The right column was completed 5 years later, shortly after his class studied the squid's external structures. Both pictures demonstrate that he had some understanding of the external structure of a squid, and we see significant growth over time. The right-hand drawing and his verbal explanation demonstrate that he knows quite a bit about squid, and that he has some ideas still developing, even in his later drawing. For instance, the chromatophores (spots) are actually grouped, not randomly spread over the squid's body. Worried that the suction cups might look like teeth, Zach labeled them.

Drawings used over time are often highly effective at demonstrating change in students' thinking and abilities. Drawings can be assessed by rubrics.

In addition to drawings, students can also complete a variety of graphic organizers, or visual displays of information where terms are grouped and represented graphically, to demonstrate what they know. One widely used organizer is the concept map (Novak, 1998). As the sample concept map in Figure 7.12 shows, a major concept or term is given at the top of the map. Beneath it, subconcepts are presented hierarchically. Each concept is related to one above it

FIGURE 7.11 *Compare the two drawings and view Zachary's knowledge as emergent: What does he know about squid structure? How has it changed over time? What does he need to understand next?*

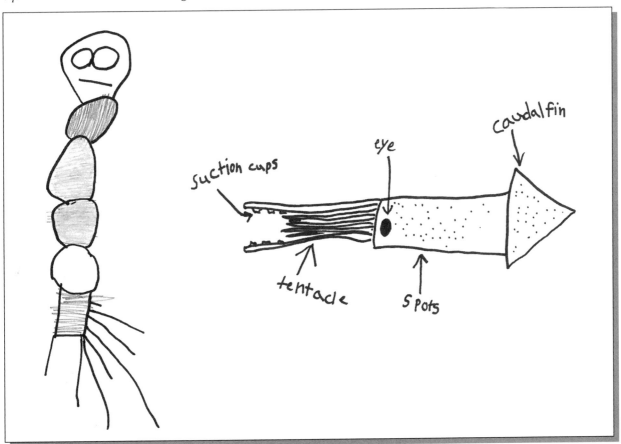

FIGURE 7.12 *A concept map shows the hierarchical organization of ideas related to a particular topic, in this case* novels.

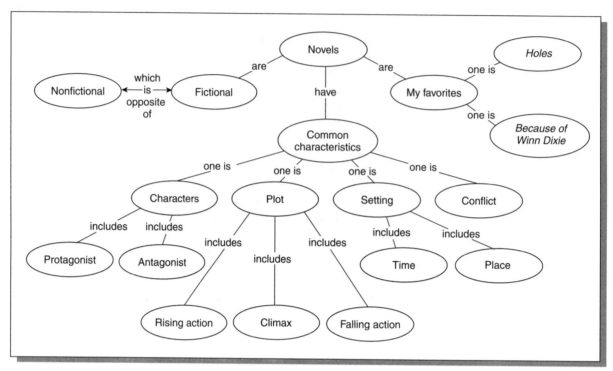

with a line or an arrow and a verb phrase that specifies the nature of the relationship between the two concepts. Often concepts are connected to more than one other concept. Before being used as assessment tools, concept maps would need to be modeled and developed during instruction. In general, the more concepts listed on a map, and the more accurately and richly connected they are, the better developed the author's thinking about that topic.

PARTING WORDS

Assessment of student progress is a messy business. Something as simple as writing a letter grade on a student paper requires us to ask ourselves difficult questions such as, "What does this letter represent? Is it growth over time, or does it show that this is one of the best papers in the stack? Does it deserve this letter when the writing is so flawed, despite that it shows understanding of the content?" Teaching is a complex moral endeavor, and the weight of an evaluator's role should be great.

You probably will not relish *every* element of the assessor's role. Guiding students to establish performance standards, commenting on their work, interpreting results, and assigning grades takes large amounts of teacher time and can feel contrary to the role most teachers *do* relish—that of coach and mentor. Figure 7.13 gives some tips to assist in some of the grading tasks that confront teachers. Try them out if you find yourself wishing that you could just say, "Open your mouth and say, 'ahhh.' "

FIGURE 7.13 *Tips on grading.*

Keeping a Grade Book and Figuring Grades

1. Computerized grade book programs can reduce work because you enter grades just once. They can also weight grades, and many include mechanisms for reporting results to students and families. Some teachers use a spreadsheet for keeping grades.

2. Find a copy of the grade report used for your level before you begin teaching and entering grades. Check the alignment of the report card with your content standards. Use the report form to structure your grading, but collect other information that is important to you and may not show up on the grade report.

3. Inform students of criteria for grades in advance. In every case possible, allow student input into grading criteria. Backwards planning (Chapter 4) can help.

4. Don't write a grade on every piece of paper. Some assignments are just for practice. In fact, many teachers judge homework assignments as complete or not and reteach to address errors. Also, feedback needs to be timely for it to be useful to the learner. Don't collect stacks of paper if you cannot return them for weeks.

5. Instead of entering percentages in your grade book, translate grades to a briefer system. Some teachers use a 1- to 12-point system, others use a 1- to 5-point system. This makes your job in adding scores easier at the end of the term and doesn't penalize students for low scores the way entering tiny percentages can.

6. After you figure grades, check again that marks accurately reflect your global assessment of each student's growth. Be prepared to defend every grade you report to parents. Be open to the possibility that you may have misgraded. Be ready to say what students will need to do differently for different marks.

7. Be careful in the words you write in the comment section of a grade report. Remember that those words will be the ones that follow students for years after they leave you. Be constructive. Point out every student's growth.

LINKS TO RESEARCH, THEORY, AND PRACTICE

Arter, J. A., & McTighe, J. (2001). *Scoring rubrics in the classroom: Using performance criteria for assessing and improving student performance.* Thousand Oaks, CA: Corwin Press.

Ashlock, R. B. (2002). *Error patterns in computation. Using error patterns to improve instruction* (8th ed.). Upper Saddle River, NJ: Merrill/Prentice Hall.

Bailey, J. M., & Guskey, T. R. (2001). *Implementing student-led conferences.* Thousand Oaks, CA: Corwin Press.

Bateson, D. (1994). Psychometric and philosophic problems in "authentic" assessment: Performance tasks and portfolios. *Alberta Journal of Educational Research, 40,* 233–245.

Benson, B., & Barnett, S. (1999). *Student-led conferencing using showcase portfolios.* Thousand Oaks, CA: Corwin Press.

Eggen, P., & Kauchak, D. (1999). *Educational psychology: Windows on classrooms* (4th ed.). Upper Saddle River, NJ: Merrill/Prentice Hall.

Hebert, E. A. (2001). *The power of portfolios: What children can teach us about learning and assessment.* San Francisco: Jossey-Bass.

Herman, J. L., Aschbacher, P. R., & Winters, L. (1992). *A practical guide to alternative assessment.* Alexandria, VA: Association for Supervision and Curriculum Development.

Howell, K. W., Bigelow, S., Moore, E., & Evoy, A. (1993). Bias in authentic assessment. *Diagnositique, 19,* 387–400.

Kohn, A. (1999). *The schools our children deserve: Moving beyond traditional classrooms and "tougher standards."* Boston: Houghton Mifflin.

Montgomery, K. (2001). *Authentic assessment: A guide for elementary teachers.* New York: Longman.

Murphy, S. (1994). Writing portfolios in K–12 schools: Implications for linguistically diverse students. In L. Black, D. A. Daiker, J. Sommers, & G. Stygall (Eds.), *New directions in portfolio assessment* (pp. 141–156). Portsmouth, NH: Boynton/Cook.

National Board for Professional Teaching Standards. (1998). The five propositions of accomplished teaching. Retrieved March 2, 2003, from http://www.nbpts.org/about/coreprops.cfm.

National Research Council. (1996). *National Science Education Standards.* Washington, DC: National Academy Press.

Newmann, V. (1994). *Math journals: Tools for authentic assessment.* San Leandro, CA: Teaching Resource Center.

Novak, J. D. (1998). *Learning, creating, and using knowledge: Concept maps as facilitative tools in schools and corporations.* Mahwah, NJ: Lawrence Erlbaum.

Popp, M. S. (1997). *Learning journals in the K–8 classroom: Exploring ideas and information in the content areas.* Mahwah, NJ: Lawrence Erlbaum.

Reineke, R. A. (1998). *Challenging the mind, touching the heart: Best assessment practices.* Thousand Oaks, CA: Corwin Press.

Ryan, C. D. (1994). *Authentic assessment.* Westminster, CA: Teacher Created Materials.

Schipper, B., & Rossi, J. (1997). *Portfolios in the classroom: Tools for learning and instruction.* York, ME: Stenhouse.

Stefanakis, E. H. (2002). *Multiple intelligences and portfolios: A window into the learner's mind.* Portsmouth, NH: Heinemann.

Sternberg, R. J. (1997a). Successful intelligence: A broader view of who's smart in school and in life. *International Schools Journal, 17*(1), 19–31.

Sternberg, R. J. (1997b). What does it mean to be smart? *Educational Leadership, 54*(6), 20–24.

Sternberg, R. J., & Grigorenko, E. L. (2002). *Dynamic testing: The nature and measurement of learning potential.* Cambridge, UK: Cambridge University Press.

Stiggins, R. J. (2001). *Student-involved classroom assessment* (3rd ed.). Upper Saddle River, NJ: Merrill/Prentice Hall.

Tanner, D. E. (2001). *Assessing academic achievement.* Boston: Allyn & Bacon.

Walvoord, B. E., & Anderson, V. J. (1998). *Effective grading: A tool for learning and assessment.* San Francisco, CA: Jossey-Bass.

WEB SITES

http://www.inspiration.com
Inspiration is a commercial software product that allows you and your students to develop concept maps and other graphic organizers. You can download a free trial version of the software at this site

http://ericae.net/
ERIC Clearinghouse on Assessment and Evaluation

http://nces.ed.gov/nationsreportcard/
The Nation's Report Card: The National Assessment of Education Progress program

http://www.cse.ucla.edu/
CRESST: National Center for Research on Evaluation, Standards, and Student Testing

http://www.ncme.org/
National Council on Measurement in Education

http://www.uni.edu/profdev/assess.html
Authentic Assessment Resources (University of Northern Iowa Professional Development Web site)

http://www.fairtest.org/
FairTest: Web site of the National Center for Fair and Open Testing, which opposes standardized testing

http://www.bigchalk.com/cgi-bin/WebObjects/ WOPortal.woa/wa/BCPageDA/sec~TH~48254~~

Assessment Strategies at Big Chalk: The Education Network (Note: This is a good site with a really long address. If it is unstable, go to the Big Chalk home page and find assessment strategies under teacher resources.)

http://www.ets.org/aboutets/issues8.html
"Debunking the Myths of Standardized Testing" at Educational Testing Service's (ETS) Web site. Also try browsing the ETS home page

http://www.nclb.gov/
The No Child Left Behind Web site

http://nces.ed.gov/nationsreportcard/
The Nation's Report Card: National Assessment of Education Progress

Also try searching with search terms for specific issues and strategies in assessment. Examples include:

Authentic assessment
Grade book programs (many sites have free downloads)
Performance assessment
Portfolio assessment
Standardized testing
Statewide achievement testing

OPPORTUNITIES TO PRACTICE

1. Pull out your stance on education from Chapter 2 and the two or three overarching goals you developed in Chapter 3 as a result of your stance. Reread your stance and goals with an eye toward assessment.

   a. As you develop your assessment system, think about what kinds of information you will need to gather as a result of your view of what is important. How can you gather that information in ways that remain true to your convictions?

   b. In evaluating your assessment system, consider the following: How does this system reflect your view of the good society? Of the purpose of education? Of teaching? Of learning? If you find little concrete evidence to link your stance toward education with your system for assessing student learning, you probably need to spend a bit more time revising the system—or the stance—to more accurately reflect your professional views.

2. Use the Assessment Analysis in Figure 7.14 to evaluate the potential of one of the instruments in use in a classroom and try it with any newly discovered assessment strategy.

3. If you are teaching, try one of the assessment strategies from earlier in this chapter. Reflect on the experience. If it provided useful information, what would you need to do to arrange your classroom to include this strategy in your assessment system?

4. Write an assessment evaluation for your students. Use it to determine how they prefer to demonstrate their learning. Ask about how teachers help them learn to assess their own work. Share your results.

FIGURE 7.14 *Assessment Analysis*

Instrument:

Intended purpose:

Criterion	Evidence	Usefulness for Intended Purpose		
1. Instrument is consistent with my stance on education.		Low	Medium	High
2. Instrument will allow me to collect information related to my instructional goals. a. Level b. Time span c. Domain(s) d. Instrument can provide information on incidental learnings.		Low Medium High a. Low Medium High b. Low Medium High c. Low Medium High d. Low Medium High		
3. Instrument will allow me to collect information systematically. a. For every student b. Validly c. Reliably		Low Medium High a. Low Medium High b. Low Medium High c. Low Medium High		
4. Instrument can be explicitly tied to instruction. a. Before instruction b. During instruction c. After instruction		Low Medium High a Low Medium High b. Low Medium High c. Low Medium High		
5. Instrument can include the learner. a. Goal setting b. Student choice c. Self-evaluation d. Evaluate instruction		Low Medium High a. Low Medium High b. Low Medium High c. Low Medium High d. Low Medium High		

Overall evaluation of the instrument:

Warm-Up Exercise for Managing the Learning Environment

Think of a store or other business that you hold in high regard: a place of business where you actually do not mind spending your time. Got it? Jot down some brief notes in response to each of the prompts.

1. Describe the physical space. What aspects of it appeal to you? Which make your life more difficult?

2. Describe how time is used within this store or business. What aspects please you? Which irritate you?

3. Describe typical interactions in this business. What do you expect? What happens when interactions are not up to your expectations?

4. You wrote the responses from the perspective of a customer. How (if at all) would your responses have changed if you wrote from the boss's perspective? Analyze whether your responses can teach you anything about the way you would like to manage your classroom.

CHAPTER *Eight*

Managing the Learning Environment

"Never before have we had so little time in which to do so much."

—Franklin Delano Roosevelt

You have so much to accomplish with your students! As you guide students' progress, you must manage them as groups within a tight space, with limited materials, and with never enough time. Just as businesspeople organize time, space, and materials for safety and productivity, so will you organize in your role as classroom manager. Dexterous classroom managers organize and maintain the business end of the classroom so that noninstructional issues interfere as little as possible with learning.

If only your sole concern as a teacher-manager were productivity, your job would be easy. However, unless your stance includes a prominent "education as business" thrust, your job is more difficult. Enacting your stance *begins* with you creating a classroom environment that clearly reflects your answer to the questions, "What do I want to accomplish? Who should these students become?" Your work as a manager reaches beyond ensuring productivity to include building a sense of community with a shared code of ethics. The environment you create should model and foster the kinds of interactions and habits you hope students will practice throughout their lives. Your job as a teacher-manager is to teach students the social curriculum, or in Charney's provocative phrase, "habits of goodness":

> When we establish a social curriculum, when we struggle to integrate ethical practice into our daily fare, we too are trying to set down habits that we want children to carry from their desks to the pencil sharpener, out into the halls, the playground, and even into the world. And we dare to envision that world far more filled with civility and honesty, with community and nonviolence than it is now. . . . We teach habits of goodness most often in the way we organize the social and academic lives of our students and in the way that we bring the children into the regular activities and ceremony of the day. (Charney, 1997, p. xiv)

This chapter encourages you to develop a classroom management plan that, through its ceremonies and rituals, shapes a sense of community that encourages learning in an environment that is both productive and humane. The chapter addresses four components of classroom management:

- Creating community: managing classroom ambience
- Managing physical space
- Managing resources: managing computers and the stuff of teaching
- Managing time

*T*he secret to winning is constant, consistent management.

—*Tom Landry*

REMEMBER THE LAW

Provide for physical safety.
Provide for adequate supervision.

Refresher from Figure 1.2.

CREATING COMMUNITY: MANAGING CLASSROOM AMBIENCE

Your central task as a teacher-manager is to start with the students and meld a group of individuals without common ground or goals into a classroom community. Kohn (1996, p. 101) defines the classroom community as

> a place in which students feel cared about and are encouraged to care about each other. They experience a sense of being valued and respected; the children matter to one another and to the teacher. They have come to think in the plural: they feel connected to each other; they are part of an "us."

Kohn's central ideas of connectedness, value, and respect are echoed in the words of numerous educators who stress democratic community (Allen, 1999; Bomer & Bomer, 2001; Hoover & Kindsvatter, 1997; Scarlett & Associates, 1998). For Gootman (2001), a true classroom community is comprised of individuals who can communicate in caring ways. To foster students' ability to converse with care, teachers must help them do three things: (1) recognize and label feelings—theirs and others; (2) communicate feelings without hurting others; and (3) listen to each other, showing interest and hearing the speaker's complete message. The teacher must serve as a model community member by listening carefully and fully to students.

Clearly, the community you and your students build sets the stage for your interactions with students and pervades each of your choices about classroom management rituals and routines. Classroom community begins to develop through the tone, or ambience, you create from the first day of school. *Ambience* refers to the mood or atmosphere of your classroom environment. Some classrooms are subdued and businesslike, some are homey, and others are full of noise and excitement. Classroom ambience can vary widely and still encourage student success. Although what works best for each of us varies, you probably want to establish an ambience that

- *Encourages students to take risks* by providing for emotional safety and a sense of belonging
- *Provides for intellectual stimulation* by including appealing visual displays, plenty of resources, and interesting real objects
- *Fosters social interaction* by providing space and opportunities for students to work together
- *Conveys a sense that school is a pleasant experience*
- *Communicates your stance toward education* without you saying a word

Metaphors and other analogies can provide a starting point for helping us think about ambience. You may recall, for instance, Jason's analogy of "teachers as pilots" from Chapter 1. Refer back to your stance on education as a guide for the kind of atmosphere you would like to establish. Skim your stance and compose a single-sentence simile: "I want my classroom to feel like a _____ ." Sample responses that may fill in the blank include the following:

- *Board room* (where powerful people meet to accomplish important things)
- *Garden* (where beautiful, dissimilar plants are given everything they need to bloom and flourish)

Teaching Tips

THINK TWICE ABOUT WINNERS AND LOSERS

Competitive games and assignments tend to be popular motivators for so
students. Don't undo the sense of community you try so hard to maintain by using
a game where one person or group wins. One winner means the rest of us are
losers. Try some alternatives: "Let's see if we can beat our best class time (or
scores)." "To win this game, each team needs five examples." "Each presentation
will receive an award. Be listening to see what each one does best."

- *United Nations* (where people from around the world work toward
  international cooperation and harmony)
- *Home* (where people who care about each other live together in
  comfortable surroundings)
- *Hospital* (a clean, safe environment where people leave healthier than
  when they entered)
- *Sports camp* (where individuals hone their skills in preparation for the big
  game)

Analogies provide very different directions for the kinds of physical arrangements, displays, furnishings, routines, and activities that teachers select in
managing their classrooms. Imagine, for example, how differently a home and
a hospital classroom would appear at first glance:

Home
- Overall atmosphere is cozy
  and calm
- Displays are personalized and
  cluttered
- Desks are arranged in groups
  for interaction
- Each group has materials at
  the center
- Several ongoing projects are
  out in view
- Lots of personal touches: fabric
  curtains, lamps, colorful rug, radio,
  potted plants, and rocking chair

Hospital
- Overall atmosphere is neat and
  warm
- Wall displays have coordinated
  backgrounds
- Desks are arranged in rows for
  efficiency
- Materials are placed out of
  sight
- All surfaces are clean and
  shiny
- Colors are limited but carefully
  used

Select a physical arrangement, time schedule, routines, and instructional
activities that build community and convey your convictions about what education should accomplish. Be forewarned, though, that you cannot establish a
pleasant ambience for the year simply by coordinating your bulletin boards and
buying potted plants before the school year begins. In fact, doing so may actually detract from a participatory community. Instead, you may build community by allowing students' voices and choices in the classroom environment.
Bomer and Bomer (2001, p. 105) suggest that the teacher may greet students
with "Welcome! We're going to spend the next week building and organizing the
classroom. How do you think it should look?" It is ultimately the *people*—the
way they treat each other and the way they care for their space—who define
the ambience.

Allow your students to contribute to the atmosphere and teach students to
help each other and to care for the room. For example, you might ask students
as homework to create a map of the perfect classroom, given the furniture and
resources available to you (Thorson, 2003).

Teaching Tips

SOME STRATEGIES FOR BUILDING CLASSROOM COMMUNITY

1. Help members get to know each other through strategies such as oral history interviews, artifact interviews, and ice breakers such as "Find someone who . . ." mixers.
2. Brainstorm a list of community characteristics that members appreciate.
3. Hold regular community circles, or **classroom meetings,** where students recognize each other's efforts.
4. Invite students to plan and create a whole class bulletin board . . . maybe to accompany the current unit or season.
5. Make a class scrapbook, time line, or Web site to capture its unfolding history.
6. Pay attention to students' moods and modify your plans based on their moods. For instance, you might take Period Three out under the trees just for today.
7. Eat together.

Students could present maps and then decide on a single map or a combination of maps to try out in your room. To review, you will actively work to build a sense of community in your classroom by:

- Forging a sense of "we" from a myriad of individuals "I's"
- Modeling genuine listening, respect and regard
- Explicitly teaching students to communicate in caring ways and then re-teaching whenever necessary
- Creating a certain ambience or tone through decisions related to physical arrangement, time schedules, routines and instructional activities
- Allowing students to contribute to the creation and maintenance of the classroom environment.

The teaching tip box gives a few examples of strategies that can encourage a sense of community. Community develops, in part, through your decisions on managing the classroom's physical space.

MANAGING THE PHYSICAL SPACE

Your choices in arranging the physical space allow you to use it to enact your convictions about how people learn and about good teaching. As you begin to map out your room, think about your goals and design the room to match. For instance, if social interaction and language development are key for you, you probably won't place the desks in rows. Visualize the classroom as "learning space" (Faltis, 2001). Breaking away from the traditional "teacher up front, students facing forward" may allow you to identify many areas in the classroom where teaching and learning can occur. Think about the different kinds of space you and your students will need. At the elementary level, these spaces typically include an area for desks or tables for seatwork, at least one area from which you can teach the whole class, small group work spaces, and an area for messy tasks. Secondary classrooms typically make fewer provisions for student movement or a variety of activities because classrooms tend to serve more specialized purposes, such as cooking rooms, weight rooms, and science laboratories. Also consider using your wall space, windows, and ceiling (if allowed) to their fullest advantage. Enrich the environment with special-interest areas such as a puzzle center (you too, high school teachers), a class library, or a music center. Keep your physical setting flexible and ensure that activities and traffic can flow easily.

As you arrange for the different areas in your classroom, be certain that you can **monitor** students at all times and that they are free from the threat of physical danger. For instance, do not allow them to stand on a chair stacked on a

desk so that they can reach a top shelf. In addition to safety, your choices for arranging the physical space can be used to enhance the spirit of cooperation. Glance around the room and see what the arrangement says about the balance of power, about student choice, about meaningful study, and about a sense of the group. Finally, when considering each option for the layout of space and resources, ask yourself two questions:

- Is it productive?
- Is it efficient?

Productivity requires that:

1. *The space allows for a balanced variety of activities.* You address students' physical, social, and emotional needs when you provide for shifts in movement. For young students especially, plan to balance seat time with floor time, whole-group instruction with individual or small-group work, and quiet activities with more boisterous ones. School tends to be a highly public place. Design an area that allows for privacy within safety constraints and crowded conditions.

2. *People can see and hear each other.* Charney (1992) contends that for students to feel safe they must feel seen. She arranges her classroom with few visual barriers so that when positioned at her work space, she can see the entire class. She reinforces her awareness of the class with comments that make students cognizant of her kind scrutiny (p. 21): "Thank you for fixing the pencil sharpener." "I notice the way Patty looks at Jamie when he speaks." You need to be able to see students, and they need to be able to see you—and each other. If students are seated in small groups, for instance, some may need to turn their desks as you provide whole-class instruction. Teach them to quickly rearrange their seats so that they can participate in the lesson. So that students can hear other members of their group during cooperative lessons, you can teach them to use "six-inch voices," which are voices that can only be heard from a distance of six inches.

3. *The students are able to focus their attention on the task at hand.* Is your directed lesson competing with a colorful bulletin board or the aquarium behind you? Are some students looking into the light because they face windows? Is the noisy science center positioned far enough away from your math group to allow students to focus on their work? Will the students working on the computers distract the others?

Efficiency in the physical layout allows you and the students to complete tasks without delays. Efficiency requires that

1. *You can get to each of the students quickly.* Physical proximity is important for encouraging appropriate behavior, providing assistance, and ensuring safety. Jones (2000) emphasizes that the greater the physical distance between students and teacher, the less likely students are to remain **on task.** Arrange your room so that you can quickly get to each of the students by positioning furniture to create wide walkways. Jones suggests that tables and desks be arranged so that the traffic pattern forms a loop, or circuit. Figure 8.1 gives a sample floor plan with the loop marked.

2. *The students can get to each other.* Student access to peers is helpful in efficient distribution of materials and in small-group and partner work.

3. *You and the students can get to the materials.* Much time can be wasted as students wait for paper or other supplies. Position materials for easy access. For instance, store materials as close as possible to the area where they will be used. Then train students how and when to distribute and use the materials. Some teachers assign two or three students to be paper passers, so that the

FIGURE 8.1 *Arrange desks or tables so that you can walk the circuit efficiently.*

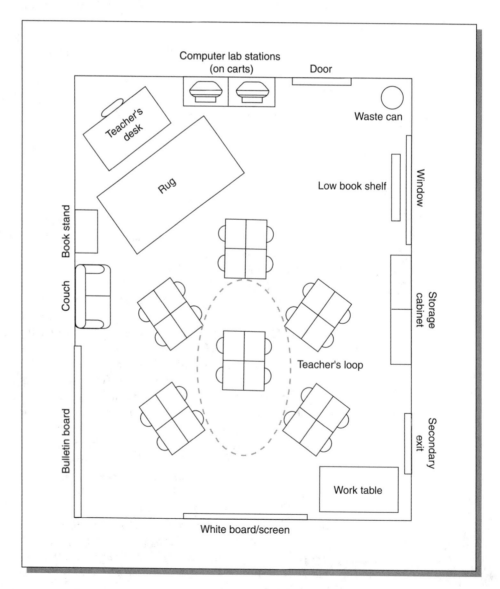

teacher gives a word and three assistants snap to work. In cooperative learning classrooms, each group typically has a supply sergeant who is responsible for gathering and collecting materials. If students fill the supply role in your classroom—and you have trained them well—let them know that if they cannot perform, they lose the job. Doing so prevents students from dawdling and allows them to take pride in a job that must be done well.

4. *You and the students can get other places easily.* Arrange furniture and work areas to avoid traffic jams. Think about areas that tend to draw crowds (the pet center, the pencil sharpener, and the drinking fountain, for instance) and provide wide margins for each. Position student seats so that these high-draw areas do not interfere with their work. Be certain that all students can reach the exits quickly in times of emergency. Figure 8.2 reviews sections of the classroom's physical space and provides guidelines to consider for each area.

FIGURE 8.2 *Checkpoints for a classroom's physical space.*

Work Areas	Checkpoints
Desks or tables for seat work	• The seating arrangement you choose speaks volumes about the kind of instruction you want to provide. Think about the instructional strategies you will employ and seat students accordingly. Does your seating arrangement mesh with your stance toward education?
	• Rows have a bad reputation, but they can be effective—especially for new teachers—if the instruction is good and desks are used flexibly. Rows may be useful, at least for the first days of school, until students have learned your expectations about talking and work times. Be careful, though, that rows do not interfere with the development of a sense of community.
	• In row configurations, short and shallow (many columns with few desks) is typically better than narrow and deep (few columns with many desks).
	• Row clusters, in which two or three desks are pushed together and yet still point forward, save space and encourage interaction. Two large, nested horseshoes serve a similar purpose and create a sense of group belonging.
	• Small clusters of desks (usually four) that face each other promote social interaction and encourage students to help each other. Slant the groups for better views of the front board. Diligence in management is essential.
	• If possible, avoid using all the floor space for desks.
	• If you assign seats, be certain that students fit their desks. Make a switch or call the janitor if they do not.
Whole-class instruction station	• Position your media equipment (e.g., white board, LCD display, and overhead projector and screen) so that all students can see when seated at their desks.
	• Use a small table to keep instructional supplies readily available.
	• At the elementary level, save enough floor space so that you can pull the entire class "up to the rug" or "over to the rocking chair" to work with all students in a more intimate setting. Reading aloud and class discussions are often more effective when students are seated in close proximity. A change of pace can be good for behavior and materials management, too. Consider alternatives if students object to sitting on the floor.
Areas for small-group instruction	• If space allows, use a round or horseshoe table for small-group instruction.
	• If space is tight, consider using space outside the classroom door or borrow from another area such as your library. Make the area off-limits, though, if you are providing instruction there.
	• Position yourself so that you can see all students. Keep your back to the wall.

continued

FIGURE 8.2 *Continued*

Work Areas	Checkpoints
Special-interest areas	• Enrich the environment by providing for learning centers such as a class library, an author's corner, a science center, a technology area, a pet area, or an art area. Even a small counter space can fit the bill. Notable examples include a claw-footed bathtub filled with pillows for reading and a tropical rain forest for independent work. • Students and their families sometimes like to contribute materials for these areas, but you will need to teach students to handle materials carefully. • Include a private area for quiet reading. This space or another may be used for students who need to be temporarily removed from the group. • Special-interest areas can be permanent or can evolve with the interests and needs of your class.
Work spaces for messy tasks	• Place the painting or art center near the sink for easy cleanup. Teach your students to place newspaper under their work and to properly care for materials. • Space outside the classroom door can be used if you can monitor all students. • Position materials for science, art, and other active lessons away from your whole-group instruction station so that you can monitor the whole group from afar as individuals go up to gather materials. It also helps to place the materials distribution center away from students' work desks, to the extent possible. • Obtain a large sheet of heavy plastic or an easy-clean rug if you need to protect carpet.
Wall space	• Use bulletin boards for instruction. Plan for displays to be interactive. Examples include knowledge charts, word walls with student contributions, and lessons related to current topics of study. • Display all students' work and change the displays frequently. • Examples of typical long-standing bulletin boards include the monthly calendar, job chart, current events, and a student work display board. • Use wall space other than bulletin boards to display classroom rules, expectations for assignments, and other items that do not change. • Make a space for your daily agenda. • Ask whether you are allowed to tape things to the walls and whether you have access to a machine that cuts out letters and other items for bulletin board displays. • It is more important for displays to be neat and to involve the students than it is for the displays to be masterpieces.
Ceiling space	• Check with your administration for rules regarding use of the ceiling. The fire marshal often restricts use of the ceiling for display space. • If allowed, take advantage of the ceiling for posting bold messages, student work that can be viewed from a distance, or artwork. • If allowed, consider suspending student work from above. Paper clips and string can do the trick.
Teacher's work area	• Find a secure place for your valuables. A purse or wallet on a desk is an invitation for trouble. • You can make your desk an instructional command center that holds resources and important information, but consider placing it at the back of the room. Your desk is not usually the best place for giving instruction, and placing too much attention on your own work space can give a distorted message about who is important in the class.
Storage areas	• Arrange for space to hold students' lunches, jackets, and backpacks. • Store paper and other materials in cupboards; keep thin stacks out for easy access. Think about balancing students' responsibility to obtain necessary supplies and the fact that you would rather not run out of construction paper in October. • Materials that present safety threats such as glue guns and craft knives should be placed well out of students' reach.

While the ideas are rolling, you may want to turn ahead to Figure 8.9 and design the physical layout of your classroom.

MANAGING RESOURCES: COMPUTERS AND THE STUFF OF TEACHING

Managing a classroom means managing all the *stuff*, to use a technical term, that inevitably goes along with teaching. One resource management question plaguing many American teachers is the dilemma of how to integrate their single classroom computer meaningfully into their instruction. Three-quarters of all American classrooms have between one and five computers in them. Teachers often struggle to use these single or few computers to their full instructional advantage.

The single computer can be used both as a teacher tool and as a student tool (Burkhardt, 1999). The teacher uses it as a tool for preparing instructional materials, communicating with families, and keeping track of student progress. If the computer can be connected to a projection system so that all can see the screen, it becomes the teacher's whole-class instructional tool. He can use it to display a slide show of the digital photos of the students at work. He can use the computer to model the writing process or to do shared writing, to draw concept maps, to present short video or audio clips that enrich the lesson, or to show still photos. Examples, for instance, include using an Internet-connected computer to show a Web-cam, real-time image of Seoul as students read about Korea in their social studies texts. A video clip can show a squid using jet propulsion to move, time-lapse images capture a storm, and pictures of rare chemical elements present difficult-to-obtain elements visually to students. In each of these cases, the computer provides students with access to information that can enhance their understanding and allow the teacher to save the products electronically. If no projection system is available, students can view images before instruction in small groups.

A single computer can also be used as a student learning tool. Individual students can provide input to larger products such as brainstorming lists. They can work in small groups to create stories, drawings, or maps. Individual students can use the computer to reinforce their lessons, for instance through drill programs that practice previously presented objectives, or by hearing content presented in their home language. Computers can be used as assessment tools, and they can be used by individuals or small groups during center time. A fifth-grade class that is learning states and capitals, for instance, may have the option of playing a "capital match" game on the computer during center time.

To ensure that all students work on the computer, their teacher creates a schedule and posts it so that small groups or partners can check and monitor their own visit. The teacher also may hang a check sheet near the computer so students check off their names as they complete their computer activities.

In addition to managing computer resources, many new teachers also struggle to stay afloat of the paperwork. New teachers, who felt otherwise well prepared, often comment that they are likely to drown under the paperwork generated in the school and classroom. One of their most important management lessons during their early days in the classroom is typically devising *systems* for managing the paper flow. They develop, for example, homework folders that go home and get reviewed periodically by families, they work with parent volunteers (when available) to organize upcoming materials and check in papers that come from home, they devise planners in which students record their assignments, and they identify spaces where students submit their work. Implementing systems for managing resources allows teachers to streamline their efforts and spend more time on instruction than one checking homework.

Morris (2000) provides an example of a system that can be useful for many such necessary management tasks: student numbers. He assigns each student a number, and this number is used for several purposes. For instance, students collect and mark homework as completed using their numbers rather than names. Their papers can be quickly collected and placed in numerical order for easy entry into the paper or electronic grade book. Materials, even individual crayons or pencils, can be marked with students' numbers for quick identification. Students can "sound off" by number at a fire drill to ensure that all are present. Numbers can be recorded on cards or craft sticks so that students are equitably called on to participate during discussions.

Experienced teachers sometimes use their resource management systems so effortlessly that it can be hard to appreciate them. Watch your mentors carefully and jot down some notes about how the teacher manages the scarce resources and plentiful paper we find in most classrooms.

MANAGING TIME

> *I* definitely am going to take a course on time management . . . as soon as I can work it into my schedule.
>
> —*Louis Boone*

Alarming studies (e.g., Jones, 1987) indicate that teachers lose up to half of their instructional time through inefficient management. Imagine wasting *half* of the precious time you have with your students. Use your classroom time as gold; wasting a single minute costs everyone in the class, and those costs can never be recouped.

Using your time as gold means that you need to *maximize* the time your students spend engaged in learning and *minimize* the time they spend in other ways in your classroom. The total amount of classroom time can be divided into three subsets: allocated time, engaged time, and academic learning time. These aspects of time are presented in Figure 8.3, which makes it clear that your job as a time manager is more sophisticated than just ensuring that students are busy at *something*. You want the bull's-eye in Figure 8.3—academic learning time—to expand so that it crowds the other two circles. Your job as a time manager is to ensure that students are experiencing success in work related to lesson objectives. Students are not using their time well if they are staring at the right page in the text but have no idea what it means. Chapters 5, 6, and 7 present principles and strategies for providing instruction and assessment to encourage student success. Poor instruction is, at the very least, a waste of time.

In addition to ensuring student success during lessons, you need to minimize the amount of time you and your students spend on business items. One guaranteed way to minimize wasted time is by using *routines* for recurring events. Routines save time and offer two added benefits (Gootman, 2001): They provide confidence and security, especially for students who are accustomed to strict family structure, are lacking in structure at home, or have physiological needs for clear and calm behavioral support. Routines also provide daily practice in appropriate behavior. You will need both noninstructional and instructional routines.

Noninstructional Routines

An initial investment in teaching your students to run the business of your classroom will save vast amounts of time over the course of the year. Students will not need to discover your procedures, and you will not need to answer 2,043 questions about where homework belongs or whether it is okay to sharpen a pencil.

Figure 8.4 lists some of the recurring "business" events that occur in classrooms for which you may wish to establish and teach set procedures. Clearly, your classroom would feel more like a penitentiary than a joyful learning environment if you were to teach and enforce rigid procedures for all of these events during the early days of school. Instead, you can teach some of the most im-

FIGURE 8.3 *The target for classroom instructional time.*

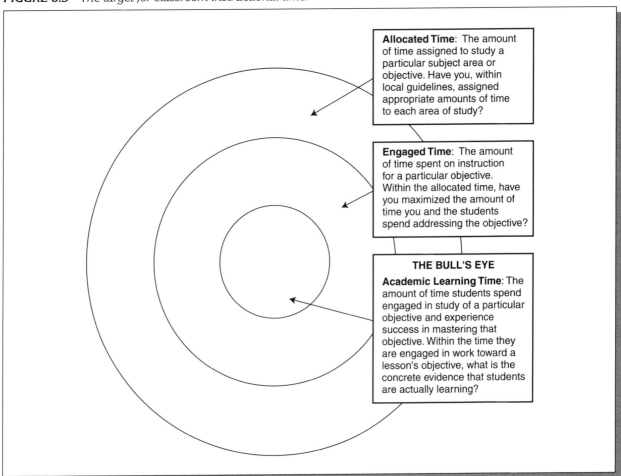

Allocated Time: The amount of time assigned to study a particular subject area or objective. Have you, within local guidelines, assigned appropriate amounts of time to each area of study?

Engaged Time: The amount of time spent on instruction for a particular objective. Within the allocated time, have you maximized the amount of time you and the students spend addressing the objective?

THE BULL'S EYE

Academic Learning Time: The amount of time students spend engaged in study of a particular objective and experience success in mastering that objective. Within the time they are engaged in work toward a lesson's objective, what is the concrete evidence that students are actually learning?

mediate routines (what students should do when they enter the classroom in the morning, how you will take roll, what is expected in each area of the classroom) early on, checking that each routine is humane, productive, and efficient. Over time students can master each of the routines that will help them run the classroom, even in your absence. The beauty of good routines is that they set the expectation that students are responsible and capable of running the show, they help students feel secure in the predictability of their environment, they reinforce your expectation that student learning is your highest priority, and they save you from countless mundane decisions.

When you teach a routine, do it purposefully with a carefully chosen instructional strategy. I have seen some teachers gracefully coax their students into routines solely through subtle modeling. More often, direct instruction (recall Figure 6.3) is employed to efficiently ensure that each student understands and can use the routine. The younger the student, the more direct instruction may be necessary. Through direct instruction, you

- Present critical information on the routine.
- Check for student understanding.
- Practice the routine with the students.
- Observe students as they practice the routine independently.

Reteaching repairs misunderstanding at any point (Wong, 1998).

For example, Ms. Garcia wants to teach her third graders to get to work immediately when they enter the classroom each morning. She clarifies her own

FIGURE 8.4 *Classroom events that could use a routine.*

- What to do when class begins
- What to do when class ends
- How to enter and exit the classroom
- Taking attendance
- Opening exercises
- Getting lunch count
- When to get a drink of water
- When to use the restroom
- How to behave in each area of the classroom
- When and how loud to talk
- When to sharpen a pencil
- Where and when to get paper and other supplies
- How to head a paper
- Where and when to submit completed work
- How to gather work for absent students
- How to complete homework when returning from an absence
- What to do if the teacher steps out of the classroom
- What to do when a visitor comes
- Who will and how to help a substitute teacher
- Who will and how to run errands for the teacher
- What to do in case of emergency

expectations and writes them on a chart. Then she teaches her students: "There are three things to be done each morning when you step into the classroom." Pointing to her chart and using appropriate hand gestures to support her message, Ms. Garcia states: "First, put your things away. Second, move your photo to the 'buying' or 'bringing' lunch string. Third, take out your journal and begin writing." After checking for understanding, Ms. Garcia provides guided practice: "Let's pretend it is morning now. Pick up your backpack and meet me in line. My bet is that all of you will be able to do each of our three morning tasks without a single reminder!" Students giggle as they indulge Ms. Garcia in her charade. She laughs along and provides plenty of praise for students as they get started on their own. If students failed to carry out one or more of the steps, she stops them, reteaches the step(s) they missed, and they try again. She leaves her chart posted for two weeks, until students have internalized the routine.

You will select noninstructional routines based on your own preferences and the ages of your students. Let's explore alternatives for one of the most common noninstructional routines: taking attendance.

Some teachers choose to call out students' names for daily roll so they have the opportunity to greet students as individuals: "Good morning, Nyguen. Good morning, Chelsea." Calling students' names in this way establishes daily positive contact with all students. However, calling each student's name aloud daily only to listen for a rote response ("Here!") is a waste of instructional time, especially for secondary teachers who have limited time with each set of students and must take attendance five or more times per day. If name-calling during roll is not used as an instructional or interactional tool, consider an alternative that takes far less time:

FIGURE 8.5 *Take roll and teach . . . at the same time.*

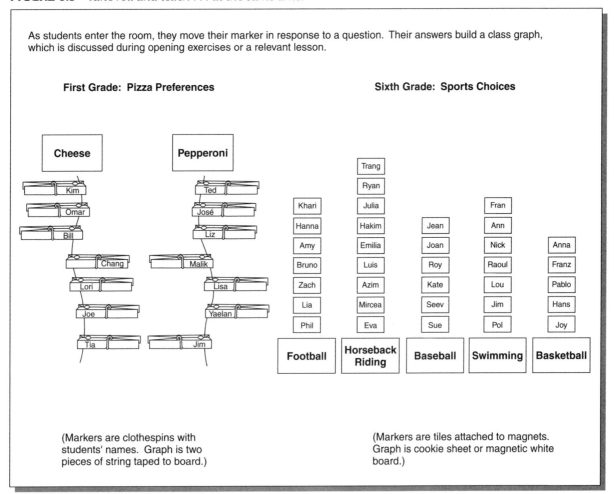

As students enter the room, they move their marker in response to a question. Their answers build a class graph, which is discussed during opening exercises or a relevant lesson.

First Grade: Pizza Preferences

Sixth Grade: Sports Choices

(Markers are clothespins with students' names. Graph is two pieces of string taped to board.)

(Markers are tiles attached to magnets. Graph is cookie sheet or magnetic white board.)

- As students work in their journals or complete some other task right after the bell, you can glance over the classroom to silently check and record absences. Some secondary teachers mark their seating charts to take roll.
- If students are in groups, one member can report absences for each group.
- Students enter the room and move personal markers—such as clothespins, cards, or magnets with their names on them—to a new area to indicate that they are present. One first-grade teacher I know photographs her students during the first week, cuts out the figures, and glues magnets to the back. Students move their photos each morning. You simply glance at the few remaining names or photos to determine absences. These photos can also be used for graphing experiences in mathematics. See Figure 8.5 for an example of how this strategy can be used to instructional advantage.

Many outstanding texts, such as those listed in the "Links to Research, The-ory, and Practice" section at the end of this chapter, can provide examples of effective management routines, as can Internet sites and experienced teachers at your school. The point is to select noninstructional routines that are appro-priate for your students, that are easily managed, and that allow you to maxi-mize the time your students have for learning.

Instructional Management and Routines

In his influential research, Kounin (1983) studied how teachers organize and manage their lessons and found that three aspects of lesson movement correlated well with management success:

- *Smoothness* Does the lesson flow from start to finish, adhering to a set focus? Are there abrupt changes in what students are asked to do?
- *Momentum* Does the lesson move along without lags created by the teacher overexplaining (the yack factor) or overdwelling (the nag factor)?
- *Group focus* Is the teacher able to concentrate on the entire group of students as a unit?

In the same way that routines can help with noninstructional issues, routines can also help smooth instructional movement wrinkles. Typical creases that can be ironed out through careful attention to instruction include the following:

- Pacing
- Transitions
- Providing assistance
- Making every minute count

Pacing   Pacing refers to the speed at which instruction is delivered. Pacing often presents difficulties for new teachers because it demands an understanding of student development, and in-depth knowledge of students grows primarily through experience. A well-paced lesson devotes just enough time to developing concepts and ideas. Lessons must progress slowly enough to ensure student understanding but quickly enough to

1. Maintain student interest and attention.
2. Minimize opportunities for misbehavior.
3. Make good use of a time within a crowded classroom schedule.

To gauge the pace of your lessons, start by watching for cues from the students. You may select a couple focus students with disparate needs, for example, a student with an identified learning disability and one who learns quickly.

An effectively managed classroom results in greater academic learning time.

Do they appear anxious? You may be moving too quickly. Are they snoozy? You may need to pep things up. Antsy? You may need to switch activities. Do not rely solely on students' body language, though, because it can be limited and misleading. Use ongoing assessments (Figure 7.4) that provide information about student learning to adjust your pacing. Active participation devices such as unison response and finger signals, for example, give quick information about student understanding during a lesson and can help you know whether your pacing is appropriate.

As you observe a variety of experienced teachers, you will note that they pace their lessons differently, depending on both their students and their own preferences. I prefer an air of productive hurrying. I like students to glance at the clock, surprised that our time is up when I close the lesson and say good-bye. To ensure that lessons do not drag, tell students how much time they have for each task and stick fairly closely to your stated limits. You may wish to use a timer to help you and the students keep track. Digital timers placed on the overhead protector are popular. Especially during group work, students of all ages seem to take as much time as they are given to complete their work. You may bend your rule a bit if they groan at your one-minute warning ("Okay, but in two minutes you will be ready to report. Hurry!"), but if you double your initial time allotment, you will teach students that they need not focus and work productively or that you can be swayed easily to relax your requirements. Send the message that time is golden.

Teaching Tips

WHAT TO DO WHEN—YIKES!— THE LESSON RUNS SHORT

As new teachers learn to gauge pacing, lessons occasionally take less time than expected. For *every* lesson you plan, have a brief, stand-alone activity ready in case the lesson runs short. Practice pages and extension activities are examples. Be certain that the extra activity is meaningful.

If you really get stuck, try some of the sponges in Figure 8.6 on page 173 or the independent activities listed in the upcoming subsection "Making Every Minute Count."

Transitions   Transitions are the periods between one activity and the next. Teachers at all levels need to switch activities efficiently *within* lessons. Teachers with multiple subjects also must manage transitions *between* lessons. Murphy must have a law to account for the fact that students—no matter the age—can remain attentive during an entire lesson and then hang from the ceiling in the two minutes between one activity and the next. To encourage smooth transitions

1. Anticipate transitions as trouble spots. Have your own materials ready. Be watchful and businesslike.

2. Plan for transitions as a mini-lesson: What exactly do you need students to do in switching activities? Tell them. Monitor their behavior and redirect as necessary ("Stop. You forgot the part about silence. Let's try again.").

3. Practice completing transitions in limited time. Challenge students to prepare for the next lesson in less than 60 seconds. Invite them to beat their previous times. Make it a wager if you are the betting type.

4. Use a change in space to ease transitions: "Finish up your cursive page and meet me on the rug by the time I count down from 20."

5. Make transitions serve double duty. For example, some teachers have primary-grade students sing as they move from one activity to the next. This keeps the students instructionally focused and limits the transition period to the length of the song. A secondary teacher may play one song on a CD to signal

the start and finish of the transition. Other options include reciting math facts and picking up trash as students move from one activity to the next.

Providing Assistance   Students often lose learning time during independent work periods because they sit and wait for the teacher's help. Make a plan so that you can provide assistance to all students who ask—before their hands fall asleep in the air. The first way to ensure that you provide timely individual assistance is to monitor the kinds of assistance students request. Imagine that you just gave instructions for a social studies assignment and eight students surround you, papers rustling, questions poised. Their presence is a sign that you need to reteach: You discover that they do not understand how to read the scale on the map. Stop answering individual questions and reteach the entire group. Or poll the class and pull aside a small group for further explanation of the map's scale. If you have developed a safe environment, students generally will not mind taking you up on your offer to join them in the back for an encore.

After ensuring that students as a group understand concepts and your directions, think about how you can make sure that students get the help they need with as little time away from learning as possible. Following are four strategies teachers find useful:

1. Use praise–prompt–leave (from Figure 6.3). When you address a student's question, give a specific compliment for what he has done right, prompt him quickly on what he needs to do next, and leave. Providing efficient help allows you to interact with more students. Jones (2000) admonishes us to spend no more than 20 seconds as we provide assistance to individuals.

2. If students are seated in groups, teach the students that there can be no *individual* question for the teacher, only a *group* question. That way, students are expected to ask two or three peers before they ask you. You not only save time but also display the expectation that students can and should help each other.

3. Check the work of one person in each row (or group) who is likely to succeed quickly. Put her in charge of answering the questions in her row.

4. Use a signal other than the raised hand. Students can stand a red card on their desks, for example, if they need your assistance. Teach them to work on another section of the task until you arrive.

Teaching Tips

RULE OF THUMB FOR RETEACHING

Choose a number, five or less, as your limit. Let's say four. If four of your students ask you for the same kind of help, do not answer individual questions; reteach the group: "I did not make this as clear as I had hoped. Many people are asking about _____. Let me explain in another way." Stick with your limit.

Making Every Minute Count   You want students engaged in learning even when you are not providing formal instruction. Make every minute count by

- Having a plan for what students should do if they finish early.
- Using "sponges" to soak up spare minutes.

Students work at different rates, and, at least at the elementary level, at some point each will approach you and say "Teacher, I finished. What should I do now?" Develop some instructionally sound responses and teach students— even kindergartners—to select and complete learning activities without your assistance. Write (or draw) acceptable choices on a chart, post the chart, and teach students to follow the chart. Add new choices occasionally. Depending on students' age, some widely applicable choices include the following:

- Read a good book.
- Write a letter to a friend in the class. "Send" it through the class post office.
- Study the globe.
- Practice skills (e.g., printing, spelling words, math facts, and vocabulary cards).
- Work at a center (e.g., for science, art, building, puzzles, or technology).
- Play a thinking skills game (e.g., chess, checkers, or a board game).
- Complete independent research. (Allow students to follow their own interests in long-term projects.)

Just as you can count on students finishing at different rates, you can bet there will be downtime, or brief periods when your class is waiting for an assembly, class pictures, or a guest speaker. Soak up those spare minutes with sponges, which are activities that encourage learning but do not require much preparation. Some sample sponges are given in Figure 8.6. Write sponges on index cards, transparencies, or in a small notebook in advance so that you can choose one and get right to work. Students can even be taught to select and lead sponge activities. While you are thinking about time management, you may choose to use Figure 8.10 to make a tentative plan for using classroom time well.

FIGURE 8.6 *Sponges for spare moments.*

1. Read student requests from a book of poetry (anything by Shel Silverstein is a sure bet).
2. Practice logical questioning with a game of 20 Questions.
3. For young students, play Simon Says to hone listening skills. Or play it in a different language.
4. Count as high as you can as a class by ones, twos, fives, tens, threes, or sevens. A variation is to count by ones and say *buzz* to replace multiples of a given number: "8, 9, buzz, 11," for example, for multiples of five.
5. Individually, in pairs, or as a class, list as many compound words, state capitals, homonyms, mammals, Cabinet members, African countries, prime numbers, chemical symbols, or anything else as you can.
6. Sharpen estimation skills by estimating and checking an unknown quantity, amount, or duration of an event. For example, "How many seconds can you stand on one foot? With your eyes closed?" "How many beans fit into my hand?" "What is the total value of the seven coins in my pocket?" "How many insects are on earth?" Use the World Almanac or a book of world records for information.
7. Write brief group stories. One person writes the opening, folds back all but the last line, and passes it to the next author.
8. Practice classification skills with "Who's in My Group?" Call students who meet an unstated criterion of your choosing (such as black hair or earrings or laced shoes) to the front of the room to be members of your group. The rest of the class guesses the rule. Be tricky and use more than one criterion. As a variation, allow students to make the rule and call up the groups. For older students, draw the dichotomous key to demonstrate your grouping.
9. Pull out a set of simple objects and list scientific observations about them. See how long of a list you can create. Then see if students locate a particular object in the pile purely by reading or listening to peers' observations. Work on improving the quality of their observations over time.
10. Bring out the map and play "I'm Thinking of a State (or Region or Island)" by allowing students to ask questions to discover your state. Allow a student to lead the next round. Or, in a less structured activity, find out how many countries are represented in the travels (or ancestries) of your students. Where is the farthest north anyone has traveled? East?
11. Tell students a story. Invite one of them to tell a story or do a trick.
12. Do some genetics research: See how many can curl their tongues, for instance. Who has a hitchhiker's thumb? Attached earlobes?
13. Try some at-your-seat gymnastics. Can students clasp their hands behind their backs if one arm reaches from next to the head and the other comes from below? Can they rub their stomachs and pat their heads at the same time? Drum their fingers starting with the pinkie, then starting with the thumb?
14. Talk about the world. What have students read on the Web today? In the paper? Seen on the news?

YOUR OWN MANAGEMENT PLAN

You have an empty room, a class list, and sets of texts. Where do you go from here? How will you establish a cohesive community? Figures 8.7 through 8.10 can help you establish an initial classroom management plan that is consistent with the major points of this book and that can set you on your way to establishing a productive and humane learning environment. Because some teachers, particularly secondary teachers, "float" from room to room rather

FIGURE 8.7 *The big view: Guiding forces in my management plan.*

1. The law:

   ☐ Reread Figure 1.2 on teachers' legal responsibilities.

   ☐ Check with administrator or mentor for expectations and sources for local laws.

   ☐ Things to keep in mind:

2. The setting:

   ☐ Check your work in Figure 1.1 to refresh your thinking about the specific locale and the expectations it provides.

   ☐ Things to keep in mind:

3. My stance toward education:

   ☐ Glance at your work in Chapter 2 to refresh your memory of your big view of teaching.

   ☐ Complete the following stems:
   A good society

   A community

   The purpose of education

   People learn by

   Good teachers

than being assigned a single room, Figure 8.11, may be helpful in helping you think about some key management issues within a single period (inspired by Emmer, Evertson, & Worsham, 2000). You will revise your plan in response to your students and your growing expertise, so use this draft to brainstorm. You may wish to first try the exercise in Figure 8.12 at the end of this chapter if you have not yet had many opportunities to observe classrooms.

FIGURE 8.8 *My plan for creating positive classroom ambience.*

☐ I want my classroom to feel like a _____ .

☐ I will foster a sense of community by:

☐ Physical arrangements to create that tone
  Work space (tables and desks):

  My instruction station:

  Small-group instruction area:

  Special-interest areas:

  Wall and ceiling space:

  My work space and storage areas:

☐ Other furnishings and strategies I will use to create that ambience:

Checkpoints

Does the room provide for

☐ Emotional safety and a sense of belonging?

☐ Intellectual stimulation?

☐ Social interaction?

☐ Pleasant experience?

☐ Student responsibility?

FIGURE 8.9 *My plan for arranging classroom space.*

The Perfect Classroom: A Map

Checkpoints

☐ Is it safe? Can I monitor?

☐ Does it encourage community?

☐ Is it productive?

☐ Is it efficient?

☐ Does it make full use of available resources?

Additional Thoughts on Particular Work Areas

☐ Work space (tables and desks):

☐ My instruction station:

☐ Small-group instruction area:

☐ Special-interest areas:

☐ Wall and ceiling space:

☐ My work space and storage areas:

☐ Computer or other technology stations:

FIGURE 8.10 *My plan for using classroom time well.*

☐ Check with administrator or mentor for requirements or guidelines on allocated time.

Sample Classroom Schedule

Routines

☐ **Some of my noninstructional routines:**

Taking attendance:

Opening exercises:

Expected behaviors for each area:

Two more routines to use (review Figure 8.4):

☐ **Instructional routines:**

Providing assistance:

Sponges:

Independent work activities:

FIGURE 8.11 *Management plan for a single period of the day.*

1. Opening Procedures

   Attendance procedure:

   Location of attendance materials such as tardy and absence slips:

   Procedure for getting work to students returning from absences:

   Instructional activity for students during attendance:

2. Rules and Procedures

   Leaving the room:

   Using classroom resources (e.g., computers):

   Getting assistance:

   Working with peers:

   Submitting work:

   Expectations on format of assignment, allowable resources, late work, extra credit:

   Recording assignments:

   What to do if teacher is occupied by a visitor:

3. Dismissal Routines

   Signal for clean-up time:

   Expectations for the room's condition upon students' leaving:

FIGURE 8.12 *Observing classroom management.*

Management Area	Observations
Ambience	**Notes**

1. This classroom feels like a _____.
 2. What things does the teacher actually do and say to create the tone?
 3. What are the big ideas about teaching and learning that seem to be conveyed by the classroom ambience?
 4. **Community:** How does the environment establish the norms of shared governance and concern?
 5. How does the tone establish
   a. Emotional safety?
   b. Intellectual stimulation?
   c. Social interaction and responsibility?
   d. School as a meaningful and pleasant experience?	

Physical Space	**Notes**

6. Observe how the teacher has structured the *physical layout* of the room.
   • Floor space
   • Wall space
   • Instruction station
   • Special-interest areas
   • Other spaces
 7. Observe how the teacher has arranged *instructional materials and resources.*
 8. How does the environment promote *physical safety?*
 9. **Productivity:** How does the environment allow for
   a. A balance and variety of activities?
   b. All students to see and hear the teacher?
   c. All students to focus on instruction?
 10. **Efficiency:** How does the environment allow for ease in
   a. The teacher reaching each student?
   b. Students reaching each other?
   c. The teacher and students reaching materials and other areas of the room?	

Time	**Notes**

11. Find the classroom schedule. How does *allocated time* encourage learning?
 12. What evidence is there that students are experiencing *success* during engaged time?
 13. How does the teacher use *noninstructional routines* effectively? List some routines you observe here to be particularly effective.
 14. If you observe *instruction*, check
   a. Pacing
   b. Transitions
   c. Provision of assistance
   d. Provisions for students who finish early	

Overall	**Notes**
15. List two or more things you learned about classroom management by observing this teacher and classroom.	

PARTING WORDS

Your painstaking efforts to maintain a pleasant and productive learning environment will not always result in a happy citizenry living in educational paradise. Sometimes a negative tone can arise if the teacher struggles with discipline, if the students begin to treat each other with disrespect, or if the class fails to establish a sense of group purpose. Chapter 9 provides suggestions for keeping the atmosphere positive, for talking through issues to encourage respect, for building community, and for managing students as a group. If you notice that your classroom is beginning to feel unproductive or unpleasant, try running through some of these steps:

1. *Get a sense of perspective.* What are you trying to accomplish with your students? What is interfering with your class's attempts to build a productive environment? A trusted outside observer may be able to offer a fresh view.

2. *Rebuild a sense of community.* Try a classroom meeting during which you set new goals as a class. Choose some high-interest activities and perhaps some positive consequences that reward students for working as a group. Allow students to make the space their own.

3. *Reestablish your expectations for student behavior.* Open your eyes wide and remind your students that you care so much about them that you cannot allow them to treat each other or their classroom in harmful ways. Clearly outline the kinds of behaviors you need to see and, if necessary, employ logical consequences to help students with their behavior.

4. *Change something.* Add quiet music. Rearrange the desks. Tape yourself and listen to your tone. Rework your routines. Flip the schedule. Laugh at the nuisances that would otherwise drive you to distraction. Have lunch with your students.

5. *Never give up.*

LINKS TO RESEARCH, THEORY, AND PRACTICE

Allen, J. B., Ed. (1999). *Class actions: Teaching for social justice in elementary and middle school.* New York: Teachers College Press.

Bomer, R., & Bomer, K. (2001). *For a better world: Reading and writing for social action.* Portsmouth, NH: Heinemann.

Burkhardt, L. (1999). *Strategies and applications for the one computer classroom.* Retrieved December 15, 2002, from http://www.lburkhart.com/elem/strat.htm

Charles, C. M. (1992). *Building classroom discipline* (4th ed.). White Plains, NY: Longman.

Charney, R. S. (1992). *Teaching children to care: Management in the responsible classroom.* Greenfield, MA: Northeast Foundation for Children.

Charney, R. S. (1997). *Habits of goodness: Case studies in the social curriculum.* Greenfield, MA: Northeast Foundation for Children.

Emmer, E. T., Evertson, C., & Worsham, M. E. (2000). *Classroom management for secondary teachers* (5th ed.). Boston: Allyn & Bacon.

Faltis, C. (2001). *Joinfostering: Teaching and learning in multilingual classrooms* (3rd ed.). Upper Saddle River, NJ: Merrill/Prentice Hall.

Gootman, M. E. (2001). *The caring teacher's guide to discipline: Helping young students learn self-control, responsibility, and respect.* (2nd ed.). Thousand Oaks, CA: Corwin Press.

Hoover, R. L., & Kindsvatter, R. (1997). *Democratic discipline: Foundation and practice.* Upper Saddle River, NJ: Merrill/Prentice Hall.

Jones, F. (1987). *Positive classroom discipline.* New York: McGraw-Hill.

Jones, F. (2000). *Tools for teaching: Discipline, instruction, motivation.* Santa Cruz, CA: Frederic H. Jones & Associates.

Kohn, A. (1996). *Beyond discipline: From compliance to community.* Alexandria, VA: Association for Supervision and Curriculum Development.

Kounin, J. (1983, November). Classrooms: Individuals or behavioral settings? *Monographs in Teaching and Learning.* Bloomington, IN: Indiana University.

Morris, R. (2000). *New management handbook: A step-by-step guide for creating a happier, more productive classroom.* San Diego: New Management.

Savage, T. V. (1991). *Discipline for self-control.* Upper Saddle River, NJ: Merrill/Prentice Hall.

Scarlett, W. G., & Associates. (1998). *Trouble in the classroom: Managing the behavior problems of young children.* San Francisco, CA: Jossey-Bass.

Thorson, S. A. (2003). *Listening to students: Reflections on secondary school classroom management.* Boston: Allyn & Bacon.

Wong, H. (1998). *The first days of school.* Mountain View, CA: Harry K. Wong Publications.

WEB SITES

http://www.ida.net/users/marie/ed/cm.html
  Classroom management and effective discipline resources for educators

http://www.csrnet.org/csrnet/management.html
  Classroom Management: CSRnet

http://newmanagement.com
  Rick Morris's Web site. Morris is known for his positive management strategies that emphasize meeting the basic needs of power, love, fun, freedom, *and safety. Be warned: This site gives articles and tips, but it also sells Morris's products*

www.pacificnet.net/~mandel/
  ClassroomManagement.html
  This site includes many classroom-management techniques for use at all levels of public schooling

OPPORTUNITIES TO PRACTICE

1. Use the observation sheet given in Figure 8.12 to observe an experienced teacher's room environment and classroom management. At the end of the observation jot down a few great ideas that are consistent with your own thinking about management. Incorporate them into your own plan.

2. Read a professional journal article on classroom management. What is the author's implied stance toward education? Are the strategies consistent with what you know about good teaching?

3. Alfie Kohn (1996) is critical of schools' overreliance on punishment and rewards and the illusion of choice it presents for students. To what extent do you agree with him? What would it take to change the practices that he sees as inhumane?

4. Start a file for promising classroom management ideas. Encourage a share session with peers. Observe more classrooms for ideas on management. Remember that every strategy you consider needs to measure up to the tough standard of your stance toward education and must encourage student learning in humane ways. Plenty of management strategies around today fall short of those criteria.

Before you begin reading Chapter 9

Take your pick of Exercise A or B . . . or, if you like, do both.

Warm-Up Exercise A: Encouraging Appropriate Behavior

Think back to a teacher you loved or admired when you were young. Briefly jot down a few notes about that teacher. What specifically did the teacher do to gain your admiration?

What lessons about classroom discipline can you draw from this teacher? (P.S. You can learn lessons from a teacher you disliked as well. Analyze a negative experience too if you like.)

Warm-Up Exercise B: Shopping List of Promising Rules and Tools

Chapter 9 asks you to develop your own discipline program, and it presents much information that can support your efforts. Use this table to keep the big picture in mind as you read Chapter nine, if you like.

Rule: Treat all learners with dignity and respect.
Tools:

Establishing a climate of dignity and respect	Responding to Behavior
❏ Celebrate and suffer	❏ Address the behavior
❏ Active listening	❏ Private correction
❏ Peer listening	❏ Hints
❏ Model and teach	❏ *I*-messages
	❏ Strength refreshers
	❏ Emotional control
	❏ Laughter
	❏ Apologies

Rule: Actively prevent misbehavior.
Tools:
❏ Meaningful curriculum
❏ Development and motivation
❏ Authority
❏ Clear expectations
❏ Anticipation
❏ Positive approach
❏ Nonverbal communication

Rule: View discipline as an opportunity to help students develop toward independence.
Tools:

Establishing a climate that promotes independence	Addressing behaviors in ways that encourage self-control
❏ Choices	❏ Talk it through
❏ Respect for decisions	❏ Self-correction
❏ Clear limits	❏ No power struggles
❏ Consistency	❏ Anger shields

Rule: Address discipline in many ways and on multiple levels.
Tools:
❏ Group size
❏ Overlapping
❏ Intensity of response
❏ Motivation for misbehavior
❏ Redirecting behavior

CHAPTER *Nine*

Encouraging Appropriate Behavior

> *"For the very true beginning of her [wisdom] is the desire of discipline; and the care of discipline is love."*
>
> —The Wisdom of Solomon 6:17

Discipline and *love* in the same sentence? Discipline is not an evil word, although it strikes fear into many a teacher's heart. What is it about maintaining classroom discipline that seems inherently troublesome for many teachers, especially novices? The need to discipline students can run counter to new teachers' need to feel loved and accepted. Also, pressing one's own will above that of the children often invokes conflict. Teachers must at times ask students to behave in ways that are at odds with the students' youthful agendas.

You will be most successful as a disciplinarian if you begin with a positive attitude. Encouraging appropriate behavior is not an act of coercion. Rather, it is an act of care and respect by a teacher who values students enough to help them make good decisions about their behavior. Nearly every teacher's philosophy includes the goal of helping students to become considerate citizens who exhibit self-control and take responsibility for their own actions. Because you respect your students, you will be eager to help them grow toward independence—not only academically but behaviorally as well. This chapter offers rules and tools for classroom discipline, and it encourages you to develop your own discipline program.

Fast Facts 9.1

Survey Says . . .

41% agree that . . . . . . student misbehavior interferes with their teaching

32% agree that . . . . . . student tardiness and class cutting interferes with their teaching

63% agree that . . . . . . rules for student behavior are consistently enforced by teachers at their school

Source: From a national survey of public elementary and secondary teachers. U.S. Department of Education, National Center for Education Statistics. (2003). "Schools and Staffing Survey, 1999–2000: Overview of the Data for Public, Private, Public Charter, and Bureau of Indian Affairs Elementary and Secondary Schools." *http://nces.ed.gov/pubs2002/2002313_1.pdf*

RULES AND TOOLS FOR CLASSROOM DISCIPLINE

You have a duty to provide a productive learning environment, and a few basic rules can provide good direction as you create and maintain a warm and respectful classroom:

1. Treat all learners with dignity and respect.
2. Actively prevent misbehavior.
3. View discipline as an opportunity to help students develop independence.
4. Address discipline issues in multiple ways and on multiple levels.

These four basic rules can be implemented through tools, or specific strategies, such as those addressed in the following sections.

> ### REMEMBER THE LAW
>
> 1. Teachers are prohibited from
>   - Humiliating students.
>   - Physically punishing students, except under strict guidelines for corporal punishment (where allowed).
>   - Using academic penalties for behavioral offenses.
> 2. Students have rights to due process.
>
> *Refresher from Figure 1.2*

Treat All Learners With Dignity and Respect

Every learner—every human—deserves courtesy and kindness. Given their lesser size and status, children in our society sometimes receive less thoughtful treatment than do adults: Fast-food workers glance over the heads of children waiting at the counter, tired parents are easily irritated, and teachers readily interrupt. Within the classroom, Curwin and Mendler (2001) emphasize, the importance of maintaining student dignity is essential; students must feel that you respect them as people, are concerned about their needs, and understand their perspectives. As you redirect misbehavior, Curwin and Mendler advise you to protect students' dignity by thinking about your own: How would you respond if a teacher used this strategy with you? By fostering respect and dignity, we offer hope. Make your classroom a refuge where students receive the same consideration as would respected adults, through both the environment you create and the ways you elect to respond to students' behavior.

The secret in education lies in respecting the student.

—*Ralph Waldo Emerson*

Following are 12 ways you can treat people with dignity and respect. The first four points establish the climate; the rest of the list show responses to behavior.

1. Celebrate and suffer
2. Active listening
3. Peer listening
4. Model and teach

Caring relationships are based on mutual respect.

5. Address the behavior
6. Private correction
7. Hints
8. *I*-messages
9. Strength refreshers
10. Emotional control
11. Laughter
12. Apologies

Establishing a Climate of Dignity and Respect You want students to know that every person in your classroom is important. The sense of community you began to establish through your work in classroom management (Chapter 8) is the starting point for your climate of respect. Use a warm and respectful voice (Kohn, 1999). Show students that you know and value their perspectives (Wormeli, 2001). Learn about the things they care about and remember to see the world from the eyes of someone their age.

| Celebrate and suffer |

1. Celebrate and suffer One way you can demonstrate respect for your students' thoughts and experiences is by sharing their successes and their slips. When students express emotions, especially sadness or despair, it is tempting for teachers to rush in, quickly analyze the situation, tell students how they should be feeling, fix things, and move on. However, this overly helpful response can serve to take away from another person's experience. You need not feel that you must provide explanations or analyses for every event that causes emotion for your students (Schneider, 1997). A quiet, sad smile, a thumbs-up, or a round of applause may be a terrific way to show students that you understand their positions and respect their experiences.

| Active listening |

2. Active listening On a more immediate level, you can show that you value students' words and ideas by practicing active listening (Gordon, 1974). In active listening, the teacher summarizes or reflects the speaker's message. For instance, a teacher may begin his reply to a frustrated student, "You seem to be saying that this homework was hard for you." A question stem such as "Are you saying that. . . ?" can also help to ensure clear communication. Active listening shows students that you value their ideas enough to be certain that you understand them correctly. It allows you to demonstrate that you believe communication involves two parties, each deserving to be heard. Gootman (2001) gives six tips for caring listening:

1. *Show interest.* Show interest and pay attention when students speak. Hold your body still and give your full attention.
2. *Hear them out.* Wait until students are finished speaking before saying anything.
3. *Separate your feelings from their feelings.* Respond to the issue, not the emotion.
4. *Look for nonverbal cues.* Body language can help you find the true meaning of the message.
5. *Put student feelings into words.* Try to interpret their message and emotions by rephrasing what you think you have heard.
6. *Don't argue with students' feelings.* Accept students' rights to feel as they do rather than suggesting that they should feel different emotions.

Gootman's tips can be equally effective for helping students listen to their peers.

| Peer listening |

3. Peer listening Silent but accepted norms teach students that they need to listen raptly to the teacher but not so carefully to each other. Students need to be encouraged to listen to each other. When we allow children to ignore their peers, we perpetuate their disrespect and interfere with the sense of community we are trying to establish. Following is a typical scenario: The class chatters over Ray as he shares his ideas. The teacher implores, "Stop, Ray, I can't hear you." When the class quiets down, the teacher repeats Ray's words for the class: "Ray was saying . . . " In this scenario, the teacher is the traffic cop who controls the conversation. Let's rewrite the scenario so that it encourages more respectful and caring interactions: The class chatters, but this time the teacher suggests, "Ray, let's wait just a second. Some of your peers can't hear you yet." The class quiets down, and the teacher urges: "Ray, why don't you repeat the last thing you said now that you have all ears on you." Now the teacher sends the message that she expects students to listen to each other. She doesn't repeat Ray's words but directly encourages students to listen to each other.

Model and teach

4. Model and teach   This scenario also highlights the importance of directly teaching students to treat others with dignity. Take advantage of the power of modeling to show learners what fairness and dignity look and feel like. When modeling is insufficient, draw students' attention to respectful treatment. If they treat someone disrespectfully, quietly and calmly point out the consequences of what they have done and help them find more dignified alternatives. For example, when students use harsh words to tease, tell them firmly that harsh words can hurt and are not allowed in your classroom. Then give them some acceptable alternatives to teasing. Each of these tools can help you build a supportive climate, but you will also need to address misbehavior in ways that maintain students' dignity.

Responding to Behavior   How you choose to respond to inappropriate behavior can teach lessons that last a lifetime. You have the power to humiliate or help. Be certain that you redirect inappropriate behavior without embarrassing learners. Remember that, as the sole adult in the classroom, you and your words can carry tremendous power. Students, especially younger ones, depend on adults for messages about who they are and what they are worth.

Address the behavior, not the person

5. Address the behavior   A child may carry your words into adulthood, so when you praise or provide correction, address students' actions and not their character. For instance, when your class has listened attentively to a guest speaker, it is more effective to praise specific behaviors ("You all watched and listened with such respect!") than to address students' value as people ("You are so good!"). When you need to correct misbehavior, do not apply words such as *lazy, thoughtless,* or *bad* to the students. Instead, provide feedback on what students *did* that was wrong: "You talked while the guest speaker was talking" instead of "You are so rude!" Say "You left the room a mess" instead of "You are so messy!" When you address behavior and not character, you send the message that students are worthy people, even when they err.

Use private correction

6. Private correction   In the instances when most of the class is fine but one student needs redirection, make it a point to speak quietly with her in private. While the others work, approach the student's desk for a calm conversation about her behavior. If you can continue providing adequate supervision, you may elect to hold your conversation in the hall or outside the door. This approach allows the rest of the class to continue without interruption and saves the student from public humiliation. Private communications also lessen the chance that students will respond defensively to your correction to save face.

Start with hints

7. Hints   When some or all of the class needs redirection, start with the lowest level of intervention possible: the hint. For example, you may have just assigned a reading task, but you notice that a few students are still working on a fun math activity. You calmly remind students what they should be doing ("Calculators should be put away now. Everyone is finding page 83."). Often no greater intervention is required, and you have shown students that you trust them to follow directions with only a gentle reminder.

Use I-messages

8. I-messages   Gordon (1974) suggests that students are often unaware of the effects of their actions on others. Teachers can use *I*-statements to state their emotions without anger or blame and without belittling the student. An *I*-statement has three parts:

1. Statement of the problem ("When people sharpen their pencils while I talk . . . ")
2. Specific effect of the problem ("Other students cannot hear me, . . . ")
3. Statement of the teacher's feelings (". . . and I am frustrated to have to stop and wait.")

Once a teacher uses an *I*-statement, the teacher and students can work on the problem together. I-statements express respect by encouraging students to pay attention to their effects on others, allow the teacher to state emotions without humiliating, and convey the teacher's trust that students can address a problem.

Refresh students' memories of their strengths

9. Strength refresher   When students are corrected by their teachers, they may lose perspective that a single mistake is just that: a *single* mistake. You can reaffirm your faith in students' basic goodness by starting your correction with a strength refresher (Schneider, 1997). In a strength refresher, you remind the student of how he typically behaves and point out that this mistake was atypical for him. For instance, when you discover that Roger spit water during a passing period, you pull him aside for a conversation: "Roger, I was surprised to hear that you spit. You usually do a super job of helping us make sure that our school is a safe and clean place." Because you demonstrate your faith in Roger's usual behavior, he will probably feel less guarded about explaining the incident to you and more eager to correct his behavior for tomorrow. Strength refreshers remind students that you see them as good people.

Model emotional control

10. Emotional control   Humans are not born with a balance between their emotions or impulses and their conscious knowledge about appropriate behavior. Emotional control or **emotional intelligence** comes through socialization (Good & Brophy, 2000). One way teachers can help children gain emotional control is by modeling it. Derek, one of my middle school students, interrupted me so frequently and so energetically that I wanted to squirt him in the face with a water bottle. Deep within, I knew that squirting a fellow human would serve as an affront to his dignity, but I was sorely tempted.

Sometimes we take personal offense at students' misbehavior, and anger is a natural human emotion. However, you need to have your emotions in check when you address students' behavior. If you are angry, you are not ready to respond to your students. Give yourself a few seconds to collect your emotions, telling students that you will be better able to address the situation when you are calmer. You may, for instance, discover that your class showed no mercy in antagonizing the music teacher. You are furious that they could act that way, and you are embarrassed that their behavior may reflect on you. Instead of yelling, though, you lower your voice and say, "I am shocked and angry to hear about this. In fact, I am so angry that I cannot discuss this with you right now. When my head is clearer, we can discuss this situation." If you lash out while you are angry, you may need to backtrack later, and you may say something hurtful. Controlling your own anger models your wishes that students do the same, and it stops you from attacking a student with your words. Further, when we are angry, other people are in control of us (Jones 2000).

Strength, according to Jones, comes from calm. By calming your body through strategies like relaxed breathing, you calm those around you and you help people get back to work.

11. Laughter   Despite your supportive atmosphere and respectful interactions, there are times when students will manage to push your buttons. It seems to be a quest that marks the progression of childhood: Some students *live* to get a reaction. If you are able to retain your sense of humor, you can use laughter to diffuse tense situations and maintain dignity—the students' and your own.

I know a teacher who entered her room to find an ugly caricature of herself drawn on the board. Instead of standing with her hands on her hips and demanding the name of the offending artist, she said, "Pretty good, but I need my glasses," and added a ridiculous version of her reading glasses to the sketch. What could have been a tense moment passed with smiles throughout the room. Using humor can show that you do not take the world (or yourself) too seriously and that you maintain a positive outlook.

When using humor to address behavior, be certain not to direct your humor at students. Humor is highly individual, and it is cultural. At least until you have a thorough understanding of your students and a cohesive group spirit, use jokes that are directed at yourself or at situations outside the students and be sure that the students see the humor as well. The point is to respond playfully to situations that might otherwise erupt into power struggles or other unproductive interactions.

12. Apologize   Finally, when despite your best attempts you offend a student's dignity, apologize. You may occasionally speak before you think and hurt feelings. Consider using a calm, apologetic message: "That did not sound at all as I had intended. I apologize if I hurt your feelings. Next time I will choose my words more carefully." You will not lessen your authority by admitting a mistake. You will probably, in fact, gain authority by displaying your willingness to disclose and correct an error: You are fair. You model the humility that you hope students will also display. You demonstrate how humans (teachers!) make a mistake, learn from it, and go on. And you acknowledge that your students deserve respect. In addition to treating students with respect, you can prevent much of the misbehavior that plagues some classrooms.

Actively Prevent Misbehavior

Some misbehavior occurs because it is human nature to press the limits, to test the predictability of our environments. However, misbehavior also occurs when students' educational needs go unmet. Albert (1996) suggests that we can create a sense of belonging that goes a long way in preventing misbehavior by using the three Cs: capable, connect, and contribute. Teachers need to help students see themselves as *capable* by focusing on success and making it acceptable to make mistakes. To help students build personal *connections* with teacher and peers, teachers can accept their students, appreciate their accomplishments, affirm students' positive traits, and show genuine displays of affection. Finally, teachers need to encourage students to *contribute* to their classroom, school, and local community.

Preventing misbehavior through the three Cs requires your thought and advance planning. Seven proactive strategies can help you forestall much of students' misbehavior:

1. Meaningful curriculum
2. Development and motivation
3. Authority
4. Clear expectations
5. Anticipation

6. Positive approach
7. Nonverbal communication

Use meaningful
curriculum

---

1. Meaningful curriculum   When students are engaged in relevant and interesting learning experiences, they are often too busy to misbehave. Do students see the purpose in what you want them to learn? Are their topics your topics? How well does school capture issues seen as vital to the students? Three-quarters of the secondary students recently surveyed agreed either somewhat or strongly with the statement, "Most of my schoolwork is busywork" (Metlife, 2002). Check your curriculum to ensure that the content is appropriate and that you are using rich learning strategies that accommodate students diverse needs. Although some topics may not spark immediate student enthusiasm, if you remember to COME IN (Chapter 5), you increase the chances of engaging students in important learning and thus forestall misbehavior. If you have assessed the curriculum and your plans and found them sound, a tougher test is to watch a videotape of yourself teaching. Is your instruction as engaging as you had hoped? If not, think about when you as a student misbehaved.

Teaching Tips

BRIDGING THE STUDENTS' WORLD AND THE SCHOOL'S WORLD

Actively pursue strategies that help *you* incorporate issues from students' worlds into your classroom and help *them* see the importance of what school has to offer. Try these activities, for instance:

1. *Listen to the issues students discuss and incorporate them into your instruction.* Some educators suggest that students' issues should be placed firmly at the center of the curriculum. Thematic planning can be used to incorporate issues that are important to students. On a more specific level, a teacher might overhear her students discussing an impending threat of small pox. She plans a brief series of science lesson that addresses the history, procedures, and ethical issues pertaining to vaccination.
2. *Use a student survey before you plan a unit to find out what students would like to know about the topic.* A survey may begin, "Students study the American Revolution in many grades, but sometimes they don't find out what they would really like to know. What do you still not know about that war?" An in-class discussion can serve the same purpose: "Let's make a list of the things we wish we knew. . . "
3. *Incorporate students' interests in sports, music, and other aspects of culture into the topics you select and the methods you use to study them.* For example, students may analyze lyrics of rap music for examples of poetic devices. In chemistry, students may make ice cream as an example of a phase change.
4. *Begin every lesson with a bridge.* Bridges pique students' curiosity and connect their interests and knowledge with the content of the lesson. A mathematics lesson might begin with an interesting problem embedded in a real life context. A literature lesson on genres might begin with a quick tally of students' favorite books. An art lesson may begin with a guided imagery session to a favorite locale for students.
5. *State the purpose of your lessons.* Tell students how this information or skill will be useful. Or, have them tell you. "You'll need this for the test" or ". . . for next year" tend not to be convincing reasons for many students.

Attend to students'
maturation and
motivation

---

2. Motivation and development   Study the characteristics of your learners and then align your expectations to their physical and emotional development. For instance, kindergartners should be expected to sit for only about 10 minutes before the activity changes, but older students can succeed with longer periods of sustained activity. Despite the fact that high school students can sit and listen for hour-long periods, as a general rule, it is useful to allow students of all ages to spend about 2 minutes actively processing information for every 10 minutes they spend listening. That means after you provide 10 minutes of information, they need a chance to discuss it. Try some of the "tell each other" strategies (Figure 5.7) to help students process information.

Also match your activities and expectations to factors such as the time of day and year. It is human to be sleepy after lunch and antsy before the last bell rings. Primary teachers are especially good at using games such as Simon Says or Copy My Clap Pattern to refocus students' attention. Secondary teachers can ensure that they provide high-interest activities when students' energy or attention may be likely to wane. They can also ask students to stand, stretch, and listen as they present a few minutes of information. Changing physical location or position gives students a break and allows them to refocus.

In addition to planning for students' developmental capabilities, you can also prevent misbehavior and encourage learning by attending to motivation. Research suggests that many elements that affect student motivation, shown in Figure 9.1, can be directly influenced by the teacher. When students lack the enthusiasm to stay focused, try tweaking one of the factors of motivation from this figure. For example, Wormeli (2001) advises middle school teachers to support student motivation through strategies such as creating an emotionally safe environment, communicating learning goals clearly, using vivid lessons, building suspense, and providing frequent feedback. These aspects of motivation can be operationalized to support student motivation through strategies such as creating an emotionally safe environment, communicating learning goals clearly, using vivid lessons, building suspense, and providing frequent feedback (Wormeli, 2001). If a student gives up upon viewing a whole sheet of tedious grammar exercises, the teacher may rip the sheet in half to affect the student's *perception of effort and probability of success*. Another teacher works hard to return students' essays shortly after they submit them. He knows *immediate feedback* can increase motivation. By ensuring that your classroom meets students' physical, emotional, cognitive, and social needs, you optimize the probability that they will engage in learning and in appropriate behavior. Although it is true that you cannot *force* students to learn, there are many ways you can tweak *your own* behavior and assignments that can directly affect students' motivation.

A QUESTION FOR SECONDARY TEACHERS:

Kohn (2001) cites research that indicates that, as students move from elementary to middle or junior high school, there is a shift from trying to figure things out to trying to achieve. Does authentic learning remain a motivation for your students?

FIGURE 9.1   *Factors of motivation.*

- *Needs and interests.* Motivation increases when physical, psychological, and social needs are met. Examples include feelings of safety from physical and psychological harm and students' perceptions that they are treated fairly.
- *Level of concern.* Motivation is optimal when there is some tension about completing a task but not enough to provoke acute anxiety.
- *Perception of required effort.* Motivation increases when individuals perceive that the amount of effort required to complete a task is reasonable.
- *Probability of success.* Motivation increases when individuals perceive that there is a good chance they will succeed.
- *Knowledge of result.* Motivation increases when individuals have specific, immediate information about the result of their efforts.

Establish yourself as an authority figure

3. Authority   When students respect their teacher as an authority, they tend to behave well. Teachers establish themselves as authorities using different combinations of power, as described by French and Raven (1959):

- *Expert power:*   The teacher is perceived by the group as having superior knowledge about the content, about teaching, and about individual needs.
- *Referent power:*   The teacher is liked and respected because she is perceived as ethical and concerned about her students.
- *Legitimate power:*   The teacher has the right to make certain decisions by the sheer power of her official role as teacher.
- *Reward power:*   The teacher has power because she can distribute rewards, including tangible items such as candy and privileges and social awards such as praise and attention.
- *Coercive power:*   The teacher has power because she can punish.

Reward power and coercive power predominate in many classrooms, probably because they are often effective for immediate control of student behavior. Examples include "changing the card" systems, table points, and candy as a reward. Unfortunately, teachers who establish no firmer authority base than the use of rewards and punishments run a strong risk of having their power collapse. Additionally, rewards and punishments have limited usefulness if they demean students' dignity, interfere with the development of self-control, or work at cross-purposes with the teachers' larger vision of education.

Instead, Savage (1999) suggests that more lasting and mutually respectful authority is based on the teacher's expert and referent power. Because both of these kinds of power depend on students' perceptions of you—as an expert and as a concerned, trustworthy adult—you can begin to earn students' respect by demonstrating your knowledge and care. Other kinds of power can be used judiciously as supplements, especially in your early years as a teacher.

Establish clear expectations

4. Clear expectations   Students make better choices about their behavior when they know what is expected of them. Start by developing a set of classroom rules, either with the students' help or on your own. Keep your list of rules down to about four or five in number and state each rule in positive terms. For instance, "Raise your hand before speaking" is more helpful than "Do not shout out." If you develop the rules without student input, be certain that students accept the rules as useful and reasonable. If you choose to have the class develop the rules through group discussion, check that their rules are reasonable and address major areas of concern for classroom behavior (when to talk, when to move around, and how to treat each other and belongings). Some teachers operationalize their rules for classroom talk with a color system: "red" for silence, no one out of her seat; "yellow" for whispers in small groups; and "green" for regular conversational level. If you elect to include explicit consequences for following and breaking the rules, be sure that they are logical and humane.

You also need to establish clear expectations for special circumstances. Before a field trip, for instance, teach your students approximately three specific behaviors you expect to see. A primary teacher might hold up three fingers, one for each expectation, and state in positive and clear terms his expectations for student behavior during the trip: "First, you need to stay with your buddy. Second, you need to keep your hands to yourself. Third, you need to stay where you can see an adult at all times." Then the teacher checks for understanding of his rules: "Let's see how many know the first special rule for today. I see 10 hands up. I will wait for another 10. . . . Good. Say it aloud." He reteaches until he is certain that all students know what he expects. Parties, assemblies, and sports activities are other situations when clearly stated expectations are critical.

*I*f you are prepared, you will be confident, and will do the job. —*Tom Landry*

CLASSROOM RULES

Jot down four classroom rules that address major areas for classroom behavior in positive and specific terms:

1.
2.
3.
4.

When you have revised these rules and are happy, include them in your own discipline program.

Anticipate and set students up for success.

Anticipate behavior

5. Anticipation   You can prevent misbehavior, too, by anticipating and thus avoiding trouble spots. You know that your students are a curious bunch, so if you leave a bowl of mealworms for your science lesson on the front table while you attempt to teach a social studies lesson, you invite misbehavior. By placing the mealworms out of sight, you help students focus their attention on the lesson at hand. Similarly, if you have passed out pointy compasses for your third-period geometry lesson, collect the compasses as students move into the next phase of the lesson. Removing distractions is a sure bet for preventing misbehavior. See Figure 9.2 for some other trouble spots that can be avoided with careful planning.

Your ability to anticipate common trouble spots will improve with experience. You can begin by planning instruction and your room environment with an eye toward setting students up for success. Charney (1992) spends the first six weeks of the school year teaching students to monitor their own behavior and use the items in the room safely through her own version of the three *R*s:

- *Reinforcing:*   Commenting on the positive behaviors students demonstrate ("I notice that you are solving that problem together.")
- *Reminding:*   Asking students to state the expectations for behavior ("Remind me, where do we put the brushes when we are finished?")
- *Redirecting:*   Pointing students toward more appropriate behavior ("Rulers are for measuring.")

FIGURE 9.2   *Anticipating and avoiding trouble spots.*

Students are more likely to misbehave when . . .

1. . . . they think you can't see them. So . . .
   - When you stand and talk with an individual, keep your back to the wall and position yourself where you can see the class.
   - Write on an overhead projector rather than the board, especially if you are left-handed.
   - Make eye contact with the students farthest from you as you work with individuals.
2. . . . they are allowed to disengage without clear expectations. So . . .
   - Plan your transitions between lessons. Think through each aspect of the transition. Make your directions very clear, and minimize the time spent switching activities.
   - Have all your materials ready to go. Lay them out at different stations for quick distribution and collection, as appropriate.
   - Prepare a student to take over if you need to speak with an adult or have another interruption during class. Practice the routine.

You will also use your knowledge of your particular students to anticipate possible misbehaviors. Then plan an appropriate response. When you have a few quiet minutes at home, rehearse your calm, productive responses to those behaviors: What will you do and say the next time students chat during a transition time? Having a response ready often helps to forestall problems.

Keep things positive

6. Positive approach Because classrooms are crowded and hurried, it is very easy to focus on those students determined to derail our lessons. However, when we emphasize misbehavior, we contribute to a negative tone and provide attention for the wrong bunch of students. Instead of criticizing the wigglers who are facing the wrong way during your **read-aloud,** glance around the group. You will probably notice that more than half are listening raptly. Concentrate on those students. Smile warmly and say, "More than half of you are eagerly listening! I really appreciate that!" Then wait and praise as the other class members give their attention. Remember, though, that false praise is probably worse than no praise at all; keep your praise genuine. Keep in mind, too, that students' reactions to public praise can vary by age level. Although some teachers use public praise effectively with older students (perhaps with a simple "Thanks, Rogelio. Thanks, Trang."), older students often view teacher praise about behavior as manipulative. Reactions to public praise also vary among individuals. Some students are embarrassed by public praise and respond better to a private word.

In public and private, praise good behavior specifically and in a way that stresses logical consequences: "Thanks for cleaning up, my friends! When you work so quickly to straighten our room, we have lots more time left for art!" That way you reinforce the notion that students' motivation to behave is not simply to please you, it is to keep the environment productive and enjoyable for all.

A praise statement keeps the atmosphere positive, builds your referent power, and serves as a gentle reminder for what all students should be doing. Emphasize what students do right and you help to prevent misbehavior. Figure 9.3 shares some strategies that can help to establish a positive learning environment—and thus curb misbehavior—from the first day you meet your students. Through effective management, a meaningful curriculum, and

FIGURE 9.3 *Establishing a positive environment from day one.*

1. *Learn students' names immediately (yes, during the first day).* Use names to address students. It is an immediate way to show your respect for them as people. One strategy is to take 10 quick minutes to go up and down the rows or through the tables, repeating students' names as you memorize them. Make it a game in which all who learn at least three new names are winners.

2. *Convey your high expectations and enthusiasm for teaching and learning right away.* Examples include enthusiastic messages about being glad for your time together, stories about you as a person to help show that you expect to connect with students as people, and previews of the exciting things students will learn and do in your class.

3. *Teach your classroom rules or have students develop them in a community.* Keep the number brief and state the rules in positive terms.

4. *Provide for learning and for student choice on the first day.* Ask students what they want to learn about certain subjects, either through private journal entries or via a class chart. See how students' ideas fit with your thinking. Teach at least one real lesson on your first day and prime your students to share what they learned when they go home that night.

5. *Immediately establish routines and effective management to prevent misbehavior.* Teach students your procedures and rules regarding pencil sharpening, leaving their seats, using the restroom, submitting finished work, and other routines right away.

genuine concern for your students, you can prevent much behavior that could otherwise distract from learning.

Use nonverbal communication

7. Nonverbal communication   Many efforts to discipline are communicated not through teachers' words but through their bearing and their actions, or nonverbal communication. Jones (2000) demonstrates vividly the power of body language. Without saying a word, Jones suggests, you can prevent misbehavior by moving purposefully throughout the room, sending the message that you mean business through your direct gaze and relaxed bearing, and by moving your body (turning it, moving it closer to students, and staying long enough to convey your message and ensure compliance, and then moving away).

Thus, you can use nonverbal communication to prevent misbehavior by informing students that you feel confident in your own abilities, that you are aware of their actions, that you care about the students, and that you will help the students make good choices about their actions (see Figure 9.4). The following four strategies might expand your communications repertoire:

- *Bearing.*   Carry yourself in a way that communicates self-confidence. Stand erect and relax. Use eye contact and facial expressions to support your verbal messages. (Remember, though, that your direct gaze may not be returned by students who do not share your cultural norms for conveying respect.)
- *Gestures.*   Like a symphony conductor, use your gestures to make requests for behavior. Pointing is rude, but you can lower both hands, palms down, to indicate a need for lower volume. A hand in front of you, palm forward, can support your message to Angela that she stop talking, as can a quiet shake of your head. Nod when she quiets down. Practice in the mirror to develop "the look" that corrects misbehavior without a word.
- *Physical proximity.*   Some teachers are stuck like glue to the front of the room . . . but not you. Move throughout the room so that your physical presence is felt by all. Teach in different parts of the room. When you see

FIGURE 9.4   *The "I mean business" look is captured not just in teachers' stare but in the message sent by their entire bearing. How is this teacher doing?*

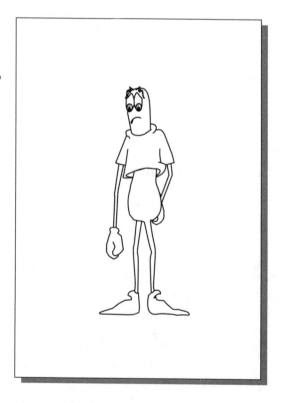

two students begin to wander **off task**, move physically closer to them but continue teaching. Often your presence alone will bring them back to attention. If not, try tapping a single finger on their desks. Only when these efforts fail do you need to send a verbal message.

- *Withitness.*   An effective teacher knows what is happening in every area of the classroom. Kounin's (1977) term *withitness* describes the childhood conclusion that teachers have eyes on the backs of their heads: Teachers need to be aware of all their students' actions all of the time. Position yourself so that you can see all students and monitor carefully. For instance, using an overhead projector, a projection panel, or a magnetic lap board instead of the chalkboard allows you to face the group as you instruct.

In sum, the powerful conclusion I hope you drew from this section is that much of student behavior is in your hands. You have tremendous power to set students up for success by thinking proactively about discipline and planning purposefully to prevent misbehavior. You can stop many unproductive behaviors before they start when you actively support students' wise decisions. When students misbehave, treat their actions as an opportunity to nudge them toward independence.

View Discipline as an Opportunity to Help Students Develop Toward Independence

Human development appears to be driven by two competing forces: (1) the need to be loved and to belong and (2) the need to do for oneself. From the minute they are born, people engage in the quest for self-determination, as evidenced by a child's struggles over time to, first feed himself, to tie his own shoes, to set his own curfew, to pierce or tattoo his flesh, and, as an adult, to make his own way. At each stage of this struggle, the child demands a different kind of loving support from the adults in his world. However, the struggle for independence and self-control appears to be a universal one.

> Children today are tyrants. They contradict their parents, gobble their food, and tyrannize their teachers.
>
> —Socrates (circa 450 BCE)

Our job as classroom teachers is to provide an atmosphere that ensures emotional security and a sense of belonging and that allows students to safely learn to control their impulses and govern their own actions (Gootman, 2001; Savage, 1999). That may sound obvious, but it may not be prevalent practice. For instance, in one study (Lewis, 2001), elementary and secondary students' perceptions were that, when faced with student misbehavior, their teachers responded by increasing their use of coercive discipline rather than using techniques that fostered students' development of responsibility.

Teachers' efforts to discipline should channel the fight for self-control so that it follows productive paths. We need to love our students enough to help them develop, and we can do so by (1) establishing a climate that promotes independence and (2) addressing their behaviors in ways that encourage self-control.

Establishing a Climate That Promotes Independence   Your instruction and physical environment should provide safe opportunities for students to think for themselves and to make meaningful choices. Try these five tools for establishing such a climate:

1. Choices
2. Respect for decisions
3. Clear limits
4. Consistency
5. Natural consequences

Offer choices

1. Choices   Within safe and acceptable limits, provide repeated and varied opportunities for students to make meaningful decisions. Arrange options so that

Here is your chance to support this student in developing self-control. What will you do?

a range of choices is acceptable. For instance, you can allow students options for the literature group they join, the reinforcement page they select in mathematics, the topics they pursue, and the tables they choose at center time. Students can also select places to sprawl during silent reading, the consequences for behavior, classroom jobs, and class fund-raisers. The more mature the student, the broader the range and number of choices he may be able to handle. When students have the opportunity to make meaningful choices, they see that they are capable of making good decisions and that you respect their ability to do so (Coloroso, 1994).

Respect decisions

2. Respect for decisions   Once students make choices, respect their decisions. Make it a point to override their choices only if they show themselves unable to follow through or if the consequence of their decisions would be harmful. Students' decisions may not match your own, but unless the consequences are dangerous, students should be allowed to experience them.

Set clear limits

3. Clear limits   Not every choice a student makes is acceptable. As children, students still need your help in internalizing standards of conduct that provide for physical safety and respect the rights of others. Gootman (2001 p. 38) calls such limits "waist high fences." Waist-high fences are expectations or rules that keep students safe and encourage enjoyable learning for all. Establish clear limits in your classroom so that students know the boundaries of permissible behavior. You can set limits through your class rules, your own modeling, and your interactions. For instance, during sixth period, Steve is a bit too relaxed, leaning back in his chair, fingers laced to cradle his head, feet up on his desk. Privately you tell him, "Steve, this is a place for learning. In this room, your feet belong on the ground and your hands belong near the desk." You finish with a bit of humor and a smile: "If this were my family room couch, you would be welcome to relax."

Setting limits is sometimes difficult for new teachers, who tend to be concerned that their students like them. However, one of the kindest things you can do for your students is to provide a stable environment with reasonable limits and to forbid travel beyond those limits. Students will push until they find your limits. When they find those boundaries, they can turn their attention to other matters. Do them—and yourself—a favor and make your limits clear at the outset. *Say what you mean . . . and mean what you say.*

Be consistent: Follow through

4. Consistency Perhaps even more difficult than setting limits is following through to reinforce those limits. Children of all ages find limits to push. One of the most effective ways you can reinforce reasonable limits is by responding consistently to students' requests and behavior. Your consistent responses will help students see that their environment is predictable and that they can rely on stable rules and expectations. When you show them that you mean what you say, you convey to students that you care enough about them to keep your promises. If you are inconsistent, students will learn that they can do as they please and that they cannot trust you to do as you say. "No" must mean "No" every single time (see Figure 9.5). This is a tough one, but your efforts will pay off. Follow through consistently.

Allow for natural consequences or arrange for logical consequences

5. Natural consequences People with self-control understand the link between their behaviors and the consequences of their actions. Unfortunately, schools often emphasize rewards and punishments that are not only unrelated to students' behavior but are also delivered by the hands of another, the teacher. Examples include discipline programs that have students copying class rules when they talk out of turn or receiving food for following directions. In programs like these, teachers retain responsibility for delivering the consequences of students' actions, and students may have a harder time establishing authentic motivation for appropriate behavior.

Help students take responsibility for their actions by arranging classroom conditions so that they face the natural consequences of their behavior. Natural consequences (Dreikurs, 1968) flow from the behavior and are not

FIGURE 9.5 *Students will push until they find your limits. When you are inconsistent, they may control you rather than controlling themselves.*

arranged by another. For instance, when a student talks while directions are given, he misses the opportunity to gather appropriate materials for his art project. A natural consequence of Ming's running in the lunchroom is that she spills her lunch.

When it would be unsafe or unfeasible for students to experience natural consequences as a deterrent to future misbehavior, provide a consequence that is at least logical. A logical consequence for Sheila's breaking Jaime's pencil out of anger, for instance, is that she supply Jaime with another pencil. Charney (1992) suggests that at least three kinds of logical consequences are available to teachers:

- *Reparations:* When a child or group breaks or loses something, it must be replaced or repaired. The situation must be fixed.
- *Breach of contract and loss of trust:* When a student or group acts in a manner that contradicts the rules of the group, rights are temporarily lost.
- *Time-outs for inappropriate participation:* When a student or group does not participate in a manner consistent with expectations for the situation, the student(s) or group is removed from the situation until better choices are made.

When students live with the consequences of their choices, they come to see that the best discipline is not enforced by an authority but comes from within: They build self-control. In sum, you can foster student self-control by providing a safe environment that allows for choices within reasonable limits and builds the connection between student behavior and its consequences. You can also nurture self-control in the ways you respond to misbehavior.

No man is free who cannot control himself.

—Pythagoras

Addressing Behaviors in Ways That Encourage Self-control Your response to misbehavior should be approached as an effort to help students to gain self-discipline. The following four tools can help:

1. Talk it through
2. Self-correction
3. No power struggles
4. Anger shields

Talk it through

1. Talk it through Wise teachers do more than put an end to misbehavior: They use misbehavior as an opportunity to teach. For example, when Tyler swings a baseball bat dangerously close to a friend's face, his teacher responds by moving forward to stop the bat and then intones: "Tyler, look how close that bat came to Dan's face. What could happen if you do not look where you swing?" The teacher guides Tyler to consider the potential harm of his impulsive bat swinging by listening openly to his honest answer and then discussing appropriate alternatives. Before he lopes away, Tyler assures his teacher: "I will go check out the baseball field because it is less crowded. I will look behind me before I swing." By guiding Tyler to consider hurtful outcomes, his teacher helps Tyler to forge the links between behavior and its consequences.

Talking it through can be difficult when you feel rushed. It takes time to teach students about good behavior. Although you may not have included behavior as a daily objective, no doubt it has a place in your long-range goals, and your time investment will most likely be a good one. Talking it through can also be difficult when you feel irritated because you *just want those monsters to stop it*. There are indeed times when belaboring an incident of misbehavior serves only to prolong it. Talk it through when there is a reasonable chance that students have not considered the potential effects of their actions. Otherwise, address the misbehavior as briefly as possible and move on.

Talking it through is useful because it (1) models the expectation that rational people use words to sort things out, (2) tightens the link between behavior and consequence without actually allowing for dangerous consequences, and (3) works to prevent similar misbehavior in the future. Talking it through can help students see their mistakes not as crimes but as opportunities to do better.

| Allow for self-correction |

2. Self-correction Your goal is that students control themselves, so whenever possible, allow students themselves to find solutions to their problems and to select appropriate behaviors. When faced with the typical barrage of tattling during rug time ("Teacher! She is bothering me!"), a wise teacher I know tells the offended child, "I am sure you can find a quieter place to sit." The student almost invariably moves quietly to another, less provocative spot on the rug, and his talking friends receive a hint about their own behavior. As another example, Doug holds a lively conversation during independent work time. His teacher approaches him for a quiet talk: "Doug, the time to chat has passed. Can you find something more productive to do, or would you like me to help you find an alternative?" Doug shrugs, "I guess I will read my ghost stories." As Doug pulls out his book, the teacher responds with an emphasis on the positive: "Good choice! I was pretty sure you would have a good idea!" The teacher joins another group but follows through by glancing at Doug to ensure that his nose is buried in his book. Allowing students to correct their own behavior provides practice—with a safety net—in controlling their own destiny.

Related to self-correction is peer correction. You need not correct every incidence of misbehavior you notice. First, sometimes drawing unnecessary attention to a fleeting or relatively minor transgression can interrupt instruction and increase the likelihood that the misbehavior will reoccur. Ignoring some misbehaviors can ensure that students are not reinforced for inappropriate behavior. Second, students can serve as a powerful influence on each other's behavior. A cold rebuff from a peer can do more to direct a poking student's behavior than can your admonitions to remember the rules against poking. If students solve problems on their own, pat yourself on the back and resist the urge to intervene.

| Avoid power struggles |

3. No power struggles Independent people have power over their fate in important ways. Children very often have less power than adults—especially in the classroom setting—and growing toward self-determination can mean questing for more power. When a student outwardly defies you and provokes your anger, you are probably engaged in a power struggle. Power struggles rarely end with satisfactory results, mainly because the student is right: You cannot *make* her do anything. Avoid power struggles in three ways:

1. *Diffuse the situation.* Use humor, greater physical distance, or a caring voice to allow the anger to dissipate: "I can see that you are angry. It may be better if we talked about this in 5 minutes. I will be back in a few moments to talk." Usually increasing your physical and emotional distance from the student helps to diffuse the student's anger and allows you to approach the situation more calmly.

2. *Let the student save face.* Offer an out so that the student can comply with your request without submitting entirely to your authority. If a student's sole choice is to do as you say, she can only lose in her own mind and in the eyes of her peers. As Linda attempts to draw her teacher into a power struggle, for instance, her teacher calmly tells Linda, "You may get out your math book, or, if you have a better idea, I am listening." Still angry, Linda replies, "Yeah! I want to do nothing!" Her teacher's wise response is to accept the student's alternative, even if it is only vaguely appropriate. "All right. Sometimes I want to do nothing, too. That is a fine choice for the next few minutes. I will be happy when you are finished with that and can join us in math. I miss you when you are gone." The teacher has allowed Linda some control, has provided her with an out so that she can join the math group with at least the appearance of her own free will, and she has reinforced the notion that Linda is a likable person with a contribution to make.

3. *Give the student the power.* A student in a power struggle may need to make one more comment after your request for quiet, or feed the hamster one more pellet after you ask him to stop. By allowing those "one mores," you convey that students do indeed have some power over *what* they do *when.* Usually a student's behavior will stop with a "one more " (Schneider, 1997). Only if it continues will you need to address the behavior again. You may also elect to abdicate your desire to control the student's behavior entirely: "I certainly cannot force you to use appropriate language, but I must insist on it in my room. You will need to use street language elsewhere." When the student realizes that you are comfortable with your own power—and its limits—he will almost certainly have a lesser need to grab for available power.

Use anger shields

4. Anger shields Expect that, at times, your students will be angry or hurt. Irate parents, similarly, may at times use hostile language with you. Although negative feelings are unavoidable, you and your class deserve to be protected from angry outbursts. Schneider (1997) suggests that you shield yourself and others with comments such as "I know you are hurt, but I care too much about our class to let you say unkind things. You need to find another way to handle these feelings. I can make some suggestions if you get stuck."

In addition, young children will need your help in putting words to powerful feelings. Help them phrase their feelings in ways that do not belittle others. Techniques such as *I*-statements can be useful even for young students.

Anger shields convey the message that every person in your room deserves dignity and respect. Schneider (1997) also suggests that anger shields (1) teach students that, although we cannot entirely control our environments, we can control how we will respond, and (2) encourage students to draw on their inner resources to handle their negative emotions.

The point of each of the mentioned strategies is to address misbehavior in ways that respect students' current power over their own emotions and behaviors and that enhance students' ability to make even better decisions in the future.

Address Discipline Issues in Multiple Ways and on Multiple Levels

Teaching looks easy . . . from the outside. To maintain a productive learning environment that supports students' bids for independence, though, you will need to draw on a rich repertoire of rules and tools that allows you to respond quickly and on different levels to different numbers of students. Your ability to integrate these different demands for maintaining classroom discipline will increase with experience, especially if you remain vigilant about growth. For now, you can begin to address behavior in multifaceted ways by thinking about (1) group size, (2) overlapping, (3) intensity of response, (4) motivation for misbehavior, and (5) redirecting behavior.

Group Size Although you will work with individuals daily, much of your time will be spent in working with groups of students. Students behave differently in groups than they do as individuals, and each group of children tends to develop its own personality. One aspect of encouraging appropriate behavior, then, is to harness the emergent disposition of your class. By working to create a sense of community in your class, you can direct students' energy in productive ways and meet the human social needs for power, affection, and emotional safety. Modeling your concern for students and requiring students to treat each other with respect form the foundation of a solid sense of community. Teachers also use strategies called class builders to create a feeling of fellowship. Community builders were introduced in Chapter 8.

Source: From a national survey of public elementary and secondary teachers. U.S. Department of Education, National Center for Education Statistics. (2003). "Schools and Staffing Survey, 1999–2000: Overview of the Data for Public, Private, Public Charter, and Bureau of Indian Affairs Elementary and Secondary Schools." *http://nces.ed.gov/pubs2002/2002313_1.pdf*

Fast Facts 9.2

Survey Says . . .

10% reported being . . .	. . . threatened with injury in the last 12 months
4% reported being . . .	. . . physically attacked in the past 12 months
5% stated that . . .	. . . physical conflicts among students were a serious problem
2% stated that . . .	. . . robbery or theft was a serious problem
1% stated that . . .	. . . student possession of weapons was a serious problem

Despite the public's fears of sensational misbehavior in American classrooms, Jones (2000) found that 80% of student misbehavior is simply talking out of turn, and that 15% is general off-task behavior. Fast Fact 9.2 reveals a relatively low percentage of reported serious misbehaviors.

For these reasons, you need to develop strategies that will maintain the group's focus. Figure 9.6 suggests some common techniques for managing the behavior of groups. Note that the tips are not punitive. Instead, they focus on positive, clear communication of expectations, careful monitoring, and specific feedback. Teachers have individual preferences, and some of these strategies (such as using tangible rewards for behavior) may undermine other elements of your stance toward discipline. Be certain to select tools that are consistent with your own convictions and with what you know about your students.

Thus, one aspect of dealing with behavior on different levels is attending to the needs of students as individuals *and* as members of a larger group. You will also need to handle more than one issue at a time.

Overlapping   To maximize the time your class spends on learning, you need to overlap your tasks. In overlapping, you address discipline issues while you continue to teach. For instance, as you respond to a student's content question, you can also move closer to two others who are embroiled in a pencil fight. While listening to a student read, you can also glance around the rest of the room to ensure that all are on task. You may need to give a "teacher look" and a shake of the head to a student who begins to fold paper airplanes while you work with another group. Through overlapping, you can prevent misbehavior by providing meaningful learning activities, nonverbal communication, and **proximity control** all at once.

Intensity of Response   Your responses to student behavior will vary by level of intensity. Canter (1976) recommends that teachers use assertive requests and that teachers match the response's level of intensity to the seriousness of students' behavior. You may start with a hint: "Everyone should be working now." If students need more support than is provided by your hint, you can use one of these increasingly intense responses:

1. Question about behavior: "What should you be doing right now?" Follow up: "Do you need help in getting started?"
2. Statement of direction using student's name: "Ivy, put away the magazine."
3. Use of eye contact and serious facial expression to match the tone and message: "Ivy, put away the magazine" while you look at her, your eyebrows raised.
4. Use of a gesture in addition to eye contact, serious facial expression, and assertive message: "Ivy, put away the magazine" as you look intently at her and gesture closing the magazine.

FIGURE 9.6   *Tips for maintaining group focus.*

1. Use a signal to gain students' attention. Don't talk while they talk.
   - Make a clear request: "Attention up here please. Let's come back together."
   - Follow through: "I'll know you're ready when your eyes are on me and your pencils are down." Or: "Thanks Miguel, I see you're ready. . . . Thanks Pat."
   - "Clap once if you can hear me. Clap twice. Clap once . . ."
   - Just wait.
   - Raise a hand and teach students that, when they see your raised hand, they need to stop talking and raise their own hand. Follow through.
   - Flash the classroom lights off then on.
   - Use a noise signal, such as a squeaker toy.
   - Lead a clapping pattern; students who are listening join in until all are with you.
   - Hold up a stopwatch and click to measure how many seconds it takes.
   - Try "Give me five" (Wong, 1998). When you say, "Give me five," students go through five steps: eyes on you, be quiet, be still, empty their hands, and listen.

2. Monitor carefully—especially the back and side edges of the room—and provide feedback on students' behavior.
   - Use hints to maintain on-task behavior: "Your group should be on the second job by now."
   - Allow for self-monitoring: "Check your noise level. Are you using quiet voices?"
   - Play soothing music quietly: "If you can't hear the music, your group needs to quiet down."
   - Use a sound monitoring device that beeps when the noise reaches a certain level.

3. Provide feedback on students' behavior as a group.
   - Use verbal statements: "Groups Two and Three, you're working especially well right now. Thanks." Or: "We are able to accomplish so much when you work this well together. Way to go!"
   - Use table points or class points that add up to time on a desired activity or other reward such as a frozen juice bar or a popcorn party.
   - Use your stopwatch to award extra seconds for a desired activity when students minimize wasted time.

4. Be fair to individuals when you deal with the larger group. Use strategies that don't penalize all students for the behavior of a few. Conversely, if everyone is talking, do not single out one or two students for consequences. If students perceive you as unfair, your expert and referent power erodes.

When student misbehavior is severely disruptive, more intense responses are appropriate. Many teachers arrange for a "time-out buddy," a fellow respected teacher who can provide a place for students to cool down if they need to be removed from the classroom. If you use time-outs, be certain to send the message that the time-out is a chance to cool down, not to suffer humiliation. Also be certain that you have a system to ensure that students arrive swiftly at the time-out room and that they return promptly. Remember that you have a legal responsibility to provide adequate supervision for every student, so be certain that students are supervised even when removed from the group. Also remember that time away from the group decreases a student's opportunity to learn.

Finally, you can vary the intensity of your response for positive behavior as well. Consider using unexpected reinforcement to show the intensity of your pleasure at students' good choices. In my sophomore year of high school, for example, my father sent a telegram to my chemistry class, congratulating me for my good grades. At the time, good grades were somewhat of a rarity for me. This surprising and thoughtful display of appreciation still draws a smile from me.

FIGURE 9.7 *Identifying and responding to mistaken goals.*

Goal	Description	What It Looks Like	How You Might Respond
Attention seeking	In attempting to gain recognition and acceptance, students behave in socially inappropriate ways.	The teacher's first reaction is to yell. The student stops the misbehavior when corrected but starts again soon.	• Persistently ignore misbehavior. • Hold a personal conference to determine how many times the student will be allowed to exhibit the misbehavior. • Monitor and provide feedback based on conclusions from the conference. • Provide attention for positive actions.
Power seeking	Students revert to unacceptable means—outwardly refusing their teachers' requests—to gain a sense of power.	The teacher's first reaction is to feel challenged. The student's reaction is defiance.	• Refuse to engage in a struggle, perhaps by instead offering a sympathetic response. • Remove the student or the audience from the situation. • Find authentic ways to allow the student to exercise power.
Revenge seeking	Students who feel that they have been wronged seek to get even.	The teacher's first reaction is to feel hurt or defeated. The student is abusive or complains of unfair treatment.	• Change the student's relationship with the teacher and peers. • Foster respect. • Help student gain social skills. • Refuse to retaliate; use matter-of-fact messages about the behavior.
Display of inadequacy	Students who feel incompetent resist help so that they can avoid even trying.	The teacher's first reaction is frustration to the point of giving up. The student does nothing.	• Never give up on the student. • Keep risks low and celebrate small successes.

Motivation for Misbehavior In addition to stopping student misbehavior, teachers need to work on the causes of behavior. When we address the motivations that underlie misbehavior, we can prevent recurrence and foster self-control. Dreikurs, Grunwald, and Pepper (1982) identify four mistaken goals that students pursue. Figure 9.7 describes each of these four goals and suggests reactions that can help you signal the identity of those goals. Dreikurs and colleagues suggest that, after you identify the student's goal, you disclose it to the student through questions such as "Could it be that you would like more attention?" Your first impulse to respond to each of these mistaken goals (as suggested in the third column in Figure 9.7) is probably the wrong one. More productive alternatives are given in the fourth column. The key is to respond in a calm and thoughtful manner that helps the student identify his mistaken goal and choose more acceptable avenues for recognition.

Whether you use Dreikurs and colleagues' ideas about mistaken goals or focus on different causes for misbehavior, the point is to realize that a student's persistent misbehavior usually has a cause and that when you and the student can identify the cause, you can work together on more acceptable alternatives.

A currently popular alternative to the Golden Rule, the Platinum Rule, can be of use as you help students move beyond their mistaken goals. The Platinum Rule admonishes us to treat others the way they would like to be treated. If, for instance, students need attention, then we can see to it that they receive attention, albeit for positive decisions they make. If students crave power, we can shape our classrooms to ensure that they have some meaningful control over what they do at school.

Short-Term and Long-Term Redirection   To work toward your overarching goal of helping students independently choose appropriate behavior, you will need to enlist strategies that address discipline issues in short- and long-term time spans. Short-term solutions focus on preventing misbehavior or stopping undesirable behavior and replacing it with less harmful alternatives. Short-term solutions are the tools you use immediately and from which you expect quick results. Long-term solutions keep in mind the broader view of your hopes for students. Long-term tools take longer to implement, and results may build incrementally over time. You will no doubt need to use more than one kind of each strategy to fully address discipline issues.

Your fifth-grade student Melanie provides an example. She rarely completes her work during class and has not yet submitted a homework assignment. She shrugs when you lecture her on responsibility and the importance of practice. Frustrated by her apparent indifference, you are determined to help. You begin with a problem-solving conference (e.g., Charney, 1992) to assess Melanie's perspective and interests and to invite her cooperation on working together. You devise a plan, taking the notes shown in Figure 9.8. Notice that your plan includes a multifaceted approach to help Melanie succeed: You will modify your curriculum, check with other specialists, include Melanie's family as part of the education team, and restructure your classroom interactions to encourage Melanie's success. In addition to these long-range approaches, also

FIGURE 9.8   *Devising a plan with short- and long-term strategies for redirecting student behavior.*

Short-Term Suggestions	Long-Term Ideas
√ Conference with Melanie to determine the cause for her not completing work (a la Dreikurs).	√ Check curriculum: Differentiate instruction by providing individual projects that tap into her interests. Use read-alouds that inspired her last year (e.g., Ramona books).
√ Call her father and get his perspective.	√ Work on elements of motivation: Break assignments into smaller pieces to increase probability of success and decrease perception of effort required.
√ Develop a contract with rewards that she finds appealing (art or science time).	√ Reorganize cooperative learning groups and begin to shift reasonable leadership responsibilities to Melanie.
√ Find high-interest, low-vocabulary books.	√ Use her parents' input about Melanie's out-of-school expertise (e.g., soccer) to build connections in the classroom.
√ Start homework sheet where she writes her assignments each day, and her dad signs nightly.	
√ Check cumulative record folder to determine if Melanie has any identified learning difficulties.	
√ Find a software program that uses reading through science (her interest).	

notice that the plan uses short-term strategies: an extrinsic reinforcer (art time as a reward for Melanie's time on task). Although you may be opposed in general to using extrinsic reinforcers, you decide that Melanie needs some immediate success and that the rewards can be dropped later as her successes begin to snowball.

By working on the apathy issue in many ways—with tools you can use tomorrow and tools that will be implemented over the year—you increase the probability of success. You may find that certain aspects of your plan are more effective than others as you work with Melanie and will drop the least effective tools.

The point is to address discipline issues along several dimensions: prevention and response, curriculum and management, group and individual focus, and cause and immediate redirection. It may sound overwhelming, but you will likely find that a few tools can serve many purposes for different learners.

So there you have it: Four rules to guide teachers' efforts in establishing and maintaining classroom control:

1. Treat all learners with dignity and respect.
2. Actively prevent misbehavior.
3. View discipline as an opportunity to help students develop independence.
4. Address discipline issues in many ways and on more than one level.

Each of these rules is supported by a number of tools that bring them to life. No doubt you will find some of these tools more useful than others, and no doubt you will also be more successful at implementing some than others, at least initially. Novice teachers tend to have similar struggles in establishing discipline. Therefore, Figure 9.9 restates a number of the chapter's tools that may be helpful in boosting you over some of the hurdles new teachers typically face

FIGURE 9.9 *Discipline boosts for new teachers.*

Direct →Check→Feedback
- Use clear, positive language to *direct* students' behavior.
- *Check* to see whether students comply. Wait and watch.
- Give specific *feedback* on students' efforts to comply.
- Redirect as necessary.

Keep It Positive
- Focus on what students do well.
- Focus on students who deserve attention for making good choices.
- Be genuine and specific in your praise.
- Be fair. Smile. Laugh.

Make Your Presence Felt
- Move around the room to teach and monitor.
- Move closer to students who are beginning to stray.
- Monitor students carefully and subtly let them know that you are aware of their actions.
- Carry yourself with confidence.

Avoid Overreliance on Rewards and Punishments
- Point systems, card systems, token economies, and marble jars can all support a positive classroom environment, but be certain that *you*—not the marble jar, not the principal—are the authority in your classroom.
- Focus on logical consequences and self-control.

as they establish and maintain a positive learning environment. You may wish to review Figure 9.9 during tough days, especially those when your principal or supervisor sits in.

DEVELOPING YOUR OWN DISCIPLINE PROGRAM

This chapter offers a number of tools that may be useful for you in fostering student self-control. Other books and experienced teachers will also propose a number of appealing tips. A few books that you may find helpful, for example, are Charles (2002), Jones (2000), and Wong (1998). However, no expert—and no book—in the world can tell you the appropriate plan for disciplining *your* students. Charney (1992) urges us to teach authentically. When we teach, according to Charney, we teach from the whole teacher, revealing ourselves every day. We accept our own limitations and mistakes. We act on personal authority: "We stake a claim in the classroom and in the larger context of schools and systems—to what is personally, intimately known and felt. . . . Authenticity involves accepting our personal authority—and the risks that go with it—so that we can be agents of the changes needed in our schools" (p. 259).

To teach authentically, you need to develop your own discipline plan based on your philosophy, personality, and preferences. That plan needs to consider the particular ages, characteristics, and strengths of your students and their families and reflect your genuine appreciation for your students as individuals.

Figure 9.10 provides a planning sheet for your discipline plan. You can begin by once again perusing your stance toward education and asking yourself the following questions:

1. What do I hope my students will be as adults? What should their character be?
2. How do students learn?
3. What does it mean to teach well?

Then jot down characteristics of your students: the range of their background experiences and their age and developmental levels are examples of characteristics that may be relevant.

Next, consider your own needs, likes, and dislikes (Charles, 1992). Draw from each of these responses to develop your own rules for establishing and maintaining classroom discipline (see Figure 9.11). Remember that "rules" are not the rules that govern the students; rather they are the rules that govern *you:* What are the principles by which you will select your actions when it comes to encouraging discipline? Borrow as you see fit from the four rules presented in this chapter or from other sources, or invent your own. Then, flesh out your plan by listing tools—specific strategies—that can help you bring each of your rules to life. Review your list and work from our chapter-opening exercises, your other readings, and your own observations of expert teachers for tools that are consistent with your rules.

Expect your list of tools to grow with your experience. You will receive many discipline suggestions and tools. Before incorporating any tool into your discipline plan, however, be certain that the tool is consistent with the rules that guide your efforts to discipline. If you cannot apply the *tool* to a *rule,* the tip is probably not consistent with your stance on discipline. Stick with the tools that are in concert with what you believe to be good for students. Expect, too, that you will reflect regularly on your plan. Does it overemphasize compliance? Rewards and punishments? Does it preserve human dignity?

Also consider other resources for your discipline program. You are part of a team responsible for educating your students. Your plan needs to respond to the cultural, developmental, linguistic, and personal qualities of your students.

FIGURE 9.10 *My personal discipline program.*

This I believe . . . *(List major points from your stance toward education.)*

My students . . . *(List characteristics of your specific students or of students in general.)*

I need . . .

I like . . .

I dislike . . .

My Rules and Some Tools
(Not classroom rules, but principles that guide my approach to discipline.)

My Rule:

Some Tools:

    Establishing an environment

    Preventing misbehavior

    Responding to behavior

My Rule:

Some Tools:

    Establishing an environment

    Preventing misbehavior

    Responding to behavior

My Rule:

Some Tools:

    Establishing an environment

    Preventing misbehavior

    Responding to behavior

FIGURE 9.11 *Formalize your own set of rules that will govern the decisions you make regarding classroom discipline.*

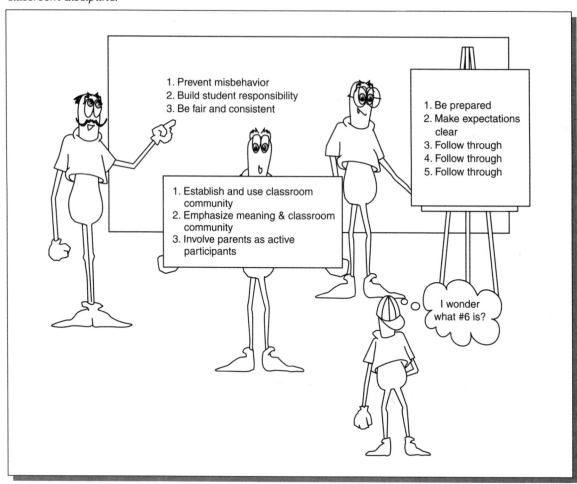

Families are experts on their children; no one knows them better. How can you appropriately tap into families' knowledge in order to learn about students and to support their growth? How will you work effectively with parents as team members to support student development? Which specialists can provide assistance? What support can you expect from your site administrators and fellow teachers? Capitalize early on the contributions each of these parties can make to the well-being of your class; do not wait until students misbehave to devise a support system. Finally, try out your discipline program. Revise the aspects that are inhumane, ineffective, or unwieldy.

PARTING WORDS

Providing positive classroom discipline is, at the least, strenuous—and it can be downright exhausting. Many, many teachers succeed at establishing fair and productive classrooms, and you can, too. Think about one of these pieces of advice on a day when you feel disheartened about the challenge of helping your students develop self-discipline:

A bad day is often followed by a good one.
Classroom discipline is said to be a series of little victories. You and your students build good discipline over time, one interaction at a time. One mistake does not mean you have lost them forever.

Remember that much of what happens in your classroom is under your control. When students misbehave as a group, ask yourself, "What can *I* do to provide a better environment, help them build skills for self-control, or prevent misbehavior?" Do something.
If your system does not work, change it.

LINKS TO RESEARCH, THEORY, AND PRACTICE

Albert, L. (1996). *Cooperative discipline.* Circle Pines, MN: American Guidance Service.

Banks, J. A. (1997). *Teaching strategies for ethnic studies* (6th ed.). Boston: Allyn & Bacon.

Canter, L. (1976). *Assertive discipline: A take-charge approach for today's educator.* Seal Beach, CA: Canter & Associates.

Charles, C. M. (1992). *Building classroom discipline* (4th ed.). White Plains, NY: Longman.

Charles, C. M. (2002). *Building classroom discipline* (7th ed.). Boston: Allyn & Bacon.

Charney, R. S. (1992). *Teaching children to care: Management in the responsive classroom.* Greenfield, MA: Northeast Foundation for Children.

Coloroso, B. (1994). *Kids are worth it! Giving your child the gift of inner discipline.* New York: William Morrow.

Curwin, R., & Mendler, A. N. (2001). *Discipline with dignity.* Upper Saddle River, NJ: Merrill/Prentice Hall.

Dreikurs, R. (1968). *Psychology in the classroom* (2nd ed.). New York: Harper & Row.

Dreikurs, R., Grunwald, B., & Pepper, F. (1982). *Maintaining sanity in the classroom: Classroom management techniques* (3rd ed.). New York: Harper & Row.

Emmer, E. T., Evertson, C., & Worsham, M. E. (2000). *Classroom management for secondary teachers* (5th ed.). Boston: Allyn & Bacon.

French, J. R. P., & Raven, B. (1959). Bases of social power. In D. Cartwright (Ed.), *Studies in social power.* Ann Arbor, MI: University of Michigan.

Good, T. L., & Brophy, J. E. (2000). *Looking in classrooms* (8th ed.). New York: Longman.

Gootman, M. E. (2001). *The caring teacher's guide to discipline: Helping young students learn self-control, responsibility, and respect* (2nd ed.). Thousand Oaks, CA: Corwin Press.

Gordon, T. (1974). *Teacher effectiveness training.* New York: David McKay.

Grant, C. A., Ed. (1995). *Educating for diversity: An anthology of multicultural voices.* Boston: Allyn & Bacon.

Hoover, R. L., & Kindsvatter, R. (1997). *Democratic discipline: Foundation and practice.* Upper Saddle River, NJ: Merrill/Prentice Hall.

Jones, F. (2000). *Tools for teaching: Discipline, instruction, motivation.* Santa Cruz, CA: Frederic H. Jones & Associates.

Kagan, S. (1994). *Cooperative learning.* San Juan Capistrano, CA: Kagan Cooperative Learning.

Kerr, M. M., & Nelson, C. M. (1998). *Strategies for managing behavior problems in the classroom* (3rd ed.). Upper Saddle River, NJ: Merrill/Prentice Hall.

Kohn, A. (1996). *Beyond discipline: From compliance to community.* Alexandria, VA: American Society of Curriculum and Development.

Kohn, A. (1999). *The schools our children deserve: Moving beyond traditional classrooms and "tougher standards."* Boston: Houghton Mifflin.

Kounin, J. (1977). *Discipline and group management in classrooms.* New York: Holt, Rinehart & Winston.

Lee, J. L., Pulvino, C. J., & Perrone, P. A. (1998). *Restoring harmony: A guide for managing conflicts in schools.* Upper Saddle River, NJ: Merrill/Prentice Hall.

Lewis, R. (2001). Classroom discipline and student responsibility: The students' view. *Teaching and Teacher Education, 17,* 307–319.

Metropolitan Life Insurance Company. (2002). *The Metlife Survey of the American Teacher. Student life: School, Home and Community. New York.* Retrieved March 15, 2003 from http://www.metlife.com/Applications/Corporate/WPS/CDA/PageGenerator/0,1674,P2817,00.html.

Savage, T. V. (1999). *Teaching self-control through management and discipline* (2nd ed.) Boston: Allyn & Bacon.

Schneider, M. F. (1997). *25 of the best parenting techniques ever.* New York: St. Martin's Press.

Wong, H. (1998). *The first days of school.* Mountain View, CA: Harry K. Wong Publications.

Wormeli, R. (2001). *Meet me in the middle: Becoming an accomplished middle school teacher.* Portland, ME: Stenhouse.

WEB SITES

http://www.disciplinehelp.com/
The "You Can Handle Them All" site. Gives discipline tips, including suggestions for addressing "117 misbehaviors" related to the categories of attention, power, revenge, and self-confidence

http://teacher2b.com/discipline/discistr.htm
The English Teacher; Methods and Practices of Classroom Discipline

http://www.proteacher.com/030001.shtml
The "Behavior Management" section of the Pro

Teacher Web site. Includes tips and articles on classic, timely, and practical topics related to discipline and management

http://7-12educators.miningco.com/cs/discipline/
The "Classroom Discipline Resources" section of the Secondary Education Teachers' Web site. Includes helpful resources, but expect many ads

http://www.teachervision.com/lesson-plans/
    lesson-2943.html
"How to Manage Disruptive Behavior in Inclusive Classrooms" provides 10 questions and answers for analyzing behavior in inclusive classrooms

http://www.BehaviorAdvisor.com
Dr. Mac's Amazing Behavior Management Advice Site. This site has many positive, useful ideas for a range of issues

OPPORTUNITIES TO PRACTICE

1. Start with the students. Try one or both of these strategies to build a discipline plan that is responsive to your learners:

   a. Determine students' preferences for how teachers should discipline, perhaps through an informal interview with questions like, "What do good teachers do?" "What advice do you have for new teachers?"

   b. Culture makes a difference too. Spend some time learning about your actual students' experiences and about general patterns for their cultural or ethnic groups. Two sources to get you started are Banks (1997) and Grant (1995). The Internet can also provide information. Use the cultural group's name as a search term.

2. Observe an experienced teacher in action.

   a. How does the room environment encourage positive behavior?

   b. How does the curriculum prevent misbehavior?

   c. List some strategies the teacher uses to provide feedback to students on their behavior, noting which messages are positive, neutral, or negative.

   d. List some strategies the teacher uses to allow students to monitor and correct their own behavior.

   e. What evidence do you see that the teacher understands and is responsive to students' perspectives?

   f. What else do you notice about the teacher's discipline system?

3. Pick any tool from this chapter. Try it out, either in your classroom or at home when the occasion arises. How did it feel to you as a teacher? To the other party? Remember that there are always effects—usually both intended and unintended. What effects did this tool have in this circumstance?

4. Arrange for a friend to mock interview you for a teaching position, focusing on your approach to discipline. Use your discipline plan (Figure 9.10) as support for the points you make. Your friend could devise difficult scenarios for you to respond to as part of the interview. (Caution: This exercise is harder than it sounds.)

5. Develop a one-page handout of your discipline program that you can share with students, parents, your master teacher, or other interested parties. You may wish to begin with a credo, or statement of beliefs. (Note: Many teachers develop professional portfolios. This one-page handout and artifacts such as notes home and photographs of children productively engaged are highly appropriate entries.) Invite input, especially from students' families.

6. Choose and respond to one of these critical incidents. Use the rules and tools in this chapter or your own to describe the problem and suggest a plan.

   a. Josh, a ninth-grader walks into fifth period 2 minutes late. His arms are full of books, papers and notebooks all awaiting a chance to spill to the ground. He gives the teacher a sheepish smile and announces, "Sorry I'm late. My backpack broke at lunch." On the way to his seat, he trips on Brittney's desk. The class bursts out in laughter. Josh's face turns red, and he alone stoops to gather his spilled belongings.

   b. Susana, a first-grade teacher drags into the lounge at lunch. "What is it, Susana?" asks fellow teacher, Brent. Susana replies: "I am fed up with my students' constant tattling: 'Teacher, he looked at me.' 'Teacher, she says I copied her.' 'Teacher she took Dylan's eraser and then put it back when she saw me.' I need this tattling to stop!"

   c. Joseph is a new fifth-grade teacher. He is feeling successful about how his students are treating each other, but their constant talking is wearing him down. When he tells them to quiet down, they do, but within 3 minutes the noise level is back to being too high. He feels like he is nagging with his constant reminders.

Before you begin reading Chapter 10

Warm-Up Exercise for Growing in Your Profession

Consider your future. Choose some of the prompts below to jot down some of the possibilities of where you hope to be . . .

- **One Year From Today**
  Professional goals:

  Personal goals:

- **Two Years From Today**
  Professional goals:

  Personal goals:

- **Five Years From Today**
  Professional goals:

  Personal goals:

- **Ten Years From Today**
  Professional goals:

  Personal goals:

CHAPTER *Ten*

Growing in Your Profession

*A*deunt etiam optima: *The best is yet to be.*

Obtaining a teaching credential and landing a job are only two very early—and happy!— stages in your professional development. *Good teachers are never finished growing.* Remember Chapter 1's discussion of the National Board for Professional Teaching Standards' core propositions on teaching (2002)? Those propositions state that accomplished teachers reflect on their practice in order to continuously improve. Further, accomplished teachers work effectively with families, communities, and other professionals in order to shape the world of education. They work creatively as members of learning communities. It is your job, starting today and for the rest of your career, to work with others and to grow professionally. In fact, some say that the day teachers stop learning is the day they are finished as classroom teachers. Through its four sections, this chapter encourages you to stretch professionally by

- Engaging in the professional community
- Working with families
- Using professional ethics as your guide
- Providing some advice from the heart

ENGAGING IN THE PROFESSIONAL COMMUNITY

 *Fast Facts* 10.1

Survey Says . . .

86% agree that . . .   . . . The principal lets staff members know what is expected of them.

83% agree that . . .   . . . Teachers in their school are evaluated fairly.

79% agree that . . .   . . . The school administration's behavior toward the staff is supportive.

78% agree that . . .   . . . There is a great deal of cooperative effort among staff.

44% agree that . . .   . . . The principal talks to them frequently about their instructional practices.

Source: From a national survey of public elementary and secondary teachers. (Responses of private school teachers are very different.) Take a look: *http://nces.ed.gov/pubs2002/digest2001/tables/dt074.asp) U.S. Department of Education, National Center for Education Statistics. (2002). "Schools and Staffing Survey, 1993–94."*

You have chosen a profession that requires you to work with people every day. Your students' success depends in part on your willingness and ability to engage with other professionals in sharing, implementing, and refining professional knowledge. In the future, you will be deeply involved in the life of your school through activities such as committee work and curriculum development. As you consider the type of school in which you would like to work, think about aspects of the school and its functioning that might be deciding factors for you. Is staff collaboration important to you? Is a strong inclusion program?

Two forms of engagement you may think about right now include professional conversations about teaching and pursuing more formal opportunities for growth.

Professional Conversations About Teaching: Seeking and Taking Advice

In some states, new teachers are provided formal support and assistance through new teacher **induction programs.** As part of an induction program, a **support provider** or mentor is typically assigned to the new teacher to offer assistance and shape professional development activities. New teachers report very clearly that the support of a trusted colleague who is officially assigned to help out is a key factor in the new teachers' satisfaction and success. Find out what types of support are offered in your state and district and determine the extent to which you can provide input into the selection of your mentor.

Even if you do not join a school with a formal support system for new teachers, chances are you will receive informal support from colleagues. Because many teachers tend to be the nurturing type, they often support the new teacher on the block. Experienced peers at your site will likely offer advice as you stand near the photocopy machine or tear off butcher paper for your bulletin boards. Some may even offer more intense help in topics such as arranging your room, offering suggestions for working with discipline challenges, or planning your curriculum. Whether the support you receive is informal or formal, plenty of teachers will be willing to offer advice. For example, Figure 10.1 gives some suggestions from new teachers whom I recently asked for words of wisdom. Their words are encouraging because, despite the fact that they allude to the challenges of teaching (teaching looks easy . . . from the outside!) they also communicate that there are many actions you can take to build your own success.

When on-site experienced colleagues give advice or offer to help, your response can be essential to your growth as a professional and for your easy adjustment to the school culture. Experienced teachers emphatically state that the fastest way for a novice to be shunned by a school staff is to act as if she knows it all and has nothing to learn. No one likes a know-it-all. As you respond to well-meaning attempts to help, remember that you bring the enthusiasm of a "new kid," no matter your age. You may be finishing an intense teacher preparation program, so you may not feel that you need every piece of advice that comes your way. Nevertheless, you need to be gracious. You

New teachers often find that talking with colleagues lessens feelings of isolation or frustration and heightens feelings of professional competence and satisfaction.

FIGURE 10.1 *Teacher to teacher: Advice for the early days.*

- "Be prepared. Plan."
- "Take a break in the middle of the day. Get out of your room. I learned early on, that, for my own sanity, I could not keep kids in during recess."
- "Don't be afraid to ask for help. Connect with another teacher."
- "The first day of teaching is scary … The second day is worse (because you know what you've gotten yourself into!). Take it a day at a time. Don't be overwhelmed by every new thing that comes your way."
- "Be flexible. Leave room in your plan book and in your head for the possibility that this may not be a normal day."
- "Don't take on too many responsibilities in your first year. After-school volunteering, student council meetings, and school board meetings will all be there next year too."

have the gift of enthusiasm; others bring the gift of experience. Find the gem of usefulness—even if it is merely the willingness to help—that each person brings to you. Offer your own advice sparingly. Establish from your first day on site that you are eager to learn and that you respect the wisdom of experienced teachers and staff.

Conversely, you may find yourself in a lonely situation with no offers of help. In this case, be the first to shake a hand, smile, and say hello. Introduce yourself and make it clear that you are thrilled about being part of the team. If you need help, ask. Find another inexperienced friend or a teacher at the same grade level or in the same subject area who is willing to talk shop.

In addition to informal conversations, you will receive structured feedback on your teaching. If you are enrolled in a teacher education program, university personnel and a site supervisor will probably observe you. If you are a paid teacher, you will be observed by your administrator at the very least, and perhaps by a support provider. Sometimes observational support for new teachers is also provided by the district office.

Some feedback on your teaching will be formal, based on an administrator's or other official's evaluation of your teaching. In formal instances, structured observation sessions often begin with a brief pre-observation conference at which you may be given the opportunity to direct the observation. The observer may ask what you would like her to focus on. Have an answer ready. If no immediate need comes to mind, consider using one of the principles of instruction: COME IN (you could even provide Figure 5.8 with elements of your choice circled). After the lesson, you will probably have a post-observation conference. The observer may begin by asking for your analysis of the lesson. Be frank and specific in assessing the strengths and weaknesses of your teaching. Then brace yourself for the evidence or advice from the observer.

It can be difficult to accept criticism about something so close to your heart as your teaching. The worst thing to do when you receive suggestions is to take a defensive posture and state immediately why those suggestions do not apply to you or will not work. The observer knows something about teaching or he could not be in the position to offer advice in this format. One of the best things to do when you receive advice (even if you hate it) is to smile, establish eye contact, and say thank you. Then you can add something sincere to show that you understand the point of the suggestions. Honest examples, in order of decreasing enthusiasm, include the following:

- "Thanks. Those are great ideas! No *wonder* they pay you the big bucks!"
- "Thanks. That just might work! I will try it tomorrow."
- "Thanks. You have given me lots of things to think about!"

> *T*he brighter you are, the more you have to learn.
>
> —Don Herold

> *I*t's okay to make mistakes. Mistakes are our teachers—they help us to learn.
>
> —John Bradshaw

- "Thanks. I appreciate your ideas. I will need to think about some ways to make them work for my situation."
- "Thanks. Tell me more about how I could make that suggestion work in my room."

Your post-observation conference will probably be helpful and positive. However, if you have limped through a painful post-observation session, you can go home and nurse your wounded pride. Chances are in a few hours (or days) you will find some kernel of wisdom or helpfulness in the words that stung initially. The point is not to be false in your reaction to criticism but to realize that every teacher has room to grow and that once you can get over a possible initial reaction of hurt, you can appreciate a fresh insight into teaching.

Sometimes advice on your teaching may not be offered, even though you eagerly ask for it. For instance, you may have a formal lesson observation for which the evaluator gives nonspecific feedback: "Wonderful lesson! Great job!" Be ready with some pointed questions that require the sharing of evidence collected by the observer. For instance, you could ask the observer whether your instruction engaged all of the students, or whether the observer noted any evidence that students were mastering the content. (Again, provide Figure 5.8 or your credo of education. Ask the evaluator to gather relevant evidence.)

You may at times need assistance of a more dire nature. For example, you may have a student who is particularly troubled or you may be struggling to meet the needs of a specific group of students. Being a classroom teacher means being part of a team, so be certain that you ask for help. Talk with your principal, mentor, or supervisor about your needs, stating them in a professional, clear way at the appropriate place and time. Do not place blame or suggest that you are not responsible for difficult situations ("I was given the roughest class!"). Your aim is to help your students learn, and you are exactly the person who is responsible for them. Have alternatives ready if you are faced with unfair or difficult practices or procedures. Be assertive and positive, with an effort to serve as part of the solution, not part of the problem. Get your needs met without sacrificing others' rights or dignity. Use *I*-statements (presented in Chapter 9). Convey your sense of self-trust that you have the ability to make a difference and your sense of eagerness to learn.

Finally, remember that learning to teach is a developmental affair. The kinds of concerns you have, the sophistication of your thinking and your strategies, and the realm of your influence will almost certainly shift as you grow with experience. Some of the works cited in "Links to Research, Theory, and Practice" at the end of this chapter include strategies for you to work with peers to improve schools for students, teachers, and the community (e.g., Bey & Turner, 1996; Donaldson & Sanderson, 1996).

Pursuing Formal Opportunities for Growth

Many teachers find that informal and formal opportunities to talk about teaching in its daily context contribute invaluably to their growth. Formal opportunities to pursue professional learning are also valuable. Seek out resources about teaching, and, as appropriate for the amount of time available to you as a new teacher, make it a point to pursue at least one formal opportunity per year. Formal professional development opportunities range broadly; Figure 10.2 lists some tips for locating and engaging in formal opportunities to learn. Note that to grow in a balanced way you will probably need to select a variety of professional development opportunities over the course of your career. The point is to

- Make better contributions to the lives of students each year
- Contribute to your profession in broader ways
- Derive satisfaction from personal and professional growth

FIGURE 10.2 *Professional development opportunities.*

Description	Benefits	Drawbacks
1. Attendance at Professional Meetings, Workshops, and Conferences		
Meetings range from general to specific conferences, to focused workshops on working with particular student needs, on specific teaching or assessment strategies, and on subject matter areas. With time, you may be ready to provide workshops that showcase your own expertise!	+ Meetings are readily available (check the teachers' lounge for advertisements). + Meetings can directly address your areas of interest or need. + Meetings can present very practical strategies for immediate implementation, which makes them especially appealing to new teachers. + Effective speakers can inspire and restore enthusiasm.	− Meetings can be expensive, especially if your district or site doesn't provide financial support. − Meetings might take you away from the classroom, which adds to your planning load and is often unpopular with students. − Meetings often do not supply the follow-up support needed to implement new techniques.
2. Professional Memberships		
Many national, state, and local organizations focus on educational concerns. A few examples of national organizations, most with local branches, include: • National Council for Teachers of English • National Council of Teachers of Mathematics • National Science Teachers Association • National Council for the Social Studies • National Association for Multicultural Education	+ Joining an organization can increase your feelings of belonging to a professional community. + You can select your level of participation, which can vary from minimal (pay your dues and read the literature) to extensive (leadership roles). + Most associations' membership fees include both practical and research journals. + Members receive benefits such as reduced conference fees and opportunities for travel and insurance.	− Dues can be considerable. − The number of organizations you may join may be limited given dues. − If minimal participation is selected, membership may have limited effects on your professional knowledge.
3. Professional Literature		
Abundant educational resources include practical texts, scholarly texts, research journals, trade magazines, and Internet resources. Check teacher supply stores, university and local libraries, and the teachers' lounge for relevant sources. Ask experienced peers for the titles of books they deem "must haves." Go to the Web sites of national organizations and search for their journals.	+ The variety of education literature is tremendous. + You can select exactly the information you need. + Electronic searches allow you to find large amounts of information specifically related to your needs. + You can read at your own convenience. + Information can be retained and revisited. + Reading can allow for greater depth than can short workshop sessions. + You can draw your own conclusions if you read primary sources.	− It can be difficult to find the time to gather materials and read. − Some research literature is not written with the classroom teacher in mind. − Reading can be a solitary endeavor unless you can find a discussion partner or study group.

continued

FIGURE 10.2   *Continued*

Description	Benefits	Drawbacks
4. Professional Travel		
• Local travel opportunities include visits to nearby classrooms, schools, and field-trip sites. • More extensive travel includes trips to faraway sites to examine schooling practices. • Educationally related field trips to distant sites to study the culture, language, history, or natural phenomena (e.g., the Galapagos Islands) can provide college course credit.	+ Travel, even to the school down the street, can help to overcome the idea that one's own practices are the only ones found to be effective. Travel broadens our experiences and views of good practice. + Travel can provide you with empathy and skills for addressing diverse learners. + Travel can increase your subject matter base and the resources you draw from in your classroom teaching.	– Seeing other schools at work usually means leaving your own students during instructional hours. – Travel can be costly and time consuming.
5. Advanced Study		
Advanced study through a university can result in: • a certificate • an advanced credential • a graduate degree	+ Advanced study is often particularly meaningful for teachers because they can draw from the background of their own teaching experience. + Advanced study is professionally satisfying when it results in a specialized set of skills and attitudes that can be used to serve students and the profession. + Advanced study provides for a greater number of professional options. + Advanced study is the typical mechanism for advancing on the salary scale in public schools.	– Advanced study requires a long-term time commitment, usually at least one year of part-time study. – Advanced study can be overwhelming as teachers balance the needs of their students and of their educational programs. – New teachers are usually highly focused upon their classrooms and may not be ready to engage in advanced study for the first year or two of their teaching careers. – Without financial assistance, advanced study can be expensive.
6. Professional Writing		
• Informal writings by teachers include private journals and handbooks for local distribution. • Many education journals and magazines, including electronic sources, welcome contributions from practicing teachers. • Findings from action research projects are useful to other professionals when published. • Practicing teachers also contribute helpful practical works to the literature (one example is Newmann's reference in Chapter 7).	+ Professional writing offers a powerful means for contributing to the profession. When teachers write, they send the message that educators are thoughtful and can build and share knowledge with each other. + Professional writing offers an in-depth way to learn about your own practice. + Professional writing allows you to share information that you find most relevant with people in your own setting. + You are a great model for your students when you write professionally.	– Writing is among the most time intensive ways to contribute to the field, in part because of the process of composing, and in part because of the procedures involved in formal publication. – Most teachers find difficulty in splitting their interests among the demands of classroom teaching and of putting ideas on paper.

FIGURE 10.2   *Continued*

Tips:
(a) Reread your warm-up exercise for this chapter. Circle some opportunities from those introduced in this figure that will help you reach your goals. Add them to the warm-up exercise.
(b) When expense is involved in professional development, ask your administrator if support is available. Check, too, with your tax advisor to determine and document legitimate professional expenses.

WORKING WITH FAMILIES

Effective teachers realize the incredible potential that strong family–home connections can have for fueling students' success. There is evidence that parent participation has positive effects on students' attitudes toward schooling and, ultimately, on their academic achievement. Yet many teachers feel that their efforts are unsupported by families. Fast Facts 10.2 notes that just slightly more than half of public elementary and secondary teachers in one survey felt supported by parents. This fact seems reflected in common teachers lounge talk where frustrated teachers begin their sentences with, "Those parents . . ." or exclaim, "They just don't value education." Teachers have a right to be frustrated by the many challenges they face in helping students learn. However, these discouraged exclamations reflect **deficit thinking,** or the belief that families are faulty in some way and need remediation. Instead, the research on parent participation indicates that:

- Parents of all races and economic levels do care deeply about their students.
- Parents do value education. What it means to be "well educated" can vary based on culture and other factors, but parents do want their students to succeed.

Based on these positive convictions, effective parent involvement programs begin with the assumption that parents are knowledgeable, influential people who have contributions to make to students and their education. According to Nieto (1996), strong parent programs hold parent empowerment as a main goal, commit to serving low-income families, and draw from the culture, values, language and experiences of the home.

Fast Facts 10.2

Survey Says . . .

In 1993–1994:

53% of K–12 teachers agreed that . . .	. . . they received a great deal of support from the parents for the work they do.[1]

In 1999–2000:

24% of K–12 teachers reported that . . .	. . . lack of parent involvement was a serious problem at school.[2]

13% of the principals agreed.

[1]*Source:* From a national survey of public elementary and secondary teachers. U.S. Department of Education, National Center for Education Statistics. (2002). "Schools and Staffing Survey, 1993–94" *http://nces.ed.gov/pubs2002/digest2001/tables/dt074.asp*

[2]*Source:* U.S. Department of Education, National Center for Education Statistics. (2003). "Schools and Staffing Survey, 1999–2000: Overview of the Data for Public, Private, Public Charter, and Bureau of Indian Affairs Elementary and Secondary Schools." *http://nces.ed.gov/pubs2002/2002313_1.pdf*

Teaching Tips

WORKING WITH FAMILIES

1. Draw on their broad and long history with their children.
2. Remember that parental ego and protection defenses can be deeply involved in parenthood.
3. Make the most helpful assumptions possible.
4. Include them as essential team members. Use inclusive language and plan for solutions together.
5. Provide different ways for families to be involved.

Families and schools should view themselves as serving on the same team in working together to encourage student growth.

Many successful examples of schools valuing families and their expertise in order to build partnerships for the benefit of students exist (e.g., Cairney, 2000; Moll, Amanti, Neff, & Gonzalez, 1992). Establishing such successful programs involves a great deal of continued effort on the part of both the family and the teacher. Common threads include:

1. An awareness that each of us is steeped in our own culture and values and a willingness to explore those values and to accept that there are alternatives to them. This awareness allows each partner to remain vigilant about remaining sensitive to others' perspectives. The greater the mismatch between a parent's experience and the culture of the school, the greater the likelihood that the parent will feel estranged from the schooling process and the more trust and support in understanding this new culture the teacher may need to establish.

2. Partnerships need to be two-way and balanced. Both parties need to be seen as having valuable knowledge and perspectives.

3. There is mutual accommodation (recall Chapter 3) in that the teacher seeks to learn about the students' communities and cultures and about how to communicate effectively with families. Home visits, translator-mediated conferences, notes home, and research are all examples of teachers learning about their students. Care must be taken not to offend families with requests that they may consider inappropriate (Davidman & Davidman, 1997).

4. There are clear, frequent, and multifaceted attempts to communicate. The communication needs to be respectful, in the language of the home, and it needs to take many forms including both written and oral messages.

5. Partnerships need to expand traditional options for family involvement. Parents who speak a language other than English need options for becoming involved, and all families benefit from involvement beyond attendance at infrequent nighttime events or classroom volunteering. Examples include literacy programs where parents join school-based writing clubs and units of study that incorporate the **funds of knowledge** of the community. Funds of knowledge are the rich understandings and networks of support that community members develop and use in daily life.

6. Partnerships need to grow over time, and as trust builds, teachers can provide suggestions for how parents may support their students' school success (Faltis, 2001).

From the start, you can work toward effective family participation by encouraging family members to play an active role on the education team. Let parents know that you value their expertise about their children and that you can teach the student together much better than you could alone. Use concrete strategies to welcome family input and to communicate openly. For instance, if appropriate, send a letter home during the first week of school asking families about students' experiences and families' hopes and wishes for their children's education. Call or send home a note, written in the home language, during the first month of school to share each student's success with his parents. Use a newsletter to keep families abreast of classroom news. Try e-mail if that is appropriate, or establish telephone trees to spread information to each family. Sometimes standing in front of the school after dismissal allows teachers to talk with parents or other caregivers. Finally, find different ways for families to be involved in education. For those who can volunteer in your classroom, arrange for activities such as small-group tutoring and materials preparation. Send projects home for parents to complete with their students. Include a range of involvement so that all families can experience success with their students. For example, parents may have the option of (a) listening to their student recount an event from the day or (b) participating in an interview about family experiences related to the day's story.

Establishing effective partnerships is long, hard work. Despite your best efforts, you may occasionally grumble about an obstinate parent. Sometimes the job may feel more difficult because of actively engaged parents. If you find yourself in this situation, it may help to remember that parents are experts on their children. They have spent years tending these young lives. They know some things about their children that teachers may never understand. They also have a right to make some choices about what they perceive as best for their children. Work to separate your own feelings from a parent's emotional demands. Whether or not you agree with the course of action suggested by the parent, consider the possibility that the parent is motivated by his or her ideas of what is best for the student. Welcome input and retain your stance as an instructional leader.

Another motivation to consider is that parents' egos and protection defenses can be deeply involved. For many parents, nurturing a child is an act without comparison. Many of us discover the depths of love when we become parents. That deep love—and some ego—can color the way parents interact with teachers and other professionals. Please be gentle with parents who defend their children in the face of a perceived threat or criticism or who live through the accomplishments of their children.

Some of the techniques you learned in Chapter 9 for encouraging humane, forthright communication may assist you as you talk with parents. Figure 10.3 recounts some promising strategies from Chapter 9 that may transfer to your informal conversations and your formal conferences.

If you feel frustrated when it appears that parents are falling short of your expectations, it can be helpful to assume the best. Instead of assuming that parents do not care about their child or they would ensure that daily homework is completed, think about what other things might account for the fact that homework is not getting finished: Does the parent perceive that the student needs to take sole responsibility? Does he view it as outside the scope of his authority so that it would be an affront to your professionalism if he were to step in? Is there a tough softball schedule? Is the student caring for younger siblings? When a parent does not come to back-to-school night, remember that school

FIGURE 10.3 *Tips for communicating with parents.*

1. Set a warm and supportive tone for your conversation.

Establish yourself as an authority figure.	Use genuine concern for students and your expert knowledge base to build trust with families. You may be new, but you are a professional.
	Be certain that the care you feel for each of your students if reflected in your words and actions.
Use nonverbal communication.	Communicate your concern for students by choosing a collegial location for conferences (not, for instance, you behind an imposing desk). Share your care and enthusiasm in your handshake, your posture, and your facial expression.
Celebrate and suffer.	Appreciate—don't evaluate—families' successes and struggles with their children. It's hard work to be a parent. Remember, your work with the students stops every day. Families are in for the long haul.
Actively listen.	Use body language to indicate that you are fully attentive.
	Paraphrase your understanding of what parents say. Show that you understand the parents' concerns.
Keep things positive. Use laughter.	Keep the tone of your conference hopeful and assertive: This is an effective team! Express shared commitment and communicate your sense of certainty that together you and the family can help the student. Use humor appropriately to keep a sense of perspective.

2. State your concerns fairly and without evoking defensiveness.

Use a strength refresher.	Begin with a statement of the students' tremendous strengths. Use that as a context for what you can work on next. We can all improve.
Use *I*-messages to communicate your concerns.	You can lessen parents' defensiveness by not placing blame. Not: "*You* aren't checking that homework is done" but "When Joey does not complete homework, *I* worry that he won't master these fundamental concepts."
Address the behavior, not the person.	Talk in specific terms about what you see the student doing and saying. Then talk about the consequences. Steer clear of phrases that label. Provide specific evidence, including work samples and grade-book marks to illustrate the student's strengths and struggles.

3. Work on addressing issues as a team.

Ask for family insights.	Draw on families' considerable years of experience: "What has been effective in the past?" Talk frankly about what seems effective and ineffective in your own efforts.
Establish clear expectations.	Give parents clear guidelines of things they can do to help. Share professional literature. Give lists of suggestions. Especially if parents are feeling ineffective, you'll need to give concrete suggestions for things to try. Remember, you need a license to be a teacher, but parents typically have no training for their role. We all can use some friendly suggestions, especially when shared by someone we trust and respect.
Offer choices and respect decisions.	Suggest for parents some specific options for strategies to help their students. When parents make a choice, respect it instead of suggesting others.
Follow through.	Do what you say you'll do. Check to see that the parents do the same. If they don't, talk about changing the system to make it more manageable for them.
Talk about addressing issues in multiple ways on different levels.	Discuss possible motivations for misbehavior. For example, are things going well for the student at home? In Scouts? In day care? Make a plan to address issues in the short run and in the longer range. Be certain the plan includes both home and school aspects.

might be an intimidating place for some. Or a parent may work at night. When you assume that parents do not care, you close the door on your chances of working with them on behalf of the student. Assume the best. Remember the powerful role you play in forming effective home–school teams and in leading learning. Teachers who think that they *can* make a difference *do*.

FIGURE 10.3 *Continued*

4. Avoid ugliness.	
Model emotional control.	Even if parents express emotions inappropriately, you need to remain calm and professional. If parents have difficulty collecting themselves, use a supportive statement that recognizes their right to feel strongly. You may want to suggest that you talk another time. Do the same if you are no longer in control: "I care so much about this issue that I'm having trouble remaining calm. I'd like to excuse myself. We can talk again tomorrow evening."
Use anger shields.	Occasionally parents become so emotional that they can no longer behave with the best interests of their children in mind. Don't talk to a parent who angrily interrupts your instruction. Instead suggest that the parent stop by the office and make an appointment to see you after school or during your conference period. If a conference takes a hostile turn, stand up and excuse yourself: "I see you care deeply about your student. However, this conversation is no longer professional. I'll be glad to talk to you at another time when the principal is able to join us."

USING PROFESSIONAL ETHICS AS YOUR GUIDE

Ethics and **morals** are the often tacit rules that govern how people should treat each other. According to Goodlad (1990), the entire enterprise of education is a moral one; the primary purposes of schools, providing access to knowledge and enculturating the young, are moral callings. Further, teachers are part of a system. When you enter this profession, you accept its code of ethics (Soltis, 1986). You take on the obligation to act in the best interest of your students, including commitments like protecting them and taking responsibility to help them learn. These are weighty responsibilities. Further, teaching is fraught with tensions and dilemmas that require you to act as a moral agent (Buzzelli & Johnston, 2001; Kidder & Born, 1998–99).

> *T*he test of the morality of a society is what it does for its children.
>
> —*Dietrich Bonhoeffer*

Finally, you have entered a career in which professionals are typically held to a higher moral standard than the general public. In each of your dealings, be certain that professional ethics inform your choices about how to act and what to say.

Using professional ethics as your guide means that you must advocate for the students and advocate for yourself. Advocating for the students means that you

Fast Facts 10.3

Survey Says . . .

24% agree that . . .	. . . they have to follow rules at their school that conflict with their best professional judgment

22% of elementary teachers agreed

27% of secondary teachers agreed

Source: From a national survey of public elementary and secondary teachers. (Responses of private school teachers are different.) Take a look: *http://nces.ed.gov/pubs2002/digest2001/tables/dt074.asp* U.S. Department of Education, National Center for Education Statistics. (2002). "Schools and Staffing Survey, 1993–94".

1. Ensure students' physical and emotional safety. Be certain that you carefully monitor the students and make reasonable efforts to protect them from bodily and psychological harm.
2. Know students' legal rights and your responsibilities. Protect students' right to privacy. Do not discuss them casually in the lounge.
3. Report suspected abuse. Your role is not to gather evidence to erase doubt. You are legally bound to report *suspected* abuse. Do not rationalize to save yourself—or the family—the pain and trouble.
4. Work to secure appropriate testing if you suspect that special services are appropriate. Be certain that you watch both male and female students and students of color to assess their potential for gifted programs and

check for your own biases when you recommend counseling or other services.

5. Build meaningful partnerships with families and others who are experts. Commit to working as part of a team in the best interests of the students.

6. Begin with the attitude that you *can* serve as a positive influence on students' lives. If you do not know an answer, you can—and will—find one. Teachers with high degrees of **self-efficacy** tend to be more effective than ones who do not believe they can effect change.

7. Think about the long-term consequences of your actions, and consider your choices from a variety of perspectives.

8. Being a professional is more than being an employee. Do everything you need to do to help students learn.

9. Even if it feels like everyone else has, never give up.

Advocating for yourself means that you

1. Know your responsibilities, rights, and benefits. Read your contract. Understand how to obtain legal representation if you need it.

2. Are careful about being alone with students and using physical contact.

3. Are a team player. Find the good in each staff member. Steer clear of those who whine or complain, instead viewing the profession with a positive outlook.

4. Volunteer for a committee or two that benefits the school. Do not sign up for every committee in your eagerness, though, because your students (and your personal life) will be shortchanged. Say "yes" to the commitments that you can accomplish well.

5. Strike a balance in your life. Your family—and your students—will benefit from your being well-rounded.

6. Choose your battles. Not every insult to your sensibilities is worth a fight to the death.

7. Are on time. Stay as late as necessary to do a good job.

8. Eat something healthy once in awhile and get enough sleep.

9. Have confidence in your ability to teach and to improve.

SOME ADVICE FROM THE HEART

You are entrusted with one of the greatest privileges I know: Shaping young lives in the classroom. My deepest hope for you is that you will approach each day in the classroom with passion and with the burning desire to do one thing better than you did yesterday. My final words of advice for you come from me as a *citizen* who trusts you to bring up the next generation as an informed, compassionate group, as a *teacher* who expects you to lead students to discover the power and beauty of knowledge, and as a *parent* who speaks for others in believing that every day, when we release to your care our cherished children, you will provide a safe and loving atmosphere where their minds and spirits will be uplifted. My final suggestions are these:

1. *Listen to your students.* Teaching is more than telling. When one of my sons was young, I needled his teacher at back-to-school night to hear some wonderful words about my precious son (remember, parents are ego involved). Her comment? "I am surprised he cannot cut." That teacher, it turns out, said many helpful, positive things about my child over the course of the school year. But at this early moment, I felt like I had been punched in the stomach. My son's teacher did not know that he sat on the couch at age 3 and sang "Nobody knows the troubles I've seen." She did not know that he asked about volcanoes on Mars. She knew he could not cut. She knew him in terms of what he could not yet do, in terms of his deficits. Please think about your students as people.

Believe in them as knowers and learners. Listen to their stories. Entertain their questions. Even 5-year-olds have lived a lifetime before meeting you.

*R*espect for the fragility of an individual life is still the first mark of the educated man.

—*Norman Cousins*

2. *Be careful with the praise you give.* When you compliment a student, be genuine and specific. Your ultimate goal is not to shore students up with a steady stream of shallow and false praise. You are not the ultimate authority. You probably do not want your students to grow dependent on you—or anyone else—for judgments of their self-worth. Self-esteem is based instead on students' own assessments of their work and abilities, on their own ability to judge a job done well. Help them recognize good work. Teach them to value themselves for who they are and what they can accomplish.

3. *Do not waste people's time.* You may be new. You may be learning. No doubt you will be better next year. But remember that this year is almost certainly the only chance at 10th (or second or any) grade that your students will ever have. I can promise that some days in the classroom will feel like survival. If you begin to experience entire weeks during which you are searching for activities to keep students occupied, you are wasting people's time. Do not try to justify the educational benefits of a steady diet of word searches. You need to do better. Get some rest and start planning meaningful learning experiences.

4. *Stay only as long as you are effective.* Classroom teaching is not for everyone, and in many cases it is not forever. It is difficult to teach. Even expert teachers have bad days . . . and bad years. If you ever hate your job each morning, you need to change your life. You can change what you do in your classroom. You can change grade levels or school assignments. You can remain in education but leave the classroom. Or you can take your own set of skills and use them in a different field. It is not a disgrace to leave teaching. You will do everyone a service if you leave when it is time to go. There are many ways for each of us to contribute to the world.

5. *Pull from inner resources.* My personal experience with classroom teaching is that it can bring tremendous emotional highs—watching a student learn can inspire awe—and lows. There may be times when even those who love you the most cannot pick you up after a tough day in the classroom. Instead, you will need to draw on your inner resources to reconsider your motivations and refresh your resolve to have a better day tomorrow. One of the devices I use when I need to encourage myself is a collection of quotes from people in my life who have helped me learn about teaching. Some of the deposits in my quote bank are shown in Figure 10.4. Try creating your own collection of quotes to provide some advice when you are in need.

*N*o bubble is so iridescent or floats longer than that blown by the successful teacher.

—*Sir William Osler*

6. *Look for the best.* Each person you encounter has something to add to your professional life. The students each offer their own funny idiosyncrasies and their fresh, rough-and-tumble view of the world. Your staff members have been in your place and have learned from it. Finally, *you* have something to contribute to the world through your teaching. Look for the best you have to offer and nurture it. Good wishes to you.

LINKS TO RESEARCH, THEORY, AND PRACTICE

Bey, T. M., & Turner, G. Y. (1996). *Making school a place of peace.* Thousand Oaks, CA: Corwin Press.

Buzzelli, C., & Johnston, B. (2001). Authority, power, and morality in classroom discourse. *Teaching and Teacher Education, 17,* 873–884.

Cairney, T. H. (2000). Beyond the classroom walls: The rediscovery of the family and community as partners in education. *Educational Review, 52*(2), 163–174.

Clark, C. M., Ed. (2001). *Talking shop: Authentic conversation and teacher learning.* New York: Teachers College Press.

Davidman, L., & Davidman, P. T. (1997). *Teaching with a multicultural perspective: A practical guide.* New York: Longman.

Donaldson, G. A., Jr., & Sanderson, D. R. (1996). *Working together in schools: A guide for educators.* Thousand Oaks, CA: Corwin Press.

Epstein, J. (2002). School, family, and community partnerships: Your handbook for action (2nd ed.). Thousand Oaks, CA: Corwin Press.

Faltis, C. J. (2001). *Joinfostering: Teaching and learning in multilingual classrooms* (3rd ed.). Upper Saddle River, NJ: Merrill/Prentice Hall.

Gill, V. (1998). *The ten commandments of good teaching.* Thousand Oaks, CA: Corwin Press.

Goodlad, J. I. (1990). The occupation of teaching in schools. In J. I. Goodlad, R. Soder, & K. A. Sirotnik (Eds.), *The moral dimensions of teaching.* San Francisco: Jossey-Bass.

Kidder, R. M., & Born, P. L. (1998–1999, December–January). Resolving ethical dilemmas in the classroom. *Educational Leadership, 56*(4), 38–41.

Kottler, E., Kottler, J. A., & Kottler, C. J. (1998). *Secrets for secondary school teachers: How to succeed in your first year.* Thousand Oaks, CA: Corwin Press.

Moll, L. C., Amanti, C., Neff, D., & Gonzalez, N. (1992). Funds of knowledge for teaching: Using a qualitative approach to connect homes and classrooms. *Theory into Practice, 31*(1), 132–141.

Nieto, S. (1996). *Affirming diversity: The sociopolitical context of multicultural education* (2nd ed.). White Plains, NY: Longman.

Sesno, A. H. (1998). *97 savvy secrets for protecting self and school: A practical guide for today's teachers and administrators.* Thousand Oaks, CA: Corwin Press.

Soltis, J. F. (1986). Teaching professional ethics. *Journal of Teacher Education, 37*(3), 2–4.

Warner, J., & Bryan, C., with Warner, D. (1995). *The unauthorized teacher's survival guide.* Indianapolis, IN: Park Avenue.

Wachter, J. C. (1999). *Sweating the small stuff: Answers to teachers' big problems.* Thousand Oaks, CA: Corwin Press.

Wormeli, R. (2001). *Meet me in the middle: Becoming an accomplished middle-level teacher.* Portland, ME: Stenhouse.

WEB SITES

http://ccsso.org/seamenu.html
The Council of Chief State School Officers. Provides links to all 50 states' Departments of Education

http://nbpts.org
National Board for Professional Teaching Standards

http://www.ed.gov/pubs/TeachersGuide/index.html
Teacher's Guide to the U.S. Department of Education. Includes explanations of services and links to clearinghouses (or storehouses of information on given topics)

http://www.nationjob.com/education
Education jobs page (listings from the NationJob Network)

http://www.bartleby.com/100/
Bartlett's Familiar Quotations, 10th ed.

http://www.teachervision.com/lesson-plans/lesson-3730.html
The Teacher Parent Collaboration section of Teacher Vision Web site offers practical suggestions for working with parents, including questionnaires and handouts that can be used for parent education

OPPORTUNITIES TO PRACTICE

1. Interview a trusted, respected colleague for some advice on professional development. Share your work from the chapter-opening exercise and ask for insights.

2. Compose a letter to families. Have your principal read it over and then send it out.
   a. Introduce yourself.
   b. Let parents know how eager you are to work with their students.
   c. Ask families some questions that help you to understand their students and their hopes for the future.
   d. Include a tear-off portion to enlist parent help.

   Or, prepare a PowerPoint presentation for back-to-school night or your own Web page.

3. Make an index card file or a spreadsheet with all of your students' names, addresses, and phone numbers as available. Develop a plan to contact each family throughout the year. Mark each card, or record a comment on the spreadsheet, as you make each parent contact.

4. Commit to one formal professional growth opportunity right now:
   a. Subscribe to one professional journal.
   b. Attend a workshop.
   c. Join a professional organization.
   d. Take a field trip to another classroom on your site (or beyond).
   e. Write a reflection on your practice. Share it with your students.

5. Develop your own quotation collection.

6. How will you know whether you are improving in your teaching? Make a list of things you will accept as evidence that you are sharpening your professional skills. Consider using the self-analysis found in Figure 1.7 to reanalyze your practice.

FIGURE 10.4 *Quotes that have helped me learn about teaching.*

(My apologies to those whose words I've misremembered over time.)

"Now that you have a child, you know how much I love you."

— LuAnn Munns Berthel, my mother, who taught me in one sentence how deeply one can love.

"They're only children."

— attributed to Gordon Guillaume, my father-in-law, by Beverly Guillaume, his wife. These words remind me that the job of a child, apparently, is sometimes purely to annoy.

"If you are committed to improving, you probably will."

— Cheryl Bloom, my master teacher, who taught me to keep working at classroom discipline.

"'Stop worrying so much about *teachers'* questions, and start worrying about *students'* questions."

— a rough paraphrase of five years with James T. Dillon, who taught me to listen.

"Interesting people do more than teach."

— Carol Barnes, who taught me that well educated people have a variety of interests in their lives.

"Assume that people are doing the best they can."

— Jodi Elmore, my student teacher, who reminds me that I should approach people with the understanding that most of us just keep trying to do the best we can using what we have.

"What you focus on will grow."

— Ernie Mendes, who reminds me to see people in terms of their strengths rather than in terms of their shortcomings.

Here's a lighter set I've composed to capture my own foibles.

Murphy's Laws for Teachers

1. Things take about two to three times longer than the time you have (or than you expected).
2. The lesson right before (or right after) the one your supervisor (or principal) observes is great.
3. Typos in memos to families are much easier to spot right after you send the papers home.
4. Someone will throw up before winter break.

GLOSSARY

access to the core curriculum With full access to the core curriculum, each student, including those acquiring English, comprehends instruction related to the academic content seen as central and makes progress in mastering that content.

accountability The idea that educators and schools should be held responsible for student mastery of the curriculum.

active participation Strategies employed by the teacher during a lesson to ensure that every student overtly engages in and responds to the lesson.

analytical trait rubric An assessment tool that allows the reader to rate components of a performance separately, using criteria that are specific to each component.

backwards planning An approach to curricular planning that begins with the end product: the envisioned student performance. With this clear vision of what students should be able to do as a result of instruction, teachers plan instructional events. Specifying performance through rubrics created with students is often a component of backwards planning.

behavior (portion of objective) That portion of the objective that specifies, in observable terms, what the student will be able to do as a result of instruction. The expected student performance.

"big idea" approach An approach to unit planning in which the teacher begins with a focus on the major ideas or generalizations related to the content and then selects activities designed to help students develop those big ideas.

certification The process by which K–12 educators gain official authorizations to teach. States vary in their certification requirements and processes.

classroom meeting A gathering in which all classroom participants have the opportunity to provide input to the agenda and the meeting itself. Classroom meetings can serve a number of purposes such as event planning, open discussion, and problem solving. The teacher facilitates, but students play an active leadership role.

concept map A graphic organizer that is hierarchically organized, presenting a major concept or idea and revealing the connections among the concept and its subconcepts.

conditions (portion of objective) That portion of the objective that specifies relevant aspects of the environment such as the materials, time, or resorces that will be available (or not) to students as they demonstrate mastery of the objective.

content standards Statements of the subject matter teachers are to teach and students are to master. Developed at different levels (national, state, and local), standards describe outcomes that students should demonstrate in given curricular areas throughout the grades.

criteria (portion of objective) That portion of the objective that specifies how well a student is to perform. Criteria provide the standard against which the student performance will be assessed. Criteria are often stated in terms of speed, accuracy, or quality.

criterion-referenced Assessments that compare students' performance to an external standard rather than to the performance of their peers.

curricular integration The combination of two or more traditional content areas in a manner that reveals the connectedness of the subject matter. There are many approaches to curricular integration.

curriculum That which students are expected to learn at school and that which they actually learn there.

deductive strategies Instructional approaches that move from general rules or principles to specific examples of those principles. Teachers present content directly, and students engage in a carefully sequenced set of activities to ensure mastery.

deficit thinking An approach to considering students or families in terms of their failings or in terms of what they do not know rather than in terms of the strengths and experiences they bring to the classroom that can serve as a springboard for further learning.

democratic classrooms Classrooms where teacher and students share power and responsibility more equally than is the case in traditional classrooms. Shared decision making through democratic processes is an emphasis.

differentiated instruction An approach to teaching that seeks to maximize student growth by beginning with each student's current knowledge and skills and offering a variety of learning experiences to help each student move forward. Experiences can vary in their difficulty level, their topic, and their allowances for students' preferences for learning and expression.

direct instruction　A deductive approach to instruction where the teacher states the major idea or skill early in the lesson and then systematically and explicitly leads students to mastery of the objective.

directed lesson　A lesson in which the teacher maintains careful control of the content, presents it explicitly to the students, and allows them to practice during the lesson as they work toward and demonstrate mastery of the lesson's objective.

dominant culture　In a region, the group of people whose ways of thinking and behaving are predominant. Factors such as historical precedence, population size, and social status influence determine which culture is dominant in an area at any point in time.

Educational Testing Service (ETS)　According to their web site (www.ets.org), ETS is the world's largest private educational testing and measurement organization. ETS develops tests and other measures to provide information to test takers and other stakeholders. Examples of their tests include the Test of English as a Foreign Language (TOEFL), the SAT I and II (formerly the Scholastic Aptitude Test), and the Graduate Record Exam (GRE).

emotional intelligence　A person's ability to understand his own emotions and the emotions of others and to use this understanding in deciding how to act appropriately.

English learners　Students who are mastering English in addition to one or more other languages spoken outside of school.

ethics　Values related to human conduct in terms of what is right and wrong.

explicit curriculum　The content (knowledge, skills, and attitudes) that schools set out to teach. It is often contained in the adopted texts and other materials as well as in the daily activities selected by teachers and schools.

funds of knowledge　The bodies of knowledge, social networks, and cultural resources found in students' homes and surrounding communities.

general education　General education classrooms are those in which students with no identified special needs are placed. Smaller numbers of students receiving special services are also typically found within general education classrooms, but general education teachers are not required to hold special certification. Instead, they work as part of a team with special educators to provide appropriate instruction for students with identified needs.

gifted　A student classified as gifted has been identified as possessing demonstrated or potential high ability in specific academic and other performance areas.

graphic organizers　Visual presentations of information. The displays are organized to reveal important aspects or patterns in the information. Graphic organizers can be developed by teachers and students at any phase during the instructional cycle.

high-stakes testing　Student or teacher assessments where the consequences are perceived to be very important to one or more groups of stakeholders. For students, grade retention or graduation are examples of high-stakes decisions that can result from their test scores.

holistic rubric　An assessment tool that allows the reader to give an overall rating to a performance. Performances are rated as being consistent with particular levels of overall quality.

implicit curriculum　The lessons students learn without their teachers having consciously selected or taught them. Students learn the implicit curriculum by drawing inferences about correct ways to think and behave based on their experiences in schools.

induction programs　Programs designed to assist new teachers through the induction, or early, years of teaching.

inductive strategies　Instructional approaches that begin with specific data and help students find a rule or pattern. Discovery learning is an inductive strategy.

inquiry lesson　An inductive lesson wherein students pursue a question or problem by using scientific processes such as observation, inference, and hypothesis testing to arrive at one or more answers.

instructional strategies　Ways of arranging parts of a lesson according to particular patterns of student and teacher behaviors to accomplish certain goals. Some examples include inquiry, cooperative learning, and direct instruction.

interactional　Phenomena wherein parties affect each other through reciprocal action.

learning styles　A combination of factors that together indicate how a person perceives information, interacts with it, and responds to the learning environment. Several schemes can be used to describe students' preferred learning styles.

linguistic　Of or pertaining to language.

local assessments　Measures used with the intent of gathering information about student performance at the classroom, school, or district level. The purpose is not to compare student performance with that of students in other places, but to gather specific information related to local curricular and instructional efforts and student learning within the immediate context.

mentors　Individuals who support the growth and development of less experienced peers, often in a partner relationship. Mentors can be formally assigned and complete a prescribed set of tasks, or they can work informally with their protegees and offer less structured support.

monitor   To actively observe students for specified purposes, often to ensure that they are safe and engaged in learning activities.

morals   Principles of right and wrong in relation to human conduct.

multimedia projects   Computer-based projects that combine different media such as sound, text, animation, and images to create an integrated product.

multiple embodiments   Varied examples of a single concept. Embodiments should be selected to portray the critical attributes of the concept.

multiple measures   A variety of assessment strategies used as part of a system to obtain a valid portrait of student performance and growth.

mutual accommodation   The notion that both the teacher and the students must actively work to learn about the members of the classroom community and the content. Through mutual accommodation, learning is not the sole responsibility of the student; the teacher must take an active role in learning about students and increasing her professional knowledge and skills to foster learning effectively.

National Board certification   An advanced level of certification available to teachers across the nation. This optional certification process compares a teacher's practices to a set of standards through performance-based assessments such as portfolios, videotaped lessons, and student work samples. It also includes a written examination. Many states offer financial compensation for the application process and some sort of incentive for certified teachers.

National Board for Professional Teaching Standards (NBPTS)   An independent, nonprofit, and nonpartisan organization comprised of teachers and other educational leaders. The NBPTS's core conviction is that the key to improving student learning is to strengthen teaching. NBPTS developed performance-based assessments of teacher performance in relation to sets of professional teaching standards. See also *National Board certification.*

No Child Left Behind Act of 2002   Federal legislation that revises the Elementary and Secondary Education Act, first enacted in 1965 and modified at several other points in history. The act is designed to fuel gains in student achievement and hold states and schools more accountable for student progress. Students in low performing schools are a special focus. The legislation increases the role of the federal government in education.

norm-referenced   Assessments that compare one student's performance with that of others.

null curriculum   The content that is not explicitly taught in schools. One example from many places in America, some may argue, is physical fitness in terms of whole body wellness and skills. General patterns for the null curriculum exist based on factors such as geographical region, local values, and historical context. The null curriculum is also a product of an individual's idiosyncratic experience in school.

off task   A description of the behaviors students exhibit when they are engaged in activities other than those specified by the lesson objective or the task at hand.

on task   A description of the behaviors students exhibit when they are actively engaged in activities related to the task at hand or the lesson objective.

Praxis   A series of Educational Testing Service tests for beginning teachers designed to measure academic skills (Praxis I, taken to enter a teacher education program), subject matter knowledge (Praxis II, taken to demonstrate competence in the subject matter related to the prospective credential area), and classroom performance (Praxis III, completed for licensure).

pre-assessment   See *preinstructional assessments.*

preinstructional assessments   Measures used before instruction begins to determine students' current knowledge, attitudes, or skills. Preinstructional assessment results help teachers plan learning experiences that most closely address students' needs.

proximity control   Based on the fact that students who are physically farthest from the teacher tend to misbehave, proximity control has teachers moving closer to students to prevent and redirect misbehavior.

read-aloud   The portion of the day in which teachers read text to the class, often for the primary purposes of fostering appreciation for the work and enjoyment in the act of reading. Can also refer to the selected text itself.

realia   Real-life materials that can support students' understanding of the content. Examples include actual objects such as coins, tools, and articles of clothing.

reliable   An instrument is reliable if it delivers consistent results. Reliable instruments yield similar results with different scorers and when given under varied conditions.

reteach   Efforts taken by a teacher to present content to students who did not master it as a result of an earlier presentation.

rubrics   Sets of guidelines that specify for the assessor the relevant criteria for a student product and indicate levels of performance.

school accountability   The notion that schools should be held responsible for student achievement, usually determined by student test scores. Accountability typically is defined through rewards or punishments at varying levels, including, for example, financial incentives for high student performance or the take-over of schools that fail to demonstrate growth in student achievement.

scope and sequence   A section in teachers' editions of classroom texts that specifies the content that is addressed in the text (scope) and suggests plans for laying out the content over time (sequence). It is typically presented in the form of a chart that displays not only the grade level addressed in the text, but also its connection to the content of the text of other grade levels as well.

self efficacy   One's own judgements of one's abilities to produce desired results, to succeed, or to control one's circumstances.

semantic   Of or pertaining to meaning.

service learning   Projects through which students continue their own learning of some content or topic by providing assistance related to the topic to individuals, groups, or organizations.

sheltered instruction   Instruction that "shelters" the linguistic demands of a lesson while simultaneously seeking to ensure that English learners master the content of the lesson. Sheltered instruction includes both discrete strategies such as teaching key vocabulary terms as well as general approaches such as building classroom environments where students feel safe to communicate.

simulation   An instructional strategy wherein students undergo a series of activities designed to replicate a real-life situation, the conditions faced within that situation, and the decision-making processes required to succeed in that situation.

social action   Planned efforts by individuals or groups to address social issues they hold as important.

Social Reconstructionism   A branch of educational thought that views schools as active agents to improve society. Schools, in this view, serve as transformers rather than as transmitters of the status quo. Notable proponents include George S. Counts and Harold Rugg.

sociocultural   An adjective that describes factors pertaining to both the social and cultural aspects of a phenomenon. Sociocultural elements describe those ways of behaving and living that are developed by people in groups and transmitted to future generations.

socioeconomic status   Some measure of a person's or group's income level and social class.

specific learning disabilities   Disabilities possessed by individuals who have adequate cognitive functioning in general and the ability to learn some things easily. Specific learning disabilities can relate to basic psychological processes involved in learning and using mathematics or in understanding and using spoken or written language.

speech or language disorders   Disorders related to the transfer of knowledge or information such as ideas and feelings. Speech disorders are specifically related to the verbal components of the communication process.

standards-based instruction   Teaching to a set of outcomes prescribed through local, state, or national content standards. Standards-based instruction may offer benefits such as uniformly high expectations for all students and close alignment among materials, instruction, and assessment. Potential drawbacks include a narrowing of the curriculum to what is prescribed in the standards and curriculum and lessons that are less responsive to local students and community needs.

student achievement   Student knowledge and skills, often as measured by test scores. Some people are concerned that achievement is currently construed too narrowly and should be more broadly conceived of through a variety of goals pertaining to student growth and how it is measured.

student-led conferences   In contrast to traditional teacher-led conferences with parents, student-led conferences ask students to take the leadership role in sharing and evaluating their work and articulating their growth. Student-led conferences seek to engage students, parents, and teachers in dialogue about student learning by shifting the power away from the teacher, who acts as a facilitator at the conference, and more equally into the hands of the student and family members.

support provider   An experienced colleague who is formally assigned to assist a new teacher throughout the induction (or early) years in the teaching profession.

task analyze   To break a complex skill or idea into its subcomponents and order those subcomponents in a logical way. Teachers task analyze academic content in order to decide how to teach the complex task effectively.

teachable moment   An often unexpected opportunity for the teacher and students to explore an event or idea that arises from daily life or classroom events.

teacher testing   Efforts to assess teachers' professional knowledge and skills. Though teacher testing has a long history in America, interest in it has heightened with current concerns over accountability.

teachers' editions   The teacher's versions of classroom texts. Teachers editions typically include many kinds of assistance for teachers, including the answers to exercises, suggested lesson sequences, prompts for using the materials with students, and suggestions for reteaching or extending the material presented in the text.

textbook adoptions   The processes by which schools commit to using particular text series. Typically, state boards of education approve works from among competing publishers, and districts select from among the approved texts those they feel are most appropriate for their local setting. The adoption cycle allows schools to obtain current materials for a variety of subject areas after a set number of years.

thematic instruction   An approach that organizes curriculum around themes that cut across traditional subject areas rather than using the subjects themselves as the organizing principle.

tracking   A practice of arranging students into stable, relatively homogeneous groups based on perceived ability or demonstrated achievement. Research on tracking suggest that it frequently does not improve achievement for students in the lower tracks, as these students often receive lower quality instruction. Conversely, many teachers feel that tracking helps them meet students' needs better by reducing the range of performance in their classes.

trade books   Commercial books, often sold in bookstores.

unit   A collection of lessons that address a common goal or topic.

valid   A measure is valid to the extent to which it measures what it is intended to measure.

INDEX